HOLLYWOOD DEATH SCENES

True Crime and Tragedy in Paradise

Corey Mitchell

OLMSTEAD
PRESS

Published in 2001 by Olmstead Press: Chicago, Illinois

Cover designed by Corey Mitchell

Text designed and typeset by the author in collaboration with
Syllables, Hartwick, New York, USA

All photographic copyright information appears on pages 322-326.

Printed and bound in the USA by
Sheridan Books, Ann Arbor, Michigan

ISBN: 1-58754-010-X

Publisher's Cataloging In Publication Data
(Prepared by Donohue Group, Inc.)

Mitchell, Corey.
    Hollywood death scenes : true crime in paradise / Corey Mitchell ; foreword by
Poppy Z. Brite ; introduction by Dennis McDougal.
    p. : ill. ; cm.
    Includes bibliographical references and index.
    ISBN: 1-587-54010-X
1. Celebrities—Crimes against—California—Los Angeles—Hollywood. 2. Crime—
California—Los Angeles—History—20th century—Case studies. I. Brite, Poppy Z.
II. McDougal, Dennis. III. Title.
HV6534.H65 M58
364.15/794/94

Editorial Sales Rights and Permission Inquiries should be addressed to: Olmstead Press, 22
Broad Street, Suite 34, Milford, CT 06460 E-mail: Editor@lpcgroup.com

Manufactured in the United States of America
1 3 5 7 9 10 8 6 4 2

Substantial discounts on bulk quantities of Olmstead Press books are available to corpora-
tions, professional associations and other organizations. If you are in the USA or Canada,
contact LPC Group, Attn: Special Sales Department, 1-800-626-4330, fax 1-800-334-3892,
or e-mail: sales@lpcgroup.com.

For Lisa
With you by my side
I fear nothing

CONTENTS

FOREWORD by POPPY Z. BRITE

I got a bad feeling about Los Angeles the first time I visited. My friends picked me up at the airport and took me straight to Barney's Beanery, which they obviously thought was Hip and Cool. They were trying to break into the Business (one of the many alarming things about this city – there's only one Business, and everybody knows what you mean when you say that word, as if any other form of business were illegitimate and probably criminal). I immediately hated Barney's Beanery as much as any place I'd ever been. The chili was shitty, the hot dogs cost eight dollars, and the sign on the wall said "NO FAGS." As a poor, chili-loving fag, I felt most unwelcome. L.A. obviously didn't care whether I felt welcome. If you can't take the heat, get out of the cesspool.

This book is about people who, one way or another, couldn't take the heat. Some of them were sucked under quickly; some managed to keep their heads above the surface for years before succumbing. But they all started with big dreams, and they all ended up on a cold slab. If you find this image clichéd, I won't argue with you. Los Angeles is a city built on clichés, possibly even a city that worships the golden, graven cliché. Death itself becomes a cliché here, the standard ending to a sad story.

Yet somehow the stories in *Hollywood Death Scenes* don't seem standard. Sad, yes; sordid, sometimes; but each one has its own fingerprints, its own blood-spatter patterns, its individual wrinkles and identifying marks. This book contains stories you've never heard as well as answers to questions you've always wondered about. It's a macabre grab-bag, a gruesome catchall.

If something in here catches your interest – and many things will – then by all means learn more about it. Put on some Sam Cooke, listen to his gorgeous voice, and feel your heart break at the stupid, useless way he died. Watch Herve Villechaize in his little-known but mind-bogglingly fabulous indie film *Forbidden Zone* and ponder how he went from the King of the Sixth Dimension to ending his life with a bullet. Read some of the many books published about the Black Dahlia and try to figure out whether any of these people have the slightest clue what really happened to Beth Short, that young, hopeful, proto-Goth party girl who finally just couldn't make ends meet. (Sorry.)

Los Angeles is a harsh place to live, especially for young people with implausible dreams. I've always thought they should erect a giant billboard of Peg Entwistle next to the Hollywood sign. Until then, this book is a fine, fascinating memorial to her and her innumerable spiritual kin – those who sank beneath the surface of Los Angeles, sometimes remembered for the lives they lived, sometimes only for their death scenes.

— Poppy Z. Brite, New Orleans, March 2001

INTRODUCTION
by
DENNIS McDOUGAL

Murder in paradise is always a puzzlement.

Each New Year's Day, when a mile or more of floral displays float down Colorado Boulevard during the annual Tournament of Roses, and iced-over football teams from the frozen North find themselves competing against tanned, content, warm-blooded California boys on the perpetually green turf of the Rose Bowl, the murder mystery renews itself:

How is homicide even possible in so blessed an Eden as is the City of Angels?

Some say it's the non-stop sunshine, superheating passions to a febrile, felonious level.

Others cite the green envy and red jealousies bred by Hollywood and the attendant money lust of Beverly Hills.

A dollop of despair cannot be denied. In a place built on hopes and dreams which have been conjured up almost by magic out of desert sand, those whose own dreams have been dashed and dashed again eventually rise up in their own way—like serfs to Czars—and seek their bloody revenge. Perhaps that is why L.A. is prone to quakes and riots and murder...not necessarily in that order.

Or perhaps, as Raymond Chandler once warned us, L.A.'s true dark secret lies in the Santa Anas – those devil desert winds with their uncanny ability to stir the Id in all of us and make hair stand up on the back of the neck, like warm static electricity. It was Chandler who observed that a stiff Santa Ana blowing hot from the north makes even the meekest housewife eye both her husband's throat and her paring knife collection with the careful elation of a mathematician who has discovered a brand new equation. These are no simple breezes, these Santa Anas. These are exhalations from the hinges of hell, and by the time they blow through the Valley, over the Cahuenga Pass, and deep into the belly of Boyle Heights, Buena Park or Brentwood, no one is safe. Doors are best double bolted from the inside.

But beware who dwells inside along with you. The revelers in Poe's "Masque of the Red Death" believed themselves safe too. A Santa Ana has no respect for walls and doors and double bolts. If there is murder in the house, the wind will find it, and all the precautions in heaven and on earth will not keep it away. Husbands kill wives, and wives, their husbands. Whole families are dispatched at once, and without any discernable reason.

As elsewhere, eternal triangles claim their share of victims, but dangerous liaisons are far more likely to turn lethal in the midst of a Santa Ana. The hedonistic culture that virtually created the "nooner" also gave rise to a frequent double dispatch of adulterers that some L.A. wags refer to as the "afternooner." In Southern California, aided by Satan's blowjob, a *ménage à trois* can become a *ménage à zip* in the blink of a bloody eye.

Hot winds notwithstanding, the hard, cold facts of the matter are that murder most foul is as inbred and permanent a part of L.A. as palm trees, surf boards, and Santa Monica

Lewinsky. It seldom shows itself at Hollywood film premieres or a telecast of the Oscars, Emmys or Grammy awards, but death lurks in L.A. Ask Bugsy Siegel, Sharon Tate, or Nicole Simpson – or any of the other men and women who came to Los Angeles to seek fame and fortune, but whose final fatal rewards are detailed in Corey Mitchell's *Hollywood Death Scenes*. Reduced to their essence, like fine brandy or snake venom, each vignette is its own morality tale, best read by firelight during a stiff Santa Ana.

Read them carefully.

Dennis McDougal

CHAPTER 1 HOMICIDAL MANIA

The culture of celebrity is like a magnet for the average person. Seeing a star on the big screen, on television, or on a stage provides a fantasy for the guy who works in the steel yard or the mother who tends to her screaming children. Actors, musicians, and artists provide a cathartic release from humdrum existence. These performers represent a form of escape and become a part of ordinary persons' lives. That is why the sudden loss of a celebrity can have such an impact. The loss is compounded even more when the star is murdered.

SAM COOKE

He was the son of a preacher man.

Sam Cooke began his musical career at the tender age of five, singing in his father's church. Over the years, he fronted gospel groups, including the Soul Stirrers with future superstar crooner Lou Rawls, and drove young female parishioners crazy.

In 1957, Cooke made a leap of faith into the secular world of pop music. Needless to say, his first hit, "You Send Me," was blessed. The song hit Number One on the charts and has sold over 1.7 million copies to date. Over the next eight years Cooke would chart 29 songs on the Top 40. He was a bona fide smash hitmaker.

Despite his chart topping success, Cooke led a less than stellar personal life. Always considered a gentleman, Cooke nonetheless had two failed marriages. He also lost his only son, Vincent, in a tragic drowning accident. This devastating loss forever changed Cooke's life. The consummate gentleman sought out solace in booze and women. It was this combination that led to his ultimate demise.

On December 10, 1964, Cooke reportedly picked up an Asian female, Lisa (Elisha) Boyer, at Martoni's restaurant, a famous music industry hangout. Cooke hit it off with Boyer and decided that they would have some fun. Instead of going to one of his swanky digs, Cooke took Boyer to a seedy motel in a bad part of town: the Hacienda Motel in South Central Los Angeles. After checking in, Cooke, intent on "twistin' the night away," stripped down to his bare essence and decided to relieve himself. While he was in the bathroom, Ms. Boyer relieved Cooke of something else. Cash. Serious cash. $5000 worth of Christmas cash he pulled out of the bank earlier that day.

Cooke stepped out of the bathroom and realized Boyer had bolted. He took off after her, sans pants. Unable to catch Boyer, Cooke reportedly banged on the door of motel manager Bertha Lee Franklin. She refused to open the door, despite the fact that she was awake and speaking to the motel owner on the telephone.

What happened next is rather fuzzy.

Franklin claimed that Cooke broke down her door and attempted to choke her. She tried to push him off but was unable to do so. So, she pulled out a .22 caliber handgun and shot Cooke straight through the heart. One shot.

9137 Figueroa Street South Central L.A.

The Hacienda Motel is now known as the Polaris Motel.

A musical legend collapsed in a bloody heap on her floor.

Boyer later claimed that Cooke had kidnapped her and intended to rape her. Others believed it was a setup orchestrated by Boyer, a hooker, and Franklin, her pimp. The cops, however, and the mainstream white press simply ignored the matter. In their minds, Cooke was "just another dead nigger."

Friends and family knew better. Muhammad Ali, a close friend of Cooke's, bemoaned the lack of investigative intensity. He said that "if this was Elvis or the Beatles" a hell of a lot more questions would have been asked. Nonetheless, the police wrote it off as justifiable homicide on Ms. Franklin's behalf. She got off scot-free.

Ms. Franklin died 18 months later. Ms. Boyer was arrested and convicted in 1979 of second-degree murder in an unrelated incident.

Sam Cooke died in body but not in the public's mind. He was one of the original ten inductees in the Rock and Roll Hall of Fame.

Not bad for the son of a preacher man.

Side view of the Polaris Motel.

9137 Figueroa Street South Central L.A.

ENNIS COSBY

The 27-year-old son of actor/comedian Bill Cosby was in the wrong place at the wrong time. While on a two-week vacation from Columbia University graduate school, Ennis Cosby decided to visit his famous father and family in Los Angeles.

On January 16, 1997, Cosby left his father's home to visit a new friend, Stephanie Crane. He headed out after midnight to visit Ms. Crane but pulled over to the side of Skirball Center Drive to fix a flat tire. Cosby called Crane, who drove out in her Jaguar clad in a fur coat. Crane pulled her sports car in front of Cosby's father's BMW and shined the lights on his car. Eventually, she got cold and returned to her car to warm up.

While in her car, a group of young thugs pulled along-side her and one of the occupants flashed a pistol. The gunman informed her that he was going to rob her and take her vehicle. Crane wasted no time in hitting the gas pedal and peeling out of there. Leaving young Ennis Cosby behind.

When she returned with a friend, it was too late. Cosby was sprawled out beside his car, a pack of American Spirits in his right hand and a long trail of fresh blood below his feet.

Two months later, a 19-year-old Ukrainian named Mikhail Markhasev was arrested for the murder of Ennis Cosby. In jail on a lesser charge, he had bragged to a fellow cellmate that he "killed a nigger" and that "it was all over television."

A year later, the former Los Angeles honor student was convicted of Cosby's murder. Apparently, it was simply a robbery gone awry. Of course, once he knew whom he had killed, Markhasev believed he was some sort of tough guy.

In reality, it was another sad case. Two young minority men with promising futures shot down because of one fatal, stupid mistake.

After the trial, Ennis's mother, Camille Cosby, wrote a scathing letter to *USA Today* condemning the people of the United States of America for breeding hatred in Markhasev. Had it not been for our racist culture, she declared, her son would still be alive today. While some readers called *her* racist, most realized that she was a grieving mother who overreacted.

In February 2001, Markhasev dropped all appeals. He confessed to the murder of Ennis Cosby and asked for forgiveness.

Skirball Center Drive South of Mulholland Drive

DOMINIQUE DUNNE

"What's happening!!!!!!!!!!!!!!" – from *Poltergeist*

Dominique Dunne, the 22-year-old daughter of film producer Dominick Dunne, sister to actor Griffin Dunne, and niece to authors John Gregory Dunne and Joan Didion, had to be asking herself what was happening.

To the untrained eye, Ms. Dunne was living the life of extreme privilege and happiness. She was an up-and-coming actress, having just starred in the box-office smash *Poltergeist* as well as working on the alien invasion miniseries *V.* She came from a well-to-do socialite family and was gorgeous in a girl-next-door sort of way. Dominique was also dating one of the top chefs in Los Angeles, John Sweeney.

Sweeney, head chef at Ma Maison after succeeding Wolfgang Puck, was not the ideal mate. He grew up in a poor family in Hazelton, Pennsylvania and had to work hard to follow his dream of cooking. He had escaped the clutches of an allegedly drunken, abusive father and was determined to make a name for himself.

One way to accomplish his goal was to be seen in the proper circles in Los Angeles. Enter Dominique Dunne.

Dunne and Sweeney met at a party in 1981. A highly charged, emotional relationship followed, along with several physical outbursts and beatings. Sweeney, unsure of himself and uncomfortable in the trappings of social celebrity, often became jealous and went off in severe fits of rage. The 6'1", 200-pound chef would often smack around the tiny, 5'2", 112-pound Dunne.

In an appearance on the acclaimed TV series *Hill Street Blues,* entitled "Requiem for a Scumbag," Dunne took on a small role as an abuse victim. When she appeared on the set, her face was swollen and purple. She would require no makeup that day for her role.

After several beatings, Dunne decided she had enough of Sweeney. She finally broke off the relationship and told him that she never wanted to see him again.

Sweeney, however, was persistent.

On October 30, 1982, he tracked her down to their former house on Rangely Avenue and spoke to her on the phone. Dunne was rehearsing with fellow actor David Packer for her role on *V.* Within minutes, an irrational Sweeney was at her front door. Dunne told Packer that she would be on the porch with Sweeney.

Packer claimed that he heard the couple argue. A sharp smack was heard, two screams,

8723 Rangely Avenue West Hollywood

and then a thud. Packer immediately called the police. He then called a friend and told him "if you find me dead tonight, John Sweeney killed me."

Packer then snuck out the back door.

As he was leaving, Packer spotted Sweeney crouching down, leaning over something. He was not sure what it was.

It was the body of Dominique Dunne.

When police arrived a few minutes later, Sweeney cried, "I killed my girlfriend and I tried to kill myself." Sweeney had brutally grabbed Dunne while on the front porch and dragged her over the driveway and into the neighbors' back yard. He then pounced on the petite actress and proceeded to wrap his huge mitts around her tiny throat. He then squeezed. He squeezed some more. He continued to squeeze. Finally, Dominique passed out and turned an unusual shade of purple.

Sweeney was quickly arrested. Dunne, meanwhile, somehow remained alive. Barely. She was whisked off to Cedars-Sinai Hospital. Five days later, despite an intense fight for her life, Dominique Dunne passed away.

The tragedy, however, had only just begun.

Eleven months after the murder, Sweeney appeared in Santa Monica Superior Court. He came into the courtroom every day with a Bible in his hand. Apparently, the façade worked. Sweeney only received a manslaughter charge and was sentenced to six years in prison.

Judge Burton Katz allowed Sweeney's attorney to besmirch Dunne's character and portray her as a lying, manipulative tramp in an attempt to justify his client's actions. The judge, however, did not allow evidence of Sweeney's history of beating a previous girlfriend. If this information had been included, Sweeney would probably have received a much harsher sentence.

Sweeney served a mere two-and-a-half years of his sentence. He actually returned to the cooking world in Los Angeles. Dominique's brother, Griffin, and her mother would have none of that. They found out where Sweeney worked and gave the patrons a chilling warning—they passed out flyers that stated, "The food you will eat tonight was cooked by the hands that killed Dominique Dunne."

It is believed that Sweeney now lives in the Pacific Northwest under another name.

8723 Rangely Avenue West Hollywood

MARVIN GAYE

*"Father, Father. We don't need to escalate.
War is not the answer. For only love can conquer hate."*
- from *"What's Going On?"*

Named after his Pentecostal preacher father, Marvin Gay Sr. (the "e" was added when his recording career began), Gaye began his singing life in church. His smooth, strong voice would raise the spirits of his fellow parishioners. Gaye soon became interested in a singing career and embarked on a successful journey.

Gaye recorded songs with Harvey and the Moonglows. By 1961, he caught the attention of Motown owner Berry Gordy and was soon signed to the legendary R&B record label.

He recorded numerous top-selling hits such as "How Sweet It Is (To Be Loved By You)," "You're All I Need To Get By," and "I Heard It Through The Grapevine." Marvin Gaye was becoming a star.

In 1968, however, the first of many tragedies would strike Gaye. While on stage in Cleveland, Ohio, his singing partner Tammi Terrell passed out. She was stricken with a deadly brain tumor and died on stage in Gaye's arms. She was only 26 years old at the time.

Though their relationship was strictly platonic, Gaye felt an immense love for Terrell and was devastated by her untimely death. He moved to London and went into seclusion to escape his pain.

Eventually, Motown came calling and reminded Gaye that he was contractually obligated to release new material. He responded with his first entirely self-penned and self-produced album, *What's Going On?* At first, the label rejected his submission. They finally relented and the album went on to become the greatest selling Marvin Gaye album ever, as well as the biggest selling Motown record of all time. Gaye's concept album dissected the ills of society—such as racial strife, environmental issues, and war—and turned them into some of the most powerful, heartfelt music of his career. The title track, "Mercy Mercy Me (The Ecology)," and "Inner City Blues (Make Me Wanna Holler)" would open the eyes of an entire generation with their dire pleas for the world to take better care of itself.

Taking care of *himself* was another story. After Terrell's death, Gaye went on a live performance hiatus. He also became addicted to all kinds of drugs. His favorite was cocaine. Gaye tried to kill himself on the island of Maui by swallowing an entire ounce of pure cocaine. He was still trying to escape the pain.

By the 1980s, Gaye had kicked his addiction to drugs, dealt with two divorces, and began

2101 S. Gramercy Place South Central L.A.

to get his career back on track. After cleaning up, he returned to the studio for the first time in years and recorded the supercharged, modern hit, "Sexual Healing." The song and album were released and quickly rose to the top of the charts. Marvin Gaye was back in business.

To capitalize on his creative and chart-topping rebirth, CBS, his new record label, decided that Marvin should return to the road. He began a yearlong tour that had him playing a gig almost every night. He soon became exhausted, as he was out of shape, so he turned again to drugs. This lethal combination led to a state of paranoia for the singer. He believed that he was going to be shot, so he hired four police bodyguards to stand on stage during his performances to protect him.

Gaye made it to the end of the tour with no major catastrophes. He was, however, exhausted. He was still required to release another album through CBS. His tour manager, Andre White, told him he should get some rest, preferably back in Europe. Gaye said he wanted to stay in Los Angeles with his ailing mother. Although White did not approve of Gaye's decision, he relented by saying, "At least your mother and father won't shoot you."

Gaye ended up living with his parents in an old Victorian mansion that he bought for them back in the 1970s. His stay there was not pleasant. Gaye's relationship with his father had always been less than stellar. Indeed, it was downright brutal. When Marvin Jr. was young, his father used to beat him. Viciously. Marvin Jr. claimed that his father had beaten him so badly that he had bruises over his entire body.

Marvin Jr. never seemed to measure up in his father's eyes. Many believe it stemmed from his leaving the world of the church for success in the secular music business. Marvin's mother says the hatred began before then. She believes that Marvin Sr. did not want his son to ever be born.

Three years of fighting with his father continued to take its toll on Marvin. He once again used cocaine to blot out the pain. He contemplated suicide often. And he purposefully confronted his father just to irritate him.

On March 31, 1984, Marvin's mother and father got into a meaningless argument over a utility bill. The argument ended.

On April 1, 1984, April Fool's Day, their argument resumed. This time, Marvin Jr. participated. Marvin Sr. began to yell at his son, and Marvin allegedly punched him.

Marvin Sr. retreated into his bedroom. He picked up a gun out of his dresser and returned to Marvin Jr.'s room. Father lifted the gun up towards Marvin and pulled the trigger. Marvin Jr. did not even flinch. He had been hit in the shoulder.

When his father saw no reaction from Marvin, he shot him again. This time, squarely in the chest. Marvin Gaye immediately slumped over on the floor in his bedroom of his parents' house. He was dead.

His birthday was the following day. He would have been 45 years old.

2101 S. Gramercy Place South Central L.A.

PHIL HARTMAN

Phil Hartman was the one funny man that everyone believed would have been passed over by the *Saturday Night Live* curse.

Sure, Chris Farley and John Belushi seemed on a crash course with destiny. But Mr. Straight, Phil Hartman?

Never.

Hartman was the plain looking Everyday Guy who nailed over 100 impressions ranging from Bill Clinton to Liberace to Barbara Bush. His weapons were his dry wit, sardonic laughter, and infectious personality. Everyone loved Phil.

The Canadian-born Hartman was educated at Cal-State Northridge where he majored in graphic design. He parlayed his education into artwork and eventually created the logo for Crosby, Stills & Nash, as well as album cover art for the Grateful Dead and Steely Dan.

Hartman was also an inspired writer and creator who helped Paul Reubens develop the Pee-Wee Herman character. Hartman was involved in *The Groundlings* comedy improv troupe on Melrose Avenue, which spawned such future stars as Andy Dick and David Schwimmer.

In 1986, Hartman hit the big time with *Saturday Night Live*. Considered "the glue" of the show by creator Lorne Michaels, Hartman made people laugh with a perfectly timed arched eyebrow and a knowing smirk. Hartman would stay with the show for eight years—a millennium in the *SNL* lifespan.

By 1994, he had appeared in several smaller comedy films. He decided to leave *SNL* and eventually landed the plum role of smarmy office guy Bill McNeal on NBC's highly praised, yet barely seen sitcom, *NewsRadio*. He was also the voice of the slimy lawyer Troy McClure on Fox's *The Simpsons*, as well as other characters on the show.

Just two years earlier, Hartman married his third wife, Brynn. The former model aspired to be an actress and screenwriter, but found herself relegated to the role of housewife and mother to their two children. Almost every one of Hartman's close friends believed that Phil and Brynn were the perfect couple. They were always happy and seemed to gaze adoringly at one another. They led a low-key, non-celebrity type of life in their modest ranch-style home in Encino.

Brynn apparently did not feel safe there. She purchased several handguns and had them placed around their home. She believed that they needed protection from any crazy celebrity stalkers that might come after her husband and their kids. It is unknown whether Phil conceded to this armament.

According to close friends of the couple, their dreamy existence slowly began to fade

5065 Encino Avenue   Encino

away. Brynn apparently became addicted to several types of prescription drugs, and also took Zoloft, an anti-depressant used to curb extreme emotions. She also was addicted to booze and had a predilection for cocaine. Hartman eventually became disillusioned with Brynn's self-destructive behavior and threatened to leave her numerous times. Others claimed his addictive nature kept him with her, in a bizarre co-dependent relationship.

On the night of May 28, 1998 Brynn set out to get plastered. It just so happened that Hartman had threatened to leave his wife for good. Brynn was not pleased. She was high on margaritas and cocaine and had also ingested Zoloft.

And she was packing heat at their suburban home.

Though no one is certain of the actual events that night, sources indicate that Brynn walked into their bedroom at approximately 2:00 AM, crept up beside their bed where Phil was sleeping in boxer shorts and a white T-shirt, and fired several shots into the comedian's head and face at point blank range.

While her two children were sound asleep in the house.

Brynn then calmly walked out of the home and across the street to their neighbor and friend, Ron Douglas. She tearfully told Douglas that she had killed her husband. Douglas consoled her for a few hours before he actually went to the murder scene and retrieved the Hartman's children. At 6:20 AM, Douglas called 911. When he told Brynn that he had called for help, she shrieked at him, grabbed the gun, and ran back into her home.

The police arrived immediately, but Brynn had barricaded herself in the bedroom. Police knocked on the door and attempted to talk her out of the room. Instead of a response, the officers only heard a single gunshot.

Brynn Hartman was dead. Her body lay next to her dead husband, Phil Hartman, whom she had murdered over four hours earlier.

5065 Encino Avenue   Encino

SAL MINEO

Twice nominated for an Academy Award, Sal Mineo had quite a career in his day. Unfortunately, he was also a member of the cast of *Rebel Without A Cause*. Many of its stars, James Dean, Natalie Wood (see p. 114), and Nick Adams (see p. 74), met untimely, violent deaths. A similar fate befell Mineo, a 37-year-old bisexual, on the downward slope of his career.

On February 12, 1976, Mineo returned from the Westwood Playhouse where he was rehearsing a play entitled *P.S. Your Cat Is Dead*. Mineo parked in his uncovered carport with script in hand. Shortly thereafter, neighbors reported hearing a chilling scream. They soon discovered the near-dead Mineo lying in the carport, bleeding profusely. He had been stabbed. A good samaritan attempted to resuscitate him, but he was too late.

A search of Mineo's apartment led to the discovery of reams of homosexual paraphernalia. Police believed at first that it might have been a kinky sex murder. It turned out to be a fatal occurrence in a string of robberies that went down in the area. Approximately ten different people had been confronted and robbed by a lowlife thug named Lionel R. Williams. After another attempted robbery, Williams was captured and confessed to killing Mineo. He claimed he only wanted to rob him.

8563 Holloway Drive West Hollywood

CHARLIE MINOR

His name may not ring many bells, but if you listened to pop radio from 1971-1995 you have heard his work. Charlie Minor was one of the most popular and successful radio promotion men in the music industry. He helped break such acts as Janet Jackson, The Police, Amy Grant, and Kenny Rogers. He was a hugely influential behind-the-scenes guy who could convince any radio program director to play the songs he was pushing. Charlie Minor, however, was not able to convince one particular person to get out of his life.

Suzette McClure was a seemingly good-natured girl, raised in a normal middle-class family in San Dimas, California. She was raised a Catholic and made decent grades in high school. She even went on to study computers at Cal Poly. By the time she graduated in 1991, she landed a position at Hughes Aircraft. She was soon pulling down good money and living a nice life for a young woman fresh out of college.

Alas, all good things must come to an end. By 1993, the aerospace industry went belly up. Sure enough, McClure fell prey to "downsizing" and was soon unemployed. She tried, unsuccessfully, for the next six months to find work but struck out left and right. Desperate and financially strapped, McClure turned to stripping. She auditioned at a prestigious "gentlemen's club" in Century City, 20/Twenty, and soon became a hit. Men were attracted to her "girl-next-door" persona and rewarded her beauty. One admirer was Charlie Minor.

Minor was born on June 6, 1948 in Marietta, Georgia. He was a gregarious child who loved to compete and, more importantly, loved to win. He was also a natural born salesman. He attended the University of Georgia where he became the band booker for his frat house. This experience translated into a love for the music business and a love for cash.

Upon graduation, Minor joined the Atlanta division of A&M Records, where he was elevated to National Promotions Director in just two years. The home base office saw potential in Minor and soon he was relocated to Los Angeles where he made a killing.

Minor was a hustler nonpareil, but a likable one. Everywhere he went, everyone truly knew his name. He garnered that reputation through hard work on behalf of his clients:

22058 Pacific Coast Highway   Malibu

Rogers, Grant, Sting, Sheryl Crow, Carole King, Nazareth, Jackson, etc., etc. He hustled, got his clients' songs played, and worked on several hits. He also excelled at partying. However, the early 90s sent him on a different pathway. He sobered up, got in shape, became a husband and father, and tried to slow down.

But he still liked the ladies.

Minor would frequent the 20/Twenty club where he met McClure. They began to spend more time together. McClure fell in love with the mogul, and referred to herself as Charlie's wife. For Charlie, it was just another notch in his belt. He would not even bring her in front of his closest friends. As far as he was concerned, she was nothing more to him than a little fuck toy.

After a few months, Minor began to tire of the stripper. He eventually met another woman and told McClure that their relationship was over. On March 19, 1995, in Minor's oceanside home, McClure decided she was going to get back together with Minor.

And to make sure she was persuasive, she brought along a tiny automatic pistol.

McClure snuck into Minor's home and hid in a closet for several hours. Minor's houseman discovered her and asked her to leave. She got out of the closet, but instead of leaving, she headed up the stairs where she passed Minor's new girlfriend and walked into his bedroom. The girlfriend claimed that she heard several shots go off in succession. She and the houseman escaped and rushed to a phone to call for help.

When the police arrived, they found Minor dead. He had been shot seven times. McClure admitted that she had shot at him several times with the weapon, rarely missing, and had hit him all over: head, shoulders, chest. There was no doubt she had killed Charlie Minor.

Minor's memorial service at A&M Records was attended by several thousands of people. It was a veritable Who's Who of the record industry.

McClure would sit in jail for nearly two years before a plea bargain was struck. She pled guilty to second-degree murder and was given 19-years-to-life in prison. She is eligible for parole in 2011.

22058 Pacific Coast Highway   Malibu

HAING S. NGOR

Haing S. Ngor was best known for his Oscar winning Best Supporting Actor role in *The Killing Fields*. He portrayed journalist Dith Pran, who wrote about the horrors of the Khmer Rouge army and the merciless slaughter the rogue dictatorship perpetrated on over one million people.

Ngor was a doctor in Cambodia who had experienced these horrors firsthand. When the Khmer Rouge began its slaughter, they targeted educated persons such as lawyers, bankers, and doctors. First, Ngor's parents were murdered. Then, his pregnant wife was forced to give birth in front of several soldiers as Ngor watched. As she began to deliver, the baby was unable to make its way out. Ngor feared that he would be singled out as a doctor and killed if he tried to save his child. He helplessly stood back as the baby was unable to make its exit. Later, the Khmer Rouge murdered his wife.

Ngor was forced to shut down his practice and attempted to flee the bloody rampage. He was captured and beaten mercilessly by the army. In addition to several beatings, he also had his pinkie finger severed.

Ngor eventually managed to escape to America. His inside knowledge of the perils in Cambodia led to his role as Pran in *The Killing Fields*. He landed other film roles and even worked with such Hollywood luminaries as Oliver Stone.

By 1996, his star in Hollywood had begun to fade. He did not let that stop him. He returned to Cambodia and built a school and a temple. His goal was to help teenagers overcome tyrannical forces.

Ngor also lived in a small apartment in downtown Los Angeles. On March 3, 1996, he was walking down the dark alley to his apartment when three young thugs accosted him. They had no idea who he was. They were simply trying to peg someone so they could get money for crack cocaine.

The three punks first took his $6,000 Rolex watch. One of the kids noticed something

945 N. Beaudry Avenue Los Angeles

around Ngor's neck. The boy demanded that Ngor give it up.

Ngor refused.

The boy, furious, pointed his .38 caliber pistol at Ngor, and pulled the trigger.

He pumped two bullets into his chest. He grabbed the locket and fled the scene. Eventually, the three young thugs were captured and prosecuted. The triggerman stated that Ngor would have lived if he had surrendered the locket.

Ngor, however, was not about to let go. The man who stood up to an entire country and an insane band of politicians was not about to back down. Especially not to give up the locket.

It contained the last known photograph of his wife.

View of downtown Los Angeles from Ngor's apartment.

945 N. Beaudry Avenue Los Angeles

NOTORIOUS B.I.G.

Christopher Wallace, more popularly known as Notorious B.I.G., or Biggie Smalls, was a famous East Coast rap artist, born in Brooklyn, New York on May 21, 1972. Wallace spent his youth in a hard part of New York as a drug dealer. He claimed he sold drugs on the corner while his momma worked everyday.

While dealing, he would also perfect his rapping skills. He put together a demo tape of his unique rhyming skills that found its way into the hands of Big Daddy Kane's DJ, Mister Cee. The tape landed on the desk of a young, hot producer, Sean "Puffy" Combs. The two first recorded together for Uptown Records and then moved to Combs's new label, Bad Boy Entertainment.

By 1994, Wallace's debut album, *Ready To Die*, was released and became a huge success. With hits such as "Things Done Changed" and the title track, Notorius B.I.G. soon became a household name in rap circles. *Ready to Die* would go on to sell 1.5 million copies and also introduced the world to other artists such as Capone and Li'l Kim.

An unhealthy rivalry began to erupt between Combs's Bad Boy Records and Marion "Suge" Knight's California-based Death Row Records. Artists from each label would attempt to belittle the other with sophomoric put-downs and high-level threats on their albums. These taunts would spill over into the press and even lead to accusations made by all of the parties involved that the others were up to no good.

This rivalry seemed to reach a saturation point in 1996 when Death Row's best-selling artist Tupac Shakur was gunned down in Las Vegas. Many believed that Combs's Bad Boy posse was responsible for the execution style murder. Wallace, who dissed Tupac on his records, was lumped into the prospective lists of enemies of Shakur.

6060 Wilshire Blvd. Fairfax District

On March 9, 1997, Wallace traveled to Los Angeles to attend the Soul Train Awards show at the Petersen Automotive Museum. He was stepping onto Death Row territory. At 12:40 AM, Sunday morning, Wallace and Little Ceaz headed out from the party. According to sources, a long car with black windows pulled up beside Wallace's rented Suburban and opened fire. Hit numerous times, Wallace was still alive. He was immediately rushed to nearby Cedars-Sinai Hospital where doctors attempted to save his life. Their attempts at resuscitation failed.

Christopher Wallace, AKA Notorious B.I.G., AKA Biggie Smalls, was dead at the age of 24.

Years later, the murderer of Wallace has not been found. Most critics dispute the theory that Wallace's murder was an East Coast/West Coast rap rivalry contract hit in return for Tupac's murder. Some people believe that a local Crips gang had been hired on for Wallace's security and did not get paid. Subsequently, they were furious and exacted revenge. This theory is usually laughed at since it is unlikely that Wallace would surround himself with the notoriously pro-Death Row Records gang.

In late 1999, the *Los Angeles Times* reported that the Los Angeles Police Department believed they knew the identity of the killer. Former L.A.P.D. Detective Tom Mack was hinted at as being the mastermind of Wallace's death. Mack, who is currently in prison on unrelated bank robbery charges, allegedly hired a hit man on behalf of Death Row Records' owner, Knight. The rival rap mogul, who was also in prison on embezzlement charges (he is expected to be released in 2001), was supposedly furious with Combs for his success and decided to take a little wind out his sails. Sources claimed that Knight told Mack to deal with it. Mack then allegedly hired Amir Muhammad, previously known as Harry Billups, to take out the rotund rapper. Both Mack and Muhammad deny the police's claims, and as of this printing, no person has been charged in Wallace's death.

6060 Wilshire Blvd. Fairfax District

RAMON NOVARRO

The silent movie star of such classic films as *Ben Hur* and *The Silver Chalice* kept many things quiet. His biggest secret was his preference for sex with men. Especially young adult males. Unfortunately, one of Novarro's peccadilloes led to his murder.

On October 30, 1968, Novarro invited over two brothers, Paul and Tom Ferguson, for a quiet night at Novarro's estate. The best friend of Rudolph Valentino was looking for a night of romance with one of the two boys. The Fergusons, however, were looking to fatten their bank accounts.

Older brother Paul had heard from another man that Novarro had a ton of money stashed away in his mansion. Novarro and Paul engaged in a sexual encounter that night. After they were done, Paul turned the tables on Novarro and demanded his secret stash.

Novarro sheepishly admitted that he had no cash on him. He even attempted to pay the Fergusons with a check. But Novarro was not broke. He was quite wealthy actually. His money, however, was tied up in the bank and the stock market. He did not like to carry cash.

This news did not sit well with Paul Ferguson. The 22-year-old hustler decided Novarro was lying. Ferguson began to beat the information out of him. For several hours, Ferguson tortured Novarro with a silver cane. He would pummel the 68-year old former movie star on the back, stomach, and groin areas. He left numerous bruises all over the actor's body. Although none of the blows proved to be fatal, Novarro eventually died by choking on his own blood.

While Paul was beating Novarro, younger brother Tom called his girlfriend in Chicago. He used Novarro's telephone and spoke to her for 40 minutes. She could hear the pitiful screams of the old man in the background.

When the police arrived, they stumbled onto a truly macabre scene. The phrase "Us girls are better than those fagits" was scrawled on the bathroom mirror with a grease pencil. Some claimed that Novarro was beaten to death with a silver lead dildo that was given to him by Valentino. Some stories claimed that the sex toy had been rammed up his rectum. Others say it was shoved down his throat. We may never know the truth.

3110 Laurel Canyon Blvd. Studio City

Police traced Novarro's phone bill and located the call to Chicago on the day of the murder. They contacted the number and the girl told them of the frightening phone call from Tom. They immediately arrested him and his brother. Both men's fingerprints were all over the house and several witnesses claimed that the men told them of the murder.

The trial of the Fergusons became a bit of a circus as Paul convinced Tom to admit to the killings. Paul believed that Tom would not receive the death penalty since he was only 17. Tom agreed to take the fall for his brother and confessed. He recanted his confession, however, when he was told that the state would seek his execution. Both brothers were sentenced to life in prison. They were paroled less than seven years later.

3110 Laurel Canyon Blvd. Studio City

REBECCA SCHAEFFER

Twenty-one-year-old fresh-faced beauty Rebecca Schaeffer was co-star of the popular 80s sitcom, *My Sister Sam*. Schaeffer had quickly climbed up the Hollywood ladder before a crazed fan, 19-year-old Robert Bardo, accosted her. Bardo had been writing her letters of admiration for months. Schaeffer was so sweet she would personally respond to each fan.

Including Bardo.

On July 18, 1989, Schaeffer was set to meet with director Francis Ford Coppola to audition for *Godfather III*. Meanwhile, Bardo had tracked down Schaeffer's home address and decided to pay her a visit. With his obligatory copy of *Catcher In The Rye* in hand (the same book found in the possession of John Lennon's assassin Mark David Chapman), Bardo staked out Schaeffer's apartment building. He rang Schaeffer's intercom, but since it was broken, she came down to answer the door.

As Schaeffer opened the front door, Bardo plugged a single bullet into her chest and casually strolled off. The aspiring actress died at the hands of her obsessed #1 fan. It was later discovered that Bardo had obtained Schaeffer's home address from a Tucson, Arizona detective agency that paid $250 to get the address from the California Department of Motor Vehicles.

Bardo hopped on a Greyhound Bus and headed back home to Tucson, Arizona. Instead of returning to his house, he went and played on a freeway. Bardo, who seemed intent on killing himself, was arrested and ticketed for jaywalking. Simultaneously, a relative of Bardo's contacted the Los Angeles Police Department when she heard the news of Schaeffer's mur-

der. She informed police that the day before the murder Bardo told her he was going to Los Angeles to visit the actress. She told them that Bardo lived in Tucson.

120 N. Sweetzer Avenue Fairfax District

The Los Angeles police contacted the Tucson Police Department and it just so happened that Bardo was in a holding cell. He was eventually extradited to Los Angeles and tried for the murder of Rebecca Schaeffer. District Attorney Marcia Clark (see O.J. Simpson p.266) successfully prosecuted Bardo for first degree murder. He was sentenced to life without parole.

After Schaeffer's murder, California Governor George Deukmejian signed a law that allows residents to prevent the DMV from releasing a person's address.

After Rebecca Schaeffer's murder, the L.A.P.D. created the Threat Management Unit. It was the first anti-stalking division in the United States. The state of California also passed the first anti-stalking law, California Penal Code 646.9, in 1990. Several other celebrities have been the victims of these crazed, lonely, psychopathic individuals.

THERESA SALDANA

Actress/model who appeared in *Raging Bull*. In 1982, she was brutally slashed by a knife-wielding obsessed fan. Arthur Jackson said he attempted to kill Saldana so that she would die, he would be executed, and they would be reunited in heaven. Saldana would become a lobbyist for the California bill limiting public access to personal information.

MADONNA

A homeless man, Robert Hoskins, claimed that the pop music icon was his wife. He threatened to slice her throat "from ear to ear" for rejecting his marriage proposals and threatened to kill her bodyguards for keeping him away from her. In one encounter, he got within ten feet of her. He was convicted in 1998.

STEVEN SPIELBERG

On July 11, 1997, the director of *Jaws, E.T.,* and *Jurassic Park* became the target of 31-year-old Jonathan Norman, who wanted to show him a lurid script he had written about "a man raping another man." Norman was sexually obsessed with the director and planned to carry out his fantasy of raping him. Norman's goal was to tie up Spielberg's wife, actress Kate Capshaw, and make her watch while he raped Spielberg. Norman was arrested with a "rape kit" which contained duct tape, handcuffs, a box cutter, and razorblades. In March of 1998, he was convicted in less than four hours and sentenced to 25 years to life.

DOROTHY STRATTEN

Dorothy Stratten came into the world as Dorothy Hoogstratten in Vancouver. At the tender young age of 17, Dorothy was spotted in a Canadian Dairy Queen scooping up a double serving of ice cream to one primo sleaze bag, Paul Snider. Nine years her elder, Snider spotted the beautiful service girl's face and figure and believed he could make a fortune off of her. He was right.

Snider began an intense courting relationship with Dorothy, and they soon became a pair. He convinced her that she was perfect *Playboy* material and that she could become famous if only she would shed her clothes. At first, the inhibited girl-next-door declined, but Snider was the ultimate huckster. She complied and Paul snapped away. He then shipped off the nudes to *Playboy* in Los Angeles, the home of Hugh Hefner. Hef took an immediate liking to young Ms. Hoogstratten. He sent for her only two days after seeing her pinups.

In no time, Dorothy, rechristened Stratten, became the celebrity *du jour* around the mansion and Hef's right hand girl. Snider decided he wanted in on the action, since he was, after all, the one with the bright idea to submit Dorothy's photos. He introduced himself to everyone as Dorothy's manager, including Hef. Hefner despised the loathsome, oily character and let young Dorothy know.

Dorothy would become the October '79 Playmate and was being bandied about as the Playmate of the Year and even the Playmate of the Quarter-Century. She was on top of the T&A heap in no time at all.

Snider was left behind.

As Dorothy's star grew brighter, Hefner decided to introduce her to some of the upper echelon of Hollywood society. At one party at the mansion, he made sure to introduce her to filmmaker Peter Bogdanovich. Bogdanovich, once a huge director of such movies as *Paper Moon*, *What's Up, Doc?*, and *The Last Picture Show*, had recently ended a relationship with another young, blond model/aspiring actress, Cybill Shepherd.

Stratten and Bogdanovich hit it off in a big way. He was ready to help her bust into Hollywood moviemaking with a serious role. She had already taken a bit role in the

10881 Clarkson Road West Los Angeles

*Barbarella*ish *Galaxina* as a sexy robot. Not a huge stretch for her. Peter wanted the world to see that his new girlfriend had more than just a pretty face and an amazing body.

Meanwhile, Snider was losing his mind with jealousy. He believed that he was responsible for Dorothy's success and that he was being ignored. Dorothy was ready to get away from Snider—everyone was telling her to do so. She felt horrible though, because she had actually married Snider earlier just to get him off of her back. Nice logic.

On August 14, 1980, Dorothy decided to meet Snider one last time, so she could sever their relationship for good. They met at Paul's apartment in West Los Angeles where the two had once lived together. Dorothy came all the way from New York, where she was in the middle of filming *They All Laughed*, directed by Bogdanovich.

One day later, Snider's apartment-mates had not heard a word from either one. Finally, one neighbor decided to peek in on the couple.

Lying face down on the bed was the body of Dorothy Stratten. She was nude and had blood smears over her entire body, including two bloody handprints on her buttocks. Her left pinkie finger was missing. So was her entire face.

Lying next to her on the floor was what was left of Paul Snider. He had a hole between his eyes, and his left eye was dangling from its socket. He was also nude.

Both were covered in ants.

Next to Dorothy was a strange apparatus. The coroner's office surmised that it was some kind of "love contraption," or sex bench. It was later discovered that Snider had created this workout bench/sex toy and hoped to market it to the porn industry. It, of course, was a failure.

Though not confirmed by the coroner's office, many speculate that Snider killed Stratten and then strapped her corpse to the bench. He then proceeded to have sex with her dead body for the next half hour. Once he was done with her, he blew out his own brains.

Dorothy Stratten was dead at the age of 24.

In a sick twist, Peter Bogdanovich married Dorothy's younger sister, Louise. They separated in 2001.

There have been two movies about the tragic life and death of Dorothy Stratten: *Death of A Centerfold* which starred Jamie Lee Curtis as Stratten; and *Star 80* which starred Mariel Hemingway as Stratten and Eric Roberts as Snider. *Star 80*'s climatic murder scene was shot in the actual apartment where the real murder/suicide took place.

10881 Clarkson Road West Los Angeles

CARL SWITZER

Better known to several generations of television fans as "Alfalfa," Carl Switzer became a star at the early age of seven on the hit comedy show, *Our Gang*. Also known as "The Little Rascals," *Our Gang* portrayed the wacky misadventures of a group of pre-adolescent kids. Switzer's "Alfalfa" stood out with his screechy, off-key singing voice, his pointy tuft of hair, and his tall, gangly body.

Switzer acted in over 60 shorts for the popular series. He did not, however, make a single dime from the show. At the time *Our Gang* was filmed, television was still in its infancy, and many considered it to be a temporary novelty. No one had even considered the concept of royalties and syndication. As a result, everyone knew Switzer, but he never profited from his fame.

As he grew older, he wound up in a series of odd jobs: tour guide, shoeshine boy, and bartender. He had to make a living while he tried to stay involved in Hollywood. By 1958, at the age of 32, Switzer seemed to be back on the Hollywood fast track. He had landed a plum comic relief role in the Marlon Brando film, *The Defiant Ones*. As a result of this film, Switzer knew that his career would take off again. Until its release, however, he still had to earn a living.

One attempt to make money had Switzer partnering up with Moses "Bud" Stiltz in a bear-hunting scheme. Stiltz fronted the money and "Alfalfa" was the hunters' guide. This venture never really took off.

Switzer once had to borrow Stiltz's favorite hunting dog. He eventually lost the dog and posted a $35 reward for the pooch. A man contacted Switzer and informed him that he had the dog. Switzer and the man met at the bar where Switzer tended. He offered to buy drinks for the man in lieu of a cash reward. The man agreed and drank a $50 bar tab. Switzer had joined the man in the celebration and soon

10400 Columbus Avenue   Mission Hills

was intoxicated. When Switzer realized that he would owe even more money to the bar due to their excessive drinking, he became enraged. He was also extremely confused.

For some unknown reason, Switzer blamed *Stiltz* for losing the $50. The reality, of course, was that Switzer lost Stiltz's dog and was responsible for getting it back—no matter how much it cost.

On January 21, 1959, a drunken Switzer and his pal Jack Piott headed over to Stiltz's home in Mission Hills to get his money. They banged on the front door. When the door opened, Switzer flashed a fake police badge and loudly yelled at Stiltz to let him in. Once

inside, Switzer informed Stiltz that he wanted his money. Stiltz told him he was crazy and to get the hell out of his house. Switzer responded by grabbing a lamp and smashing it over Stiltz's head.

Battered and bloody, Stiltz retreated to the bedroom and retrieved a pistol. Switzer snatched the gun out of Stiltz's hands and a shot was fired. Neither man was hit. Switzer forced Stiltz into a closet and shut the door. Switzer said that he was going to kill Stiltz if he did not get his money. Stiltz charged out of the closet and knocked the gun out of Switzer's hand. Stiltz grabbed the gun, but did not shoot right away. He claimed that Switzer then pulled out a knife and charged him. In self-defense, Stiltz pulled the trigger and shot Switzer in the chest.

Alfalfa was dead. Over a lost dog and a $50 bar tab.

10400 Columbus Avenue   Mission Hills

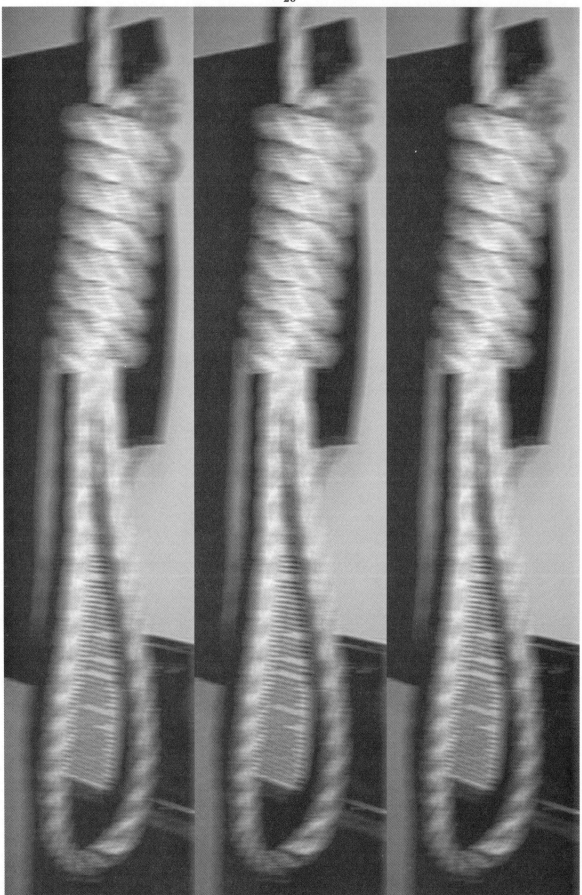

CHAPTER 2
SUICIDAL TENDENCIES

The pressure of being a celebrity can often seem overwhelming. The desire to make it big in Hollywood can consume an individual. Most "overnight" stars spent years attempting to reach the pantheon of success. The ability to maintain that level of success, especially in the midst of a fickle public, is a true challenge for many creative types. The inability to hold onto the public's adoration has driven many performers to despair. Sometimes, the pressure of success is too much for many of these creative souls to handle during their ascent to fame. Often, it is the end of a once blinding rise to the top that causes many celebrities to take their own lives.

RAY COMBS

In 1988, former Mormon missionary and standup comedian Ray Combs took over as host of the newly revived *Family Feud*. Combs stayed with the show for six years until the producers decided they needed to hire former host, Richard Dawson. Combs's firing was the beginning of the end.

After being forced off the *Feud*, Combs was involved in a devastating car wreck. He would constantly wince in pain from chronic disk problems as a result of the accident. In addition to physical pain, Combs suffered from financial hardship as well. Two comedy clubs that he owned in his former home state of Ohio went belly up. Finally, his marriage of 18 years to his wife, Debra, was on the rocks. She filed for divorce in 1995, they reconciled later that year, but she filed again the next year.

On June 2, 1996, the 40-year-old Combs called his wife. She claimed that her husband sounded delirious and morbid. He told her that he loved her and asked her to say goodbye to their six children for him.

Debra called the paramedics who took Combs to a hospital in Burbank. He was released into Debra's custody that same day. Upon leaving the hospital, Debra drove from the hospital to her home in Glendale. She stopped at a red light and Combs darted out of her car. He made it to the Ventura Freeway and hitched a ride. He later showed up at Debra's home, babbling incoherently. He was also bleeding from his forehead. He told his wife that he had fallen into a Jacuzzi.

fallen into a Jacuzzi.

Debra called the cops this time, and they escorted Combs to the Glendale Adventist Medical Center. Combs was placed on an intense 72-hour suicide watch.

It was not very effective.

At 4:00 AM the next morning, Combs took his bed sheet and made it into a noose. He hung himself in a closet.

Survey says? R.I.P.

DARBY CRASH

Darby Crash, frontman for the seminal Los Angeles punk rock band The Germs, was born Jean Paul Beahm in the suburb of Pomona. Bored with school, he formed the genesis for The Germs with high school buddy Pat Smear (Nirvana, Foo Fighters). Neither one knew how to play an instrument, but they were determined to form a punk rock band.

After a succession of Spinal Tap exiting drummers (including the former GoGos lead singer Belinda Carlisle), The Germs set out to terrorize L.A. club owners. Though they played poorly, their live shows were full of aggression and passion. Concert goers were never sure what the over-the-top Crash might do next—stick his mic in a jar of peanut butter, throw food at the audience, refuse to sing, or jump into the crowd, long before the moshpit became a concert staple.

The Germs were rude, crude, and obnoxious; and their fans loved them. As they played more often, they were able to make something close to coherent music with such anthems as "Manimal" and "Lexicon Devil."

By 1980, Darby took a flight to England. He returned a changed man. He had witnessed the ascent of Adam and the Ants, before anyone in the States had heard of them. Crash was especially fond of the Indian face paint favored by Adam. He also took on the three-feet high Mohawk look. The fans loved it.

Despite fan loyalty, The Germs never hit it big. To compound matters, Crash had a serious alcohol addiction and heroin problem. He could never fully shake his internal demons.

On December 6, 1980, just two weeks after The Germs' final show, Crash and a recent hanger-on named Casey Hopkins, AKA Casey Cola, decided to celebrate. They used the money from the final show to go on an alcohol and heroin binge. Cola and Crash both injected themselves with large amounts of heroin. Crash seemed to take more than Cola. They both passed out, overdosing on the drug. One problem: Crash never  woke up. He died in the garage in the back of his house at the age of 22.

Many of his friends believed it was an accident. Soon after his body was discovered, however, a note was found. It was a hastily scratched will bequeathing all of his worldly possessions to friends. He gave no reason for the suicide.

137 North Fuller Avenue Los Angeles

PEG ENTWISTLE

This little-known aspiring starlet has come to symbolize the dark side of Hollywood. Born in England in 1908, Lillian "Peg" Entwistle migrated to America and began a seemingly promising career on Broadway. After six years of success in the theater, she hit a bad spell during the 1931 season and decided to head west and try her luck in the film business.

Entwistle immediately landed a few bit roles in the movies as well as a contract with RKO Studios. Her first role for the company was in *The 13 Women*. Unfortunately, Entwistle's role hit the cutting room floor, and soon thereafter, the ungracious production house dropped her.

Feeling despondent over the sudden demise of her acting career, Entwistle opted to end it all. On September 18, 1932, she took off from her home directly beneath the Hollywood sign to make her final appearance. After making her way up the hillside, through the thick brush, Entwistle set out for one of the letters of the famous landmark. At the time, the sign spelled out HOLLYWOODLAND. Some claimed she headed straight for the "H," others claim that it was the second "D." Using a worker's ladder, she climbed up the backside of the letter and perched herself on top. On this particularly dark autumn night, she probably gazed at the City of Angels beneath her. More than likely, she realized it was a perfect place to commit suicide by leaping. According to her death certificate, she died from massive injuries suffered from a broken pelvis.

An anonymous female discovered Entwistle's personal belongings, wrapped them in a bundle, and left them on the Hollywood Police Department's front steps. The bundle contained a suicide note. It read, "I am afraid I am a coward. I am sorry for everything. If I had done this a long time ago, it would have saved a lot of pain. P.E."

The day after her death, her uncle opened a letter addressed to Peg. It was from the Beverly Hills Playhouse. They had offered her a lead role in a play. The story was about a woman driven over the edge, to the point of suicide.

The double irony is hard to escape.

Hollywood Sign Look for it...I think you'll find it

MARGAUX HEMINGWAY

Margaux Hemingway's parents named her after an expensive wine, which led to a night of passion and her creation. Granddaughter of one of America's greatest twentieth-century writers, Ernest Hemingway, Margaux was raised as a farm girl in Ketchum, Idaho. She would be spotted at the age of 17 and catapulted into the world of fashion modeling. Hemingway was the first model, before Cheryl Tiegs, Cindy Crawford, or Claudia Schiffer, to receive a million dollar contract.

She was gorgeous, easy-going, and not very talented.

Hemingway tried to expand her repertoire with acting. In 1976, she starred in the pathetic rape drama *Lipstick* and received across-the-board negative reviews. To make matters worse, her younger sister Mariel, who was cast in the movie by accident, received glowing reviews that led to a successful television and film career.

Margaux, by contrast, merely glowed on the club circuit. Her glimmer, however, would be blunted by excessive alcohol and drug usage. Too many late nights at the infamous Club 54 left her only asset in a sorry state. Hemingway also battled weight issues and the inevitable aging of her appearance. With no obvious acting talent, and a declining physical appearance, she fell into the ultimate model trap.

Hemingway tried to rejuvenate her sagging career by posing nude for *Playboy* magazine in 1990. The move did not pay off, however, and by 1994, she was working for a psychic hotline to make a buck.

On July 1, 1996, Hemingway finally seemed to be getting her act together. She landed a hosting role for the Discovery Channel show *Wild Animal* and had moved into a quaint little studio apartment near the beach in Santa Monica. Many of her friends and associates believed she had turned the corner. She had controlled her weight problem, looked trim and healthy, and had a positive outlook on life.

Thus, it was a surprise when her friend, Judy Stabile, began to worry about not hearing

139 Fraser Avenue Santa Monica

from Hemingway for a few days. Stabile finally stopped by Hemingway's apartment and knocked on her door. Not getting a response, she asked a couple of construction workers to see if they could help her. One of the workers used a ladder to peek into Hemingway's upstairs bedroom. He told Stabile that he saw a woman lying peacefully on the bed. They knocked on the door, but still received no answer. The men busted into her apartment and went upstairs. They discovered Hemingway lying in her bed. Dead. She was so badly decomposed that dental records were required to identify her.

Most of her friends pointed to her recent successes and believed she did not kill herself on purpose. Instead, her friends believed that she had probably taken too much of her epilepsy medicine and accidentally killed herself.

These friends seemed to forget the Hemingway legacy that was passed down to Margaux. On July 2, 1961, her grandfather, Ernest, stuck a shotgun to his head and exited the world. His brother, sister, and father had also committed suicide. This was not a new concept for the Hemingway clan. Her friends also failed to observe the significance of the date. Margaux had died on the eve of the 35th anniversary of her famous grandfather's suicide.

After several months of speculation, the coroner's office indeed confirmed that Margaux Hemingway had committed suicide. She had purposefully swallowed an excessive amount of Phenobarbital.

139 Fraser Avenue Santa Monica

BRIAN KEITH

This respected actor appeared in over 80 films and worked with such film industry stalwarts as Sam Peckinpah, Peter Bogdanovich, John Huston, Bette Davis, and Marlon Brando. Brian Keith, however, will forever be remembered as Uncle Bill on the television series, *Family Affair*.

Keith starred opposite two precocious child actors, Johnny Whitaker and Anissa Jones. Keith's role as the Manhattan bachelor/single father ran on CBS from 1966-1971. *Family Affair* was a Nielsen ratings bonanza, finishing as a Top Five rated show for three consecutive years.

By 1997, the coarse but lovable actor was caught in a downward spiral. He had been diagnosed with lung cancer and emphysema, despite having quit smoking ten years earlier. He was undergoing difficult chemotherapy treatments that constantly made him sick. Compounding matters, his daughter Daisy committed suicide in April. She had placed a gun to her head in her Hollywood Hills home and ended her life. Some reports also stated that Keith had suffered serious financial setbacks earlier that year.

The combination of a loss of a loved one, financial problems, and failing health seemed to contribute to Keith's last resort. On June 29, 1997, the 75-year-old actor placed a gun to his head in his luxurious Malibu Colony home and pulled the trigger. He died instantly.

Malibu Beach shoreline where Keith's home is located.

23449 Malibu Colony Road   Malibu

FREDDIE PRINZE

He was born Freddie Pruetzel on June 22, 1954 in the Bronx to parents of Puerto Rican and Hungarian ethnicities. Young Freddie grew up as a chubby, self-proclaimed "Hungarican." Though intelligent, he would only focus on things that excited him. The thing that excited him the most was laughter. Making others laugh. It was also a defense mechanism to keep bullies away.

Freddie parlayed his creative talents and comedic abilities into securing a slot in the New York City High School of the Performing Arts. His focus, however, shifted to the local nightclub comedy circuit. At the tender age of 15, Freddie was beginning to make a name for himself at some of the city's most famous clubs, such as The Improv.

He developed a Puerto Rican accent and a self-deprecating humor that had audiences eating out of his hand. He also became bored with school. By the time the Jack Parr television show asked him to perform, he was ready for bigger and better things. He changed his name to "Freddie Prinze" and became the self-proclaimed Prince of Comedy.

Prinze, only 17, was soon spotted by one of Johnny Carson's scouts and was asked to perform on the late-night talk show king's television program. This was Prinze's big break. He was whisked off to Los Angeles to perform live in front of millions of television viewers. What he did was unprecedented.

Prinze's five minutes were electrifying. He was so confident, funny, and likable that Carson waved the young comedian over to his couch. It was the first time that Carson had ever had a comedian come sit next to him and chat. Prinze leapt at the opportunity and continued to shine in his one-on-one with the legend.

Prinze's few minutes in the spotlight would open more doors than he could ever have imagined. Carson asked him back numerous times, and eventually, staffers at NBC would recognize the young comedian's talent. In 1974, Prinze was offered a co-starring role in *Chico and The Man*, opposite acting legend Jack Albertson.

While not the funniest show on the air, it was one of the most popular. *Chico and the Man* became an immediate hit, mainly due to the charm, humor, and good looks of Prinze. At the age of 20, Freddie Prinze had a Top Five rated television show. He was a star. His face graced the covers of numerous magazines, such as *People*, *US*, and *Rolling Stone*.

Chico and the Man also had sociological importance. Prinze's character was the only Hispanic lead role on a television series at the time. Though respected by many people, others resented Prinze for the same reason. Many viewers in the Mexican community were up in arms that a Puerto Rican, and not a Mexican, was playing the role.

Despite Prinze's happy-go-lucky nature, he also felt the pressures from the Hispanic community, the network brass, and his adoring fans. Women were crawling all over the young Latin stud. So were the drug fiends, who often populate the entertainment fringes, like pilot fish feeding off the detritus left over from sharks.

Prinze became addicted to the ladies and the pills. To overcome the female problem, he decided to settle down. He met a beautiful cocktail waitress named Kathy Cochran and quickly got hitched. Kathy became pregnant and gave birth to their only child, Freddie Prinze Jr.

Prinze, however, could not shake his other addiction.

Pills. Specifically, Quaaludes.

Prinze's love for the little monsters led to his break-up with Kathy. She filed for divorce, yet Freddie forged on. *Chico and the Man* was riding high. He also secured several high-profile gigs in Vegas, and he performed at the inauguration ball for then-President Jimmy Carter.

One month later, on January 28, 1977 at 3:00 AM, Prinze phoned up his manager "Dusty" Snyder from his West Los Angeles hotel room (at what is now known as the Beverly Hills Hotel Plaza). He told Snyder that the end was near and he was going to go out with a bang. Snyder rushed to Prinze's hotel room and confronted his obviously drug-altered client. Prinze invited Snyder inside and began to tell him that he was going to end it all. He wrote down what was considered to be his suicide note and handed it to his manager. Snyder got on the phone with Prinze's psychiatrist who assured him that Freddie was merely seeking attention and had been acting this way all week.

Prinze slipped into the bedroom to make a phone call of his own. Kathy Prinze claimed that Prinze said he was going to "end it all." When Prinze returned to the living room, he sat down on his couch across from Snyder. He reached under the sofa and pulled out a .38 caliber revolver. Snyder attempted to grab the weapon but retreated when Prinze waved the gun ominously towards him. Snyder again begged and pleaded for Prinze to put it away.

Prinze did not. He placed the large weapon next to his temple, looked Snyder in the eyes, and pulled the trigger. The walls of his apartment were spray-painted with blood and gore.

But Prinze was not dead.

10300 Wilshire Boulevard West Los Angeles

Snyder frantically called for help and Prinze was immediately rushed to the UCLA Medical Center. Prinze, however, was in a vegetative state and kept alive by machines. After more than 33 hours of artificial life, his family opted to pull the plug. Freddie Prinze had succumbed to a self-inflicted bullet wound to the head.

Initially ruled a suicide, court authorities went back to look at his death a few years later. Kathy Prinze was sure that her husband was in too good of spirits to have killed himself. Also, it was learned that Prinze had met with his secretary Carol Novak that same day and played a cruel trick on her.

When Novak arrived at the apartment earlier that day, Prinze smiled at her, pulled the same .38 caliber pistol from his waistband, and placed it against his head. As Novak helplessly looked on, Prinze pulled the trigger and flopped to the floor. Novak screamed as she saw Prinze's body spazzing on the floor. Prinze immediately broke up in heaving fits of laughter, elated that his prank had gone so well.

Upon hearing this evidence, the courts decided that Prinze had attempted another prank on Snyder when he unexpectedly ended his life. The combination of Quaaludes and firearms indeed proved lethal. Freddie Prinze's death certificate states that his cause of death was suicide. The courts, however, ruled that the young comedian's death was an accident.

10300 Wilshire Boulevard West Los Angeles

SAVANNAH

Savannah was the little farm girl who rose to the upper echelon of the porno industry, only to come crashing down.

Born Shannon Wilsey on October 9, 1971, she moved to Los Angeles to follow some of her favorite rock stars. A certifiable rock star groupie, Wilsey first hooked up with aging Southern-rock legend, Gregg Allman. She was 17, he was 42. Allman introduced her to the L.A. music scene, parties, and drugs. By the time their relationship ended, she was hooked on heroin. Wilsey soon would hook up with more rock stars including Billy Idol, Vince Neil of Mötley Crüe, and both Slash and Axl Rose from Guns 'N' Roses.

Wilsey loved to have sex—especially with longhaired rockers. She also needed to make a living. Her career choice—pornography. She began with still photography in men's magazines. Her flawless, model-like face won her several opportunities. People in the porn industry began to take notice. Eventually she would break into X-rated films and her career took off.

From 1991 to 1994, Wilsey made approximately 85 adult films. Her first screen name was Silver Kane. She would later change it to Savannah. Though usually considered to be a lackluster performer, Savannah's wholesome good looks thrust her to the top of the heap. She was soon making several thousands of dollars a day for her "acting."

Unfortunately, the star began to act like one. She was labeled the "Ice Queen" by her co-workers and fell out of favor with the powers that be. After riding high in the industry for over a year, Savannah soon found that her reputation preceded her and most filmmakers shied away from hiring her.

As a result, Savannah turned to the stage. Not theater—the traveling strip club circuit. Former porn stars often hit the road to pocket serious amounts of cash. Their work on celluloid can translate to big bucks in the topless clubs across the country. Most of the patrons of these fine establishments did not care about someone's attitude on a movie set—

3802 Multiview Drive Universal City

they wanted a pretty face, jacked-up tits, and the fantasy of being able to take home their favorite dancer at the end of the night.

Savannah had all of these qualities.

But she would lose them all on the night of July 11, 1994.

Savannah was gearing up for a cross-country trip to the Big Apple where she had a high-dollar stripping gig at Goldfinger's. While tooling around in the Hollywood Hills of Universal City, Savannah smashed head first into a pole. Reportedly she cut her face and broke her nose. The porn princess was shattered. She believed that the disfiguring accident would prevent her from attending the potential lucrative stint.

She contacted her manager, Nancy Pera, and began crying about the wreck. This was around 2:15 AM. Less than half an hour later, Pera showed up at Savannah's leased home. Fire trucks and paramedics were waiting when she arrived.

Savannah lay on the floor of the old garage in an ever-increasing pool of blood. She had placed a .45 caliber pistol, given to her by a friend for protection, to her right temple and squeezed the trigger. Her aim was far from perfect as she lay there, still breathing.

Savannah was rushed to St. Joseph's Medical Center in Burbank. Medical authorities could do nothing for the young beauty and placed her on a life-support system. Eight hours later, her father, who had not seen her in four years, gave the order to pull the plug.

3802 Multiview Drive Universal City

DEL SHANNON

Del Shannon was one of the most under-appreciated musical artists to come from the 60s and 70s. Fitting somewhere in the gap between Elvis Presley and The Beatles, Shannon made his mark by being a creative songwriter, diverse instrumentalist, and unique vocalist. Shannon wasn't a manager/label-made prefab teenybopper, but rather a multifaceted talent whose work was appreciated by fans and fellow musicians alike.

Born on December 30, 1934 as Charles Westover in Coopersville, Michigan, Shannon was a shy kid whose father hated musicians. His father's demand to get rid of his guitar only fueled his curiosity. Eventually, he became more than efficient on the six-string and began a series of barhopping gigs with piano player Max Crook. While in Michigan, Westover changed his name to Del Shannon and seriously embarked on a career as a musician.

It was a smart move.

In March of 1961, Shannon and Crook cooked up a unique ditty that would forever change Shannon's life. Together they penned the classic "Runaway." The song became a smash hit and stood tall at the top of the *Billboard* charts for four weeks. Over the next four years, Shannon would continue with a string of hits that included "Hats Off To Larry," "Keep Searchin'," and "Little Town Flirt." He was the first musician to record a Beatles cover with his 1963 version of "From Me To You," released before the Beatles blew up stateside.

By the late 1960s, however, Shannon's style of music was falling out of favor and his career seemed to fade into oblivion. He was also making good friends with the bottle. By 1979, Shannon checked himself into Alcoholics Anonymous. He was in his early forties.

The drying up session seemed to help as Shannon rebounded with a successful cover of Phil Phillips's "Sea of Love" in 1981. In 1986, producer Michael Mann commissioned Shannon to re-write his hit song "Runaway" for use on the television series *Crime Story.* The show, as well as Shannon's music, could be seen and heard every week through 1988.

Sadly, by 1990, Shannon had fought his demons and isolation for too long. On February 8, 1990, in his lovely Canyon Country estate, Shannon took a gun and placed it next to his temple. The 55-year-old musical legend pulled the trigger and ended his life.

15519 Saddleback Road Canyon Country

JASON THIRSK

Co-founder and bassist for the seminal Hermosa Beach punk-rock band Pennywise, Jason Thirsk was a positive contributing force to the indie rock pioneers. His contributions can be found on four albums including *Pennywise* and *Unknown Road*.

Despite his positive outlook on life and in his lyrics, Thirsk struggled with a dependency to alcohol. The freewheeling, partying lifestyle of the punk rock band caught up with the young bass player. In the summer of 1995, Thirsk left to sober up. He went to rehab several times, but he was unable to shake his addiction.

On July 29, 1996, the 27-year-old Thirsk was hanging out in the backyard of his Hermosa Beach home. According to police authorities, he had been drinking. While under the influence, he grabbed a small caliber pistol and began to shoot the weapon. He fired the gun towards his house, and the bullet went through his refrigerator. He then turned the weapon on himself, firing a bullet into his chest. He bled to death.

While police and the coroner's office ruled Thirsk's death a suicide, the members of Pennywise disagree. They believed that Thirsk was turning his life around and was actually happy. Guitarist Fletcher Dragge pointed out that Thirsk had taken his bass in for repairs that day and was heading out to the river with his girlfriend the following day.

Dragge further elaborated when he said, "It's not like he shot himself in the head or wrote a suicide note. If you knew how he partied, then you know when he gets hammered, he's the kind of guy who would fall off a balcony backwards. So it's pretty conceivable that it was an accident."

How comforting.

1214 Bonnie Brae Street Hermosa Beach

HERVE VILLECHAIZE

"I dread dying. But I will die. In not too many tomorrows." - Herve Villechaize

Herve Villechaize, best known as the diminutive sidekick to island entrepreneur Mr. Roarke on ABC television's *Fantasy Island*, was born in Paris. He began his artistic career as a painter and soon shuttled overseas to New York City at the age of 20 to pursue his painting. He became embroiled in the art world and branched out into acting in a series of off-Broadway plays.

The 3'11" Villechaize got his big acting break when he played the role of Nick Nack, a conspiratorial henchman of Christopher Lee's in the 1974 James Bond thriller, *The Man With The Golden Gun*. His success in the romp led to his break for which he was most well known—Tattoo.

Villechaize played the hoarse-voiced right hand man on *Fantasy Island* from 1978 until 1983. The show was a winsome addition that aired after that other definitive 70s series, *The Love Boat*. Villechaize became a pop-cultural icon with his weekly opening catch phrase, "De plane! De plane!," which greeted each of its celebrity guests.

By 1983, Villechaize sought more money for the role, but was turned down by the show's creator, Aaron Spelling. He was let go that same year. The show would never be the same without Tattoo and was cancelled the following season.

Unfortunately for Villechaize, the need for vertically-challenged, French-accented actors was not abundant. He was limited to minimal roles in B-flicks and eventually to commercials that played down to his small stature. The most memorable commercial was a Dunkin' Donuts ad wherein Villechaize pointed at the donut counter and when asked what kind of donut

11537 West Killion Street North Hollywood

he wanted responded, "De plain! De plain!"

After *Fantasy Island*, Villechaize developed a fascination for guns and drugs. Unlike most of the other stars in this book, Villechaize's drug addiction came as a result of chronic pain. As a young boy, he was poked and prodded by numerous doctors. His small size led to numerous physical impairments, both externally and internally. By the early 90s, he had suffered a few minor strokes, massive ulcers, a spastic colon, and a near fatal bout with pneumonia.

On September 4, 1993, Villechaize decided he could not take the pain anymore. He went to the movies to see Harrison Ford in *The Fugitive*. He then returned to his modest home, grabbed a gun, and headed out to the small, cluttered backyard. He sat down on the patio in front of the back window and placed the gun to his chest. He squeezed the trigger and keeled over.

Villechaize was later discovered by his common-law wife and rushed to Medical Center of North Hollywood. At 3:40 PM, he passed away at the age of 50.

11537 West Killion Street North Hollywood

JAMES WHALE

The director of the horror classics *The Invisible Man*, *Frankenstein*, and *Bride of Frankenstein* was born in Dudley, England on July 22, 1889. James Whale was a frail man, who hated hard labor, yet he fought in the First World War for his country. After being captured and imprisoned for 15 months, he was released. He turned to the arts and his life changed forever.

By 1929, his anti-war play *Journey's End* had become an internationally sought-after piece that would be translated into 29 languages. One of those countries that came calling was the United States.

Broadway. James Whale was headed for the big time.

The Broadway version of his play was a huge success and opened the doors to Hollywood. By 1930, Whale was ensconced in Los Angeles, ready to make his big-screen debut for Universal Studios. The film, *Journey's End*, proved profitable and opened even more doors. He soon directed some of the most revered horror film classics ever committed to celluloid.

After Whale's string of horror hits, he moved into non-genre fare, including the classic film *Show Boat*. By 1937, the existing regime at Universal moved out and with it, Whale's clout disappeared. He was offered what he considered to be inferior scripts and lost any directorial control on his films. He decided that enough was enough and left the film business in 1949. He retired to his home and focused on his painting.

During Whale's success in Hollywood, he also became rather notorious for his openly gay lifestyle. In 1930, he met and moved actor David Wells into his Pacific Palisades home. The two lived together for more than 20 years, although it was considered a taboo relationship at the time.

788 Amalfi Drive Pacific Palisades

In 1951, Whale met a man by the name of Pierre Foegel while on a trip to Europe. He brought Foegel home with him, kicked Wells out, and set up his new lover with a gas station. The two men lived together for the next six years.

In 1956, Whale suffered a debilitating stroke that left him without the ability to draw or read. He became despondent over his physical condition. On Memorial Day, May 29, 1957, Whale woke up, showered and shaved, and penned a two-sided note claiming that he was tired of his poor condition and ready to end it all. He got dressed and walked out to the backyard of his home. He then dove headfirst into the shallow end of the pool, apparently knocking himself unconscious. Despite having a pool in his backyard, Whale could not swim.

Upon discovery of his body, the coroner's office noted that only a small abrasion appeared on the director's forehead, indicating that his swansong dive probably did not knock him out. The coroner concluded that Whale had purposefully swallowed copious amounts of water that filled his lungs and led to his drowning.

Whale left a rather whimsical, yet morbid touch to his final production. On the nightstand, next to his bed, was a book. Its title: *Don't Go Near The Water*.

788 Amalfi Drive Pacific Palisades

ROZZ WILLIAMS

Born Roger Allen Painter in the Los Angeles suburb of Pomona, Rozz Williams is often referred to as the Grandfather of Goth Rock. Williams founded the group Christian Death at the tender age of 16 and went on to underground acclaim and adulation in the United States and especially in Europe.

Christian Death, which rose from the ashes of T-Rex, Joy Division, and punk rock, had often been cited as a major influence on rockers such as Trent Reznor of Nine Inch Nails and Marilyn Manson. Williams's image was enhanced by his fiery cross-dressing apparel, dramatic face paint, and heretical onstage behavior.

Christian Death's first album was *Only Theatre of Pain*, which was recorded in 1982. The original band would break up as soon as the record hit the shelves. One year later, a band known as Pompeii 99 approached Williams. They wanted to join forces with Rozz as the new Christian Death. They would go on to record such seminal Goth classics as *Catastrophe Ballet* and *Ashes*. Christian Death, however, never made it to a huge level of mainstream success, and this new line-up eventually disbanded.

Williams felt somewhat trapped in his own creation. He believed that many of the followers of the Goth scene were adamant about never expanding themselves. Williams wanted to break the stereotypical Goth mold and experiment with his craft. He created several side projects such as Premature Ejaculation, Heltir, and Dream Home Heartache. He also recorded an album of spoken word material.

In the early 1990s, Christian Death experienced a resurrection when indie label Cleopatra Records re-issued their early recordings. Williams would reform the band and release one

1208 N. Fuller Avenue West Hollywood

more album of new material. He would, however, continue with his side-projects, including Shadow Project, which he created with his former wife Eva O.

On April 1, 1998, April Fool's Day, Williams's roommate found him hanging in his closet in his West Hollywood apartment. There was no note. Most of his friends acknowledged that he had battled a heroin addiction for years and that he loved his booze. No one, however, sensed that he was in a bad state of mind.

Rozz Williams was 34 years old.

Small closet door from which Williams hung himself.

The actual door is on display at the Museum of Death.

1208 N. Fuller Avenue West Hollywood

CHAPTER 3
CHEMICAL
IMBALANCE

Drugs and alcohol. The fuel for creative expression or the destroyer of one's soul? Hollywood provides an interesting backdrop for the question of illicit substances and how they help or hinder the mind of a creative individual. Unfortunately, too many performers have met an early end to their lives with an overindulgence of drugs or alcohol. Whether they passed on because of an actual overdose of a chemical, or were assisted in their deaths due to a severe state of intoxication that led to an accident, many artists cannot seem to steer clear of mind-altering substances.

JOHN BELUSHI

In 1978, *Saturday Night Live* featured a short film that starred John Belushi entitled *Don't Look Back in Anger*. In the short, Belushi played a septuagenarian who visits the graves of all of his fellow cast members from the legendary comedy show at the Not Ready For Prime Time Cemetery. Belushi chuckled as he recalled that his fellow actors thought he would go first, because "I was one of those live-fast, die-young, leave-a-good-looking-corpse types. But I guess they were wrong."

The fact that Belushi would even be considered an over-the-top kind of guy is unusual given his background. He was born on January 24, 1949 in Chicago, Illinois to Adam and Agnes Belushi. His father, who migrated from Albania, owned and operated two restaurants that everyone assumed John would take over. John, however, was more interested in sports than serving lunches and avidly pursued a career in football. To keep in peak physical shape, he steered clear of any and all illicit substances: no smoking, no drinking, no hard drugs. He was a determined, aggressive young man who knew he would be successful at whatever he pursued.

Belushi was so talented at football that he received a scholarship offer from Western Illinois. He was conflicted, however, because he had recently performed in a musical and fell in love with the thought of becoming an actor. He was so passionate about acting that he turned down the football scholarship and enrolled instead at Illinois Wesleyan. Belushi then bounced around to two more colleges until he earned an Associate Arts Degree in General Studies from the College of Dupage in 1970.

While in college, Belushi also received an additional form of education. The sheltered, clean-living former jock discovered the so-called virtues of alcohol. His time spent partying increased and he often became the center of attention at group gatherings. He also understood the power of making people laugh—and he was good at it.

After graduation, Belushi turned down an offer from his father to take over the restaurants. Instead, he auditioned for the Chicago-based comic troupe Second City. He had been working on a killer imitation of then musical superstar Joe Cocker, complete with facial tics and excessive body twitches, and won over the bosses of Second City. He was hired on the spot and became the youngest performer of the group as well as the youngest to ever make it to their main stage.

The work was hard—six days a week—and the partying was harder. Belushi cozied up to such fellow performers as Harold Ramis and Christopher Guest and experimented to his heart's fullest content. He dabbled into more than just booze; marijuana, LSD, mushrooms, and speed became a part of his repertoire. Amazingly, the drugs did not seem to have a negative impact on his work. Belushi was constantly stealing the limelight from the other performers with his manic energy, his arching eyebrows, and a charisma that seemed to latch onto anyone who was in the same room.

Eventually, Belushi sought even greener pastures. He found them in New York City. In 1972, *National Lampoon*'s Tony Hendra (the manager in *This Is Spinal Tap*) was informed about the brilliant kid from the Windy City. Belushi was perfect for Hendra's Off-Broadway production of *Lemmings*, a scathing satire of the hippie-generation of Woodstock. Hendra was blown away by Belushi's Cocker imitation and knew he would be perfect for the role. He was. Another rising comedian joined Belushi on the stage; his name was Chevy Chase. *Lemmings* lasted more than a year and further thrust the blustery Belushi into the limelight.

A little over a year after the end of *Lemmings*, John Belushi got the break he had worked so hard for. He was asked to audition for a new live television sketch show that was to air on NBC. It was to be called *Saturday Night Live*. He was excited about his prospects, not only because he knew he was funny, but also because Chase had already been hired as a cast member. If Chase could get the job, Belushi knew he was a shoo-in. Producer Lorne Michaels, however, was reluctant to hire Belushi because he thought he was too loud, obnoxious, and arrogant. Indeed, on the day of Belushi's audition, Michaels made the former footballer wait for hours before allowing him to perform. Coiled up with anxiety, Belushi felt he was getting the shaft. He was about to explode when he finally got his call. He then donned a bathrobe, grabbed a stick, tied his hair up in a topknot, and became the "Samurai Warrior." He blew everyone away, especially Michaels, and was given the job on the spot.

Belushi created some of the most memorable characters of the show's history during his four-year stint: Elizabeth Taylor choking on a chicken bone, a killer bee (which he despised), the Greek hamburger cook, Mozart, and The Thing That Wouldn't Leave.

He also created an amazing character on the big screen. As John "Bluto" Blutarski in 1978's *National Lampoon's Animal House*, Belushi helped define college life for many restless and clueless young Americans with his brilliant performance as Bluto. The role made Belushi a star.

Belushi's stature was raised to an even higher level when he and fellow *SNL* player Dan Aykroyd created the mythological characters of Jake and Elwood Blues AKA "The Blues Brothers." Their appearance on *SNL* led to a record deal and eventually a Number One album.

Belushi was riding high. He had the top-rated late night television show, the Number One movie in America, and the Number One album in the country. Nothing could stop him— nothing except his ego and a lust for drugs.

8221 Sunset Blvd., Bungalow #3, West Hollywood

After the fourth season of the show and the release of the full-length feature movie, *The Blues Brothers*, Belushi and Aykroyd decided to leave *SNL*. They wanted to become even bigger stars. It turned out to be a horrible choice.

The Blues Brothers movie had under-performed. Both actors also appeared in the Steven Spielberg debacle, *1941*, which was a huge flop. Belushi then tried his hand at a serious drama in *Continental Divide*, which was also a disaster. The two then re-teamed for *Neighbors* in which Aykroyd would play the conservative neighbor who was pushed over the edge by Belushi's obnoxious counterpart. It sounded good on paper, but the two actors decided to switch roles right before filming started. The switch proved disastrous and, once again, the film bombed.

As Belushi tried to establish a film career, he continued to battle drugs and alcohol. He would get loaded and then swear off drugs altogether. Simultaneously, his weight ballooned up to ridiculous proportions. He cut back on his food and worked with a fitness expert, who even got him off drugs for over a year.

By 1982, Belushi lost control. He had been peddling an inferior punk rock script around town called *Noble Rot*. It was poorly written, and most people offered to work with him on it hoping to get something better out of him later. Belushi was desperately trying to make a stab at a serious film career. Instead of working harder as he used to in his younger days, Belushi turned back to drugs. He began hanging out with a less than savory crowd as well—namely, one Cathy Smith, a former back-up singer for The Band, who had become a strung out addict and drug dealer.

On March 4, 1982, Belushi, Smith, and former *SNL* writer Nelson Lyon spent the evening partying together. The trio ingested massive quantities of liquor and snorted even larger quantities of cocaine. They stumbled all over West Hollywood looking for the next party and ended up at the secret nightclub above The Roxy called On The Rox. From there, they walked next door to The Rainbow Room and ate. Belushi began to feel nauseous and asked Smith to take him back to his room at the Chateau Marmont.

According to Smith, Belushi asked her to shoot him up with a needle full of drugs several times that night. Belushi, who was deathly afraid of needles, seemed to like the high, she claimed. While the couple sat around in a dazed state, two famous persons stopped by to see them. Comedian Robin Williams popped in and snorted a few lines of coke, but was creeped out by Smith. He thought she was a little too crusty for Belushi and wondered what he was doing with this lowlife. Williams bolted and told Belushi, "If you ever get up again, call." Sometime after 3:00 AM, actor Robert DeNiro knocked on Belushi's door. He had been playing tag with Belushi all night. The scene inside the room was not pretty, so DeNiro decided to not stick around.

Belushi and Smith continued to shoot up until Smith decided she had to leave. She helped Belushi shower and put him to bed before taking off in his Mercedes. She noticed on the way out that he was breathing funny.

8221 Sunset Blvd., Bungalow #3, West Hollywood

The next morning, Belushi's personal trainer, Bill "Superfoot" Wallace, attempted to check on his friend. When he received no answer on the telephone, he went over to Belushi's bungalow. Inside, he found his friend

in the fetal position on the bed, sheets twisted, and a pillow over his head. When Wallace threw the pillow aside, he saw Belushi's tongue sticking out of his mouth and a horrid discoloration of his body on one side where all of his blood had settled. Wallace attempted to resuscitate Belushi but to no avail. Belushi was dead.

The official coroner's report stated that John Belushi died from "acute cocaine and heroin intoxication." He was only 33 years old.

Cathy Smith was arrested and charged with first-degree murder for her role in the injection of the lethal doses that killed Belushi. She later bargained down to manslaughter and spent 18 months behind bars.

CURSE?

Some people claim that Saturday Night Live *is cursed. In addition to John Belushi, other* SNL *cast members have met untimely deaths:*

Gilda Radner (1946-1989) Original cast member known for her roles as the angry old newscaster Emily Litella and the politically incorrect Italian Roseanne Roseannadanna. Married to actor Gene Wilder. Died of ovarian cancer at the age of 42 on May 20, 1989.

Chris Farley (1964-1997) Larger-than-life comedian known for his roles as motivational speaker Matt Foley and the "finger quote" guy before he made the transition to the big screen. Farley, like his idol Belushi, died at the age of 33. His body was found in his 60th floor apartment of the John Hancock building in Chicago on December 18, 1997, where he overdosed on cocaine and booze.

Phil Hartman (1948-1998) One of *SNL*'s most talented and versatile actors known for his uncanny impersonation of Frank Sinatra and hundreds more characters. Also starred on the modest hit sitcom *NewsRadio*, and provided the voices for several characters on the wildly popular animated sitcom *The Simpsons*. Murdered by his wife Brynn Hartman with a shotgun in his Encino home on May 28, 1998 (see p. 9).

8221 Sunset Blvd., Bungalow #3, West Hollywood

LENNY BRUCE

On the evening of August 3, 1966, several police officers and reporters carelessly stepped over the lifeless body of 40-year-old comedian and satirist Lenny Bruce. Photographers' flashbulbs popped as they captured the harrowing vision of Bruce's naked corpse, lying still on the bathroom floor next to a toilet, a sash around his arm, and a box of syringes near his hand. The authorities had him right where they wanted him, and they were not afraid to display the gruesome spectacle to the world. They were almost gleeful.

But why?

Lenny Bruce was born on October 13, 1925 as Leonard Alfred Schneider near Long Island, New York. His father, Mickey Schneider, was a successful podiatrist. His mother, Sadie Kitchenberg, was a dancer and later comedienne who went by the stage name of Sally Marr. Lenny's parents divorced when he was eight years old, and he began a roller coaster experience of entertainment with his bawdy, but intelligent mother.

Marr introduced young Lenny to burlesque and jazz, and the people involved in those worlds became his greatest influences. At the age of 18, Bruce enlisted in the Navy on October 19, 1942. Three years later, he was sick of the restrictive lifestyle of the military, so he claimed to have an affinity for women's clothes and also that the idea of homosexuality was intriguing. His superiors suggested that he leave.

Upon his dismissal from the armed forces, Bruce turned to comedy. He started off like any regular hack comic with his humor revolving around impressions and lame mother-in-law jokes. Despite his inauspicious debut, he did catch the eye of several influential media figures, including Arthur Godfrey and later Steve Allen.

Bruce began to change his routine, as he felt compelled to discuss his views of life around him. For five years, he honed his skills on the strip club circuit where he was required to bring the girls on stage. Despite the poor pay and the worse audience reaction, Bruce relished his role, because he knew he could say whatever the hell he wanted. No one was looking at the puffy-eyed Jewish kid with the dirty mouth; they just wanted naked female flesh.

In 1951, Bruce met and married stripper Honey Harlow. After two years, he convinced her to stop shedding her clothes and to concentrate on becoming an actress. Bruce was determined that he and his wife succeed as entertainers, so he packed up all of their possessions and headed to Hollywood. While in Tinseltown, he tried his hand at screenwriting and acting, but he failed miserably.

8825 Hollywood Blvd. Hollywood Hills

He was good at telling the truth and doing it with a wicked sense of humor. He was becoming known as a "sick" humorist and people began to pay attention—not just club owners and club patrons but the authorities as well. Bruce's routines had taken on serious topics such as racism, drug use, religion, and hypocrisy. He developed a devoted following of people who respected his insightful humor and his ability to address any subject, no matter how risqué or controversial.

He also began to experience problems with Honey. Though he dabbled in drugs, his wife became a full-blown heroin junkie. Even the birth in 1955 of the couple's beautiful daughter, Kitty, did not slow Honey's drug habit. By 1957, the problems between the two were beyond repair. They divorced and Bruce retained full custody of their daughter.

Instead of staying home and taking care of his daughter, Bruce took his act on the road. He became even more vitriolic as he mixed his personal anger with his astute, razor-sharp observations of society. He became a hit. He was booked all across the country and opened minds wherever he went. He also upset a lot of people.

In 1961, he was arrested at the Jazz Workshop in San Francisco for violating the California Obscenity Code. Someone objected to his use of the word "cocksucker" and filed a complaint. He was later acquitted of all charges.

A year later, he was arrested at The Troubadour (9081 Santa Monica Boulevard) in West Hollywood for obscenity. Once again, he was acquitted. Two months later, he was arrested for obscenity at the Gate of Horn club in Chicago, Illinois.

By now, Lenny Bruce was a pariah. The authorities had it out for him, not so much for the curse words he used, but for the scathing insights he provided on the hypocrisy of certain groups in the United States. In 1964, Bruce found it harder to get a gig. Club owners feared that if they booked him, they would lose their liquor licenses. He found it harder and harder to make money doing what he loved to do.

He did, however, get booked at Café Au Go Go in New York City in April of 1964. Unfortunately for Bruce, the authorities had been following his every move. He had been arrested 15 times in the last two years, and they were not about to back off. Bruce played to a packed house that also included undercover police. After the show, he was arrested yet again for violating the obscenity laws of New York.

Bruce's mounting legal fees nearly bankrupted him. In 1965, after his 40th birthday, he asked the courts in San Francisco to declare him a pauper. He claimed that he only made $2,000 that year due to the unwillingness of club owners to book him. Despite his shattered financial circumstances, Bruce became single-minded in his obsession with his case. He began to pour over legal texts and became an expert on freedom of speech rights. When he was able to work, he would bore his audiences by reading from the transcripts of his numerous legal fights. He was obsessed.

Poor, frustrated, and addicted to drugs, Lenny Bruce seemed to run out of options. On August 3, 1966, Bruce had a small group of friends over to his home in the Hollywood Hills. The home was the only thing that he maintained from his years as a comedian. It

8825 Hollywood Blvd. Hollywood Hills

had once been his castle. It had become his fortress. When he stayed there, he was able to keep the outside world away. It is also where he shot himself up with heroin.

Apparently, Bruce's friends all left at the same point during the day to run various errands. When they returned hours later, John Judnich and Bob Balliet could not find Bruce. They looked all over until they found him in his bathroom. Lenny Bruce lay sprawled on the floor, naked. Mucus had run out of his nose. He was not breathing.

When the police eventually arrived, they provided no sense of decorum at the scene. Although they cordoned off the lot to outsiders, they still allowed a number of reporters and photographers to traipse around the house. Police escorted two reporters at a time into the bathroom to document the death scene of one of the most brilliant satirists who had ever lived. The man who influenced generations of comics such as George Carlin, Richard Pryor, Cheech and Chong, Eddie Murphy, Sam Kinison, Dennis Leary, Dennis Miller, Bill Hicks, Chris Rock, and Carlos Mencia was merely treated as a warning to all who dared to stand up to authority. The picture of Bruce's naked corpse was bandied about all across America as some sort of twisted moral lesson.

The real joke came two years later. Lenny Bruce was vindicated in his New York obscenity case when a jury found that he was not guilty of violating any laws. In death, Bruce won the biggest court battle of his life.

The official coroner's report stated that Bruce died from an overdose of heroin. His friend and legendary record producer Phil Spector cited another culprit. He claimed that the revolutionary comedian died from "an overdose of cops."

8825 Hollywood Blvd. Hollywood Hills

DOROTHY DANDRIDGE

This classic beauty was a rarity in her time: a major black sex symbol. But Dorothy Dandridge possessed more than just good looks. She could dance, sing, and act. She burst onto the entertainment scene with the Dandridge Sisters and performed regularly at the Cotton Club.

Dandridge got her first big break in the film industry with a role in the 1937 Marx Brothers classic, *A Day At The Races*. She later achieved critical acclaim in two of director Otto Preminger's greatest films: *Porgy & Bess* and the all-black musical *Carmen Jones*, for which she received an Academy Award Best Actress nomination. She was the first African-American woman to receive a Best Actress Oscar nod.

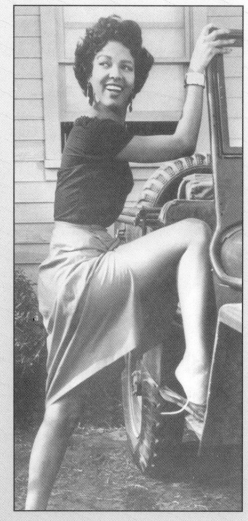

As is so often the case in Hollywood, Dandridge's career declined with her increasing age. After *Porgy & Bess* in 1959, her phone quit ringing. By 1965, however, Dandridge's career seemed to be on the rebound. She had met with producers in Mexico about two new films and had a series of singing engagements booked at New York's famous nightclub Basin Street East. On September 8, 1965, Dandridge was set to fly out to the Big Apple for that gig, but she never made it.

Dandridge's manager Earl Mills attempted to call her twice that morning. Fearing the worst, he rushed to her apartment. He found Dandridge's door unlocked, but the chain was still latched. Unable to enter, Mills broke the chain with a tire iron and let himself in.

What he found mortified him.

Dorothy Dandridge's body was lying facedown on her bathroom floor. Except for a blue scarf that adorned her head, she was completely nude.

A controversy surrounded the cause of Dandridge's death. Just one week earlier, Dandridge

8495 Fountain Ave. #D2 West Hollywood

tripped while exercising and fractured her toe. This information was enough to convince a Los Angeles Medical Examiner to officially declare that Dandridge had died as an indirect result of this accident. He claimed that fat from the fractured toe had created a blood clot that raced to Dandridge's brain and caused an embolism, killing her.

But this was before the Los Angeles Coroner's Office had sufficient toxicological examination equipment. Subsequent tests conducted on Dandridge's internal organs disputed the embolism finding. Results showed a trace amount of a new drug, Tofranil, which she had taken for depression. With this new information, some officials believed there was

sufficient evidence to claim that Dandridge had overdosed. Others believed there was not enough of the drug in her system to actually kill her.

One more aspect compounded the mystery of the death of Dorothy Dandridge. Six months earlier she sent a sealed note to Mills. After her death, he opened the envelope and was stunned by what it said. "In case of my death–to whoever discovers it–don't remove anything I have on–scarf, gown, or underwear–cremate me right away..."

Dandridge had $2.14 in her bank account when she died.

WILLIAM HOLDEN

William Holden defined the essence of the macho actor with roles in such famous movies as *The Bridge on the River Kwai* and *Stalag 17*. He could not, however, control one weakness—alcohol.

Holden was born William Franklin Beedle Jr. on April 17, 1918 in O'Fallon, Illinois. His family moved to California, and by 1938, at the age of 20, Holden graced the Pasadena Work-shop Theater stage. He was spotted by a talent scout from Paramount and was soon making movies. The following year he starred in *Golden Boy* with silent film star legend Barbara Stanwyck. She took the aspiring actor under her tutelage and helped him become a house-hold name.

Holden made a number of movies until World War II broke out. He enlisted and served from 1942 until the end of the war in 1945. When he returned, it took eight months for him to land a role. But when he did, he blossomed.

Holden's breakthrough role came in 1950 in the Hollywood-skewering film, *Sunset Boulevard*, directed by Billy Wilder. He followed that success with his Oscar-winning role in *Stalag 17*. Holden would work in over 80 films including *The Wild Bunch*, *The Towering Inferno*, *Network*, *Damien: Omen II*, and his final film, *S.O.B.*

Many people thought Holden was an SOB. In reality, he was a man who enjoyed his privacy. His desire for solitude, however, may have contributed to his death. Holden's body was found in his Shorecliff Towers apartment on November 16, 1981. He had a two-and-a-half inch gash on his forehead and pools of blood around his body. His apartment was immaculately kept, so only a few clues were necessary to determine that Holden had died from a drunken fall.

Holden apparently had drunk an entire bottle of vodka and was working on a second one. He then slipped on a throw rug in his bedroom and fell face first into a coffee table. The impact was so strong that it wedged the heavy wooden table into the wall. Despite the hard

535 Ocean Avenue #43 Santa Monica

impact, Holden remained conscious. Lying next to his body were eight bloody tissues. The coroner's report concluded that Holden had used the tissues in an attempt to stop the bleeding.

Holden's desire for privacy may have been the reason why he did not use the telephone right next to him. He hated the tabloids and did everything in his power to keep his name out

of them. If he called 911, Holden may have feared that the call would air over a police scanner and be picked up by tabloid reporters. The coroner's report estimates that Holden lived for at least 30 minutes after his fall, plenty of time for medical assistance to arrive. However, in his inebriated state, Holden must have concluded that it was more important to maintain his privacy than to seek help.

It was a fatal choice. William Holden bled to death.

The actor's body was not discovered for four days. By the time the apartment manager located Holden, he was in an advanced state of decomposition, with maggots rearing their ugly heads.

It seems unusual that no one noticed that a world-renowned actor was not around, especially his girlfriend, actress Stephanie Powers. Her *Hart to Hart* co-star Robert Wagner comforted her, but the consolation was short-lived. Ten days after the discovery of Holden's body, Wagner's wife, Natalie Wood, drowned off the shores of Catalina Island (see p. 114).

535 Ocean Avenue #43 Santa Monica

JANIS JOPLIN

"Freedom's just another word for nothing left to lose." – from *"Me and Bobby McGee"*

Born in the Golden Triangle of Port Arthur, Texas, Janis Joplin was an intelligent, creative child who grew up into an ugly duckling. By the age of 14, Joplin developed severe acne that left her exterior pockmarked and, many believe, her interior as well. The Port Arthur kids were tough and rejected Joplin.

She thought she would have the last laugh.

Once rejected, she decided to reject the "normal society." Joplin, who spent many of her teenage days crossing over the Louisiana border to hear the Cajun bands and blues cover artists, set out to find herself. She headed out west—first to Houston, then Los Angeles, then came back to Austin, Texas. Joplin realized she had one hell of a voice and worked on it endlessly.

By 1966, the year before the Summer of Love, Joplin headed back to California. She hooked up with Chet Helms, who introduced her to the San Francisco band Big Brother and the Holding Company. She auditioned for the lead singer spot and got the gig. Big Brother soon became the house band at the historical Avalon Theater.

One year later, Janis Joplin became a star. Big Brother graced the stage at the Monterey Pop Festival in Monterey, California. In front of 250,000 people, Joplin cast a spell with a spirit-invoking performance. Clad in velvet, with necklaces and bangles dangling from every inch of her body, she exploded like a whirling dervish. Her energy was unavoidable. Now, everyone wanted a little piece of Janis Joplin.

One of her suitors was Columbia/CBS Records. They signed Joplin and Big Brother to a

7047 Franklin Avenue #105 Hollywood

lucrative contract (to this day, Columbia will not reveal the amount of money involved). Joplin and Big Brother's first major label release, *Cheap Thrills*, was considered a bust. Even though it graced the top of the *Billboard* charts for several weeks, the label did not see enough sales to warrant the pricey advance paid for it. More importantly, Joplin believed the record was a failure. Her Monterey Pop experience opened her eyes to the power she held within her vocal chords. She complained that Big Brother was holding her back, fighting against her musically instead of providing the canvas for which her voice could paint perfection. So, Janis fired Big Brother and sought out greener musical pastures.

Her salvation was found in the hands of her new band, The Kozmic Blues Band. They recorded the album *I Got Dem Ol' Kozmic Blues Again Mama*, which featured the classic "Try (Just A Little Bit Harder)." Joplin, however, was still not satisfied with her life. While on stage, she became unbridled, human fury—passionate, sexual, and untamed. She was the Goddess of Rock. Offstage, she was riddled with insecurities about her looks and taunted about her sexuality. To compensate for the pain, she turned to drugs; her chemicals of choice were booze and heroin. She had a continual love-hate relationship with these drugs, often heading in and out of rehabs.

Still unsatisfied musically, Joplin again sought an upgrade in her backing band. She believed that she truly found the right musicians known as the Full-Tilt Boogie Band. Elated with her new band, Joplin once again stopped using smack. She was excited about recording a new album that would truly showcase her talents. Joplin and the band headed down to Los Angeles to record *Pearl*. The album's title came from the affectionate nickname given to Joplin by her closest friends.

Joplin's sobriety did not last long. She returned to heroin and drank extensively. During the recording of *Pearl*, the Full-Tilt guys commented that Joplin was always prepared and never showed up stoned. She was a relentless perfectionist who constantly rehearsed and knew exactly what to do when she recorded. They later discovered that she would wait until after the demanding recording sessions to shoot up. Joplin would usually head to her hotel room #105 at the Landmark Hotel to take her drugs.

On October 3, 1970, with just a few weeks of recording left, Joplin left the studio. She downed a few drinks at Barney's Beanery on Santa Monica Boulevard before returning to her temporary home at the Landmark Hotel (now known as Highland Gardens). She entered her tiny, plastered-wall hotel room and pulled out her ever-present hypodermic needle kit. Joplin injected herself using a method known as skin-popping, which works slower than an intravenous injection. A normal intravenous injection sends the drugs directly into the user's veins and causes an instant high. With skin-popping, the drug enters the skin and takes its time to find the appropriate receptacle. The high takes roughly 90 minutes before it takes affect.

While waiting for the heroin to kick in, Joplin went to the lobby,

Highland Gardens HOTEL 7047 Franklin Ave.

bought a pack of smokes, and said "Hello" to the nighttime clerk. He did not notice anything wrong with her. Joplin then returned to her room and stripped down to her panties and a T-shirt. What happened next is mere speculation. The coroner's report indicated that the drug must have kicked in and caught her off guard. Joplin fell forward, cracking her nose on the dresser. Her body was not found until the next day, almost 18 hours after she had died. She was wedged between the dresser and the bed, facedown; blood from her nose had dried on her face.

Joplin had always bought heroin from the same dealer every time she used. He was discreet and careful, using a chemist to check the purity of his drugs. On the weekend he sold this last hit to Joplin, his chemist had gone on vacation. The batch of heroin was nearly 40-50% pure, too strong for most users to withstand. In addition to Joplin, several of the dealer's other clients also passed away that weekend.

The Full-Tilt Boogie Band was stunned by Joplin's death. They decided, however, to forge onward with the album, since Joplin had already laid down several vocal tracks. The band spent two more weeks finishing *Pearl*. It is now considered her most successful commercial and artistic achievement. The album spawned such hits as "My Baby," "Mercedes Benz," "Trust Me," and the rock-classic "Me and Bobby McGee."

Coincidentally, Joplin died only two weeks after rock-guitar legend Jimi Hendrix choked to death on his own vomit. Less than a year later, Doors frontman Jim Morrison was found dead in a Paris bathtub. Three legendary figures of rock had all died tragic deaths within a single year. They were all 27 years old.

7047 Franklin Avenue #105 Hollywood

DIANE LINKLETTER

The Shoreham Towers has been the home to many celebrities over the years, including David Lee Roth and Neil Sedaka. Diane Linkletter, daughter of *Kids Say The Darndest Things* TV game show host Art Linkletter, was once a resident.

On October 4, 1969, the 20-year-old Linkletter dropped out on a permanent basis. Linkletter had taken an overabundant supply of LSD and decided she could fly. After she confided in her best friend about some horrible hallucinations, Linkletter dashed towards the kitchen.

One problem.

The kitchen had a window that led outside. Six stories high.

Linkletter's friend slowly realized what was happening and lunged for her. The friend grasped Linkletter's belt loop but could not hang on. Linkletter, doing her best Superman impersonation, plummeted 60 feet to the hard concrete below. She died upon impact.

Check out underground trash film god John Waters' non-commercially released feature film, *The Diane Linkletter Story*, for an interesting and humorous interpretation of the ill-fated daughter's demise. The lovely transvestite actor Divine stars as Linkletter.

8787 Shoreham Drive West Hollywood

RIVER PHOENIX

Born River Jude Bottom on August 23, 1970 in the tiny town of Madras, Oregon, River Phoenix led the life of a chameleon. His ability to morph into the type of person necessary to fit his surroundings served him well in his chosen profession: acting. But the inability to truly understand who he was may have played a part in his death.

River was named after the river of life from the Herman Hesse self-improvement novel, *Siddhartha*. His middle name came from the classic Beatles song "Hey Jude." He was the first of five children born to John and Arlyn Bottom, a classic hippie couple who preferred to live outside of the mainstream.

The Bottoms took their clan all over the country in an effort to find themselves through various spiritual movements. By the time River was seven, they had become enthralled by a religious sect known as The Children of God. The group practiced a non-materialistic, free love philosophy, and the Bottoms bought into it big time. They traveled all over the world to spread the news of their cult. After some time, River's parents realized that the Children of God was a negative influence and separated themselves from the group. The Bottoms moved to Florida and rechristened themselves with a new last name: Phoenix.

The family, however, needed money to survive. Phoenix, and his sister Rain, contributed by singing songs for passersby on local street corners. The duo was so talented that their parents decided to get serious about their future. They moved to Hollywood so the precocious youngsters could "make it."

It worked. After years of playing on the corners in Westwood, River began modeling. This led to television commercials, and eventually a co-starring role on CBS's *Seven Brides For Seven Brothers* when he was only 11 years old. He expanded his résumé to include theat-

8852 Sunset Boulevard West Hollywood

rical film with a starring role in 1985's *Explorers*.

By 1986, River Phoenix began a quick ascent in Hollywood with his role in the Rob Reiner-directed version of a Stephen King short story about a group of kids that discover a dead body. That movie was *Stand By Me*.

Up until the filming of *Stand By Me*, Phoenix had led a clean life. He did not smoke, drink, or curse. He was also a devout vegan who did not eat meat, fish, or dairy products of any kind and eschewed all leather products. His co-stars on the film were Keifer Sutherland and Corey Feldman. It is not clear who introduced the idealistic actor to illicit substances.

Phoenix followed up *Stand By Me* two years later with a stirring portrayal of a son of fugitives who are on the run in *Running On Empty*, co-starring Christine Lahti and Judd Hirsch. Phoenix's powerful portrayal caught the eye of the industry elite, and he was nominated for a Best Supporting Actor Oscar. He lost the award to Kevin Kline, but he ascended the ladder several more rungs. Not only was he a fan favorite with the teenage girls, but he now also received a greater modicum of respect from his peers and the insiders in the business.

Phoenix seemed to put his newfound fame and respect to good use. He bought a ranch for his family in the small town of Micanopy, Florida. He became more politically active with groups such as People for the Ethical Treatment of Animals. He even bought several thousands of acres of rain forests. Offscreen, Phoenix seemed to be making adult choices well beyond his years.

Onscreen, Phoenix steered clear of mainstream filmmaking. His acting preference was epitomized by his role as a gay, narcoleptic hustler in avant-garde director Gus Van Sant's *My Own Private Idaho* in 1991. Filmed near his original birthplace in Oregon, Phoenix allegedly began to dabble in harder drugs. Rumors were rampant that heroin was widespread on and off the set of the gritty tale.

After the shoot, Phoenix's Hollywood persona developed a harder edge. He was increasingly annoyed with reporters, and his responses to their queries become short and almost always cynical. He often stated that he lied in interviews just to make it interesting for himself and to irritate the media. According to the Hollywood rumor mill, the young, healthy vegan actor was becoming dependent on drugs. But no one stopped him.

Phoenix starred in a series of flops after *My Own Private Idaho* including *Dogfight, Sneakers,* and *The Thing Called Love*. By 1993, however, he seemed to regain his footing in the business. He was filming the lead role in a thriller entitled *Dark Blood* with actor Jonathan Pryce and was signed on to star as "The Interviewer" in *Interview With A Vampire* with megastars Tom Cruise and Brad Pitt.

On October 30, 1993, Phoenix completed a rigorous day of filming for *Dark Blood*. The film already shot about two-thirds of the script, and Phoenix had spent a grueling session shooting his death scene. He went back to his room at the Hotel Nikko (465 South LaCienega

Boulevard) in Beverly Hills and was greeted by his brother Leaf (now Joaquin Phoenix), his sister Rain, and his girlfriend, actress Samantha Mathis. Allegedly, the foursome spent several hours in Phoenix's room partying. They then got ready to hit the town.

They first went to a party in the Hollywood Hills where it is assumed that Phoenix continued to imbibe. They left the party and headed for the infamous Sunset Strip in West Hollywood. There, they entered actor Johnny Depp's nightclub, The Viper Room, so they could catch Depp's band, P, which was comprised of the *21 Jump Street* star, Flea from the Red Hot Chili Peppers (see Hillel Slovak p. 68), and Butthole Surfers lead-singer Gibby Haynes. Allegedly, Phoenix had been leaning against the stage and swaying precariously back and forth while waiting for the band to perform. A bouncer was concerned for the 23-year-old celebrity and escorted him to the restroom.

Sources said that while in the restroom, an individual handed Phoenix more drugs, which he ingested. Soon thereafter, other patrons came into the restroom and saw Phoenix shuddering violently. They threw water on his face to try to calm him down.

Around 1:00 AM, Leaf Phoenix and Mathis grabbed River and dragged him out of the

front door of the club onto the sidewalk next to Sunset Drive. Actress Christina Applegate saw the young star fall to the concrete and begin to moan. She stood there, frozen. As did Leaf and Mathis.

Finally, at 1:10 AM, Leaf snapped out of his reverie and ran towards the closest pay phone. He frantically dialed 911 and begged for help. He was vague in his description as to what was wrong with his brother, mentioning "Valium" at one point.

The ambulance arrived in four minutes and began routine procedures on Phoenix. Paramedic Ray Ribar claimed that Phoenix was dead by the time he arrived on the scene; however, he rushed the actor into the ambulance and headed out to Cedars-Sinai Hospital. Flea jumped in with his friend as well.

It was too late. The doctors at Cedars-Sinai attempted a full resuscitation, even cracking open his chest in an attempt to jumpstart his heart, but to no avail.

River Phoenix, 23, was officially pronounced dead at 1:51 AM.

The coroner's examination discovered that Phoenix had indeed taken several drugs that night. He died from "acute multiple drug intoxication," which included lethal levels of heroin, Valium, cocaine, marijuana, and ephedrine. The overdose of drugs had caused a full cardiac arrest and killed the rising star.

8852 Sunset Boulevard West Hollywood

DON SIMPSON

The second most notorious Simpson in Los Angeles, Don Simpson, was the aggressive half of the famed Bruckheimer/ Simpson film production company that created the box office smashes *Beverly Hills Cop*, *Top Gun*, and *Flashdance*.

Simpson was born and raised in Anchorage, Alaska. He claimed his parents were devout, strict Christians who abused him. He escaped the snowy confines of his domestic prison and headed for the sunny climes of California. Eventually, he would make his way to Hollywood, write scripts, and become a part of the movie-making machinery. By 1982, Simpson and his friend Jerry Bruckheimer formed a partnership that would dominate the movie industry.

Simpson and Bruckheimer were considered Hollywood Gods in the 80s when their films grossed over $1.5 billion dollars. Simpson played the creative, overbearing screamer in the partnership. He would send writers through countless re-writes of scripts. He would also live and die by the test screenings. His movies were critically lambasted as too polished and saccharine, but they made a hell of a lot of money. And in Tinsletown, cash is king. Don Simpson was riding high on his Hollywood throne.

Simpson and Bruckheimer's success in the 80s led to a huge production deal with Paramount to make five pictures for $300 million bucks. The first film under this deal was the Tom Cruise race car flick, *Days of Thunder*. The movie ran notoriously over budget and, while not a box-office failure, was a major disappointment to the studio. It seemed to be the beginning of the end for Simpson.

The duo lost their deal with Paramount, but quickly signed on with Disney. No movies were made, however, for the next three years, and the industry magazines began to ask the old death knell question, "What Ever Happened To?"

What happened to Don Simpson is simple yet tragic. He overindulged. He went too far. He sated all of his appetites. Food, sex, drugs. You name it, he did it.

Food. He had a constant battle of the bulge. Sometimes fluctuating 50-75 pounds in a short period of time. He always wanted to stay fit and trim, but he loved his tuna sandwiches and entire jars of peanut butter. To battle his oncoming obesity, he would often ship himself off to a fat farm. Later in life, as his battle became more difficult, he opted for liposuction.

Sex. According to Joanne Parrent in her Hollywood exposé, *You'll Never Make Love in This Town Again*, Simpson loved his hookers. Since he worked so many hours, he did not care for the mating ritual of dating. He needed to get off and do it right away. What better way to do that than with some high-priced hookers? He was a favorite client of Madame Alex, the most well known pimp in Hollywood until her protégée Heidi Fleiss took over the crown.

685 Stone Canyon Road   Bel Air

Simpson would frequent Fleiss's girls as well. Simpson did not just go for the usual missionary position. He was into dress-up, make-believe, bondage, humiliation, and videotaping.

Drugs. We'll get to that in a minute.

By 1995, Simpson and Bruckheimer rebounded with a splash. The buddy movie, *Bad Boys*, with Will Smith and Martin Lawrence, was a box-office smash followed by two more mega-moneymakers, *Crimson Tide* and *Dangerous Minds*. Don Simpson was back in top form, and the Hollywood elite was once again answering his calls.

Despite these successes, Simpson's self-destructive behavior did not go away. In the summer of 1995, Simpson sought to control his drug addictions. He hired a friend and aspiring screenwriter Dr. Stephen Ammerman to help him kick his numerous habits. Dr. Ammerman's idea of treatment was to prescribe even more drugs for Simpson. Ammerman believed that the dry-out process would be too painful for Simpson as he was weaned off the drug, so he would give him another drug to compensate. Soon, Simpson would become addicted to the new drug.

On August 15, 1995, Ammerman was discovered dead at Simpson's estate. His body lay in the shower of Simpson's backyard pool. A hypodermic needle was found nearby. Ammerman had overdosed on several drugs including cocaine, diazepam, venlafaxine, and over four times the lethal amount of morphine.

The straight-laced Bruckheimer had seen enough. He had constantly been trying to get Simpson to clean up his act. The death of Dr. Ammerman was the final straw. If he were to continue his association with Simpson, Bruckheimer believed his reputation would be forever tarnished. On December 20, 1995, he informed Simpson that their partnership was over. He hoped this might be the catalyst for getting Simpson to go straight.

Simpson did not. He continued his drug abuse and battled with his weight. On January 19, 1996, however, he appeared to make a turn for the better. He spent three hours on the telephone speaking with his friend and filmmaker James Toback. They were planning on working together on Toback's script *The Harvard Man*. Toback reported that Simpson sounded like his old, upbeat, film-knowledgeable self.

A few hours later, however, Don Simpson was dead. His body was found on the toilet. He had his reading glasses in one hand and a copy of the Oliver Stone biography, *Stone: The Controversies, Excesses, and Exploits of a Radical Filmmaker* in the other.

Upon further inspection, detectives found a pharmacy of drugs in Simpson's house. All legal. He had over 2,000 pills in prescription bottles that were all alphabetized. It was later discovered that Simpson had obtained 15,000 pills from over 15 physicians and eight pharmacies. The coroner further ruled that he died from a lethal combination of cocaine, Unisom, Atarax, Desyrel, Tigan, Compazine, valium, Vistaril, Librium, and Xanax.

Don Simpson was 52 years old.

HILLEL SLOVAK

The original guitarist for alternative funk-rock band The Red Hot Chili Peppers was born in Haifa, Israel on April 13, 1962. He migrated to Los Angeles at the age of five. Slovak would later attend Fairfax High School with future Chili Peppers singer Anthony Kiedis, bassist Tony "Flea" Balzary, and original drummer Jack Irons.

Slovak was a self-taught guitarist who loved the crunchy sounds of KISS, Led Zeppelin, and especially Jimi Hendrix. Together with Irons, Slovak started his first band, Chain Reaction. They moved on to another band called Anthym and would later change the name to What Is This? That band would later include the most famous future Chili Peppers, Kiedes, and Flea. The Chili Peppers would splinter off from What Is This? and make some headway, even though Slovak stayed in both bands.

In 1983, the Chili Peppers signed a major label contract with EMI. Slovak, however, stayed with What Is This?, which also signed a major deal. He would not rejoin the Chili Peppers until 1985. In the meantime, Slovak developed a mean heroin habit.

Slovak appeared on the Chili Peppers's albums *Freaky Styley* and *Uplift Mofo Party Plan*. The young, versatile guitarist blew away producer George Clinton, who claimed that Slovak was as fluid and diverse as anyone the funk legend had previously recorded. Despite his

talent, however, his drug problem did not escape the band's eye. They constantly wanted to kick Slovak out, but they also had a strong bond with their friend.

Slovak stayed with the band. By 1988, the Peppers had recorded the *Abbey Road* EP and were ready for their next album. Everything seemed to be running smoothly. Slovak, however, had not kicked his drug habit. On June 27, 1988, Slovak was found dead in his apartment. He had overdosed on heroin.

The Red Hot Chili Peppers replaced Slovak with 17-year-old John Frusciante and recorded the album *Mother's Milk*. The album and the song "Knock Me Down" were both dedicated to Slovak. *Mother's Milk* went on to sell over 500,000 copies and was followed by the top-selling Chili Pepper album, *Blood Sugar Sex Magic*, which sold over 4.5 million copies. The band is now an international phenomenon.

6141 Afton Place #114   Hollywood

LUPE VELEZ

The precursor to Jennifer Lopez, Salma Hayek, and Penelope Cruz, Velez was born in 1908 in San Luis Potisi, Mexico, as Guadalupe Velez deVillalobos. She moved to San Antonio, Texas and was raised in a convent as a little girl.

Velez was interested in theater and dance. She eventually moved to California and was discovered by Douglas Fairbanks Sr., who cast her in the film *El Gaucho*.

Velez's voluptuous personality, smoldering good looks, beautiful singing voice, and tremendous acting talent catapulted her into the top tier of actresses. She worked for such famous directors as Cecil B. DeMille, D.W. Griffith, and Hal Roach. Some of her co-stars included Fairbanks, Lon Chaney, and Gary Cooper.

The only thing that seemed to match Velez's on-screen talents were her off-screen relationships. She bedded some of the top movie stars and sports personalities of her time such as Cooper, Fairbanks, Charlie Chaplin, Jack Dempsey, Jimmy Durante, and Tarzan himself, Johnny Weismuller, whom she married in 1933. Their marriage was a tumultuous affair that lasted for five years.

Soon after her divorce from Weismuller, Velez rebounded with a series of B-movies. She is best known as *The Mexican Spitfire*. From 1940 to 1943, Velez made seven *Mexican Spitfire* movies. Often reviled as stereotypical, the series kept her in the public eye. By 1944, another event would make her the center of attention.

Velez met and fell in love with bit-part actor Harald Ramond. They had a fiery romance

732 N. Rodeo Drive Beverly Hills

that led to an unexpected pregnancy for Velez. In the 1940s, however, unwed motherhood was considered taboo, especially for a high-profile Hollywood starlet. When Velez expressed her desire to marry Ramond, he rejected her. Distraught, Velez made the decision to end it all.

On December 13, 1944 Velez summoned her hairdresser and personal make-up girl. They dolled her up for her final performance. Velez was determined to end her life and do it in style.

Velez created the ultimate suicide scene. She was perfectly made up and dressed in a beautiful silk gown. She decorated her bedroom with flowers. And, she had a bottle of pills beside her bed.

Velez crawled into her huge bed and prepared to make her final headline. She opened the bottle of pills, which contained Seconal, and grabbed a handful—75 to be exact. She swallowed all of the pills, lay back on her pillow, and closed her eyes.

The pills seemed to work, perhaps too well. Earlier that day, Velez ate her final meal. It consisted of a hearty Mexican dish of enchiladas and burritos. Her lunch, however, did not mix well with the Seconal.

Velez began to get sick. She leapt from her bed and made her way to the bathroom. She wanted to throw up. She did not make it to the facilities, before she unleashed the first torrents of vomit. She left a trail from her bed to the bathroom.

From here, the truth is a little unclear.

Some claim that as Velez made her way into the bathroom, she went for the toilet. She wanted to release her nauseating concoction. Apparently, she slipped on her vomit before she could complete the release. Velez landed face first in the toilet and drowned. Another version has Velez hitting her head on the toilet bowl and breaking her neck. Still another version claims she landed on the bathroom floor and choked to death on her own vomit.

However it happened, the spitfire's death will never be forgotten.

732 N. Rodeo Drive Beverly Hills

DENNIS WILSON

The only Beach Boy who surfed actually died in the water.

Dennis Wilson was the drummer for the massively successful fun-bunch who recorded a slew of historic rock tracks in the early 60s, including "Surfin' USA," "Surfin' Safari," "Surfer Girl," "Help Me, Rhonda," "California Girls," "I Get Around," "Fun, Fun, Fun," and "Good Vibrations." His brothers, Brian and Carl Wilson, cousin Mike Love, and family friend Al Jardine joined him. Together, the quintet ushered in the surf rock sound and became a worldwide phenomenon. Dennis Wilson was also beset by a slew of problems his entire life: mainly women, drugs, and alcohol.

Born on December 4, 1944, in Hawthorne, California, Wilson was subjected to verbal and physical abuse by his father his entire life. By the age of 16, he was able to escape the pain by joining the Beach Boys. He never escaped his father's clutches as Murry Wilson acted as the band's manager in its earliest stages.

As hit after hit rolled in for the Beach Boys, Wilson gobbled up the women and the illicit substances. He was married five times to four women. He also ran with a less-than-savory crowd in the late 60s. A small, charismatic hippie named Charles Manson (see p. 183) was the leader of that crowd. Manson and his followers, sometimes referred to as "The Family," took over Wilson's upscale Pacific Palisades home on Sunset Drive during the spring and summer of 1968. Manson's gang practically destroyed Wilson's home, wrecked his Mercedes Benz, and stole more than $100,000 from the rock star.

By 1983, Wilson's career was on the decline. The Beach Boys had been reduced to a touring "Greatest Hits" nostalgia act and meant little, if anything, in the modern era of rock. The other members of the band had asked Wilson to not tour with them due to his erratic behavior. He had lost his 62-foot yacht due to nonpayment of bills. He had also married an 18-year-old girl by the name of Shawn Love. Yes, she was his second cousin and Mike Love's daughter. Wilson would continue to deal with his demons by snorting more cocaine and drinking more booze.

On December 28, 1983 Wilson slipped over the edge, literally and figuratively. He had been in and out of various rehabilitation clinics the previous week. Nothing, however, could keep him from the bottle. He returned to the marina where he used to dock his old boat. He spent the day drinking with another boat owner, Bill Oster. By noon, he had already con-

13929 Marquesas Way Basin C-1100 Marina Del Rey

sumed an entire fifth of vodka. He then came up with the brilliant idea of diving for treasure—with nothing more than shorts and a mask.

Wilson began to descend 13 feet below to retrieve items from his former boat slip. He was able to gather several trinkets he had tossed overboard in previous fits of anger. He pulled up such items as a rope, battery parts, and a picture frame that once held a picture of him and his former wife Karen Lamm (who would later befriend crime victim Kitty Menendez—see p. 81).

Wilson later had a sandwich and returned to the water. His friends were not worried, since they knew Wilson was a prankster. He loved the water, and he loved to show off. He dove down one more time to pick up more junk. He never surfaced again.

Dennis Wilson's body was recovered at 5:45 PM directly below his former boat slip. Los Angeles Coroner Thomas Noguchi claimed that Wilson's blood alcohol level was .26, well over California's legal intoxication limit at the time of .10. Noguchi's report stated that Wilson had experienced a state known as "nitrogen narcosis." Scuba divers who dive too far below the surface often experience this sensation. The pressure from being that deep causes a sense of giddiness or euphoria. Those who suffer from nitrogen narcosis tend to dive deeper due to their relaxed state and sometimes never resurface.

It is rare for nitrogen narcosis to occur in 13 feet of water. Wilson, however, experienced it due to his intoxicated state, not the depth of the water. When the narcosis kicked in, Wilson believed he could stay under longer, but he eventually ran out of breath. By that time, he had swallowed too much water and could not make it to the surface.

Wilson's family received special permission from former California Governor and then-President of the United States Ronald Reagan to bury the drummer at sea. Reagan was a longtime Beach Boys fan.

13929 Marquesas Way Basin C-1100 Marina Del Rey

CHAPTER 4 MYSTERIOUS CIRCUMSTANCES

In a town built on lies and fabrications, it should come as no surprise that there have been multitudes of unusual occurrences in Hollywood. During its storied history, Hollywood has been witness to several unsolved crimes, unimaginable human horrors, and the flat-out bizarre. From gangster assassinations, murder for money, and questionable suicides, Hollywood has a history rife with scandals that continue to fascinate the world.

NICK ADAMS

Nicholas Aloysius Adamshock was born on July 10, 1931, in Nanticoke, Pennsylvania. His father was a Lithuanian émigré coal miner. Nicholas grew up in Jersey City, New Jersey in some of the rougher areas of the city. He dreamt that one day he would escape the rough confines of the city and become a movie star like his idol, James Dean. His dreams, and nightmares, would come true.

Adamshock changed his name to Nick Adams, moved to Manhattan, and was determined to make it as a stage actor. He befriended actor Jack Palance who set him on the path of theater. He garnered a few small roles and then decided to hit the road for Hollywood. Adams withdrew $350 from his bank account, stuck his thumb out, and hitch-hiked cross-country.

Adams was quick with the hustle. He busted his ass working a multitude of menial jobs until he finally got his big break. He convinced director John Ford that he was perfect for a role as a sailor in *Mister Roberts*. In less than 24 hours, he was whisked off to Hawaii to play opposite Jack Lemmon, James Cagney, and Henry Fonda.

Adams parlayed his success in *Mister Roberts* into a role in one of Hollywood's most infamous productions, *Rebel Without A Cause*. Adams fulfilled his dream of meeting his idol, James Dean, even sharing dialogue with the young, hard-edged icon. Unfortunately, Dean would die in a car crash the same weekend the movie opened. The formerly law-abiding Adams, despondent over Dean's death, turned into a troublemaker. He received nine speeding tickets that same year.

Adams's career swayed back and forth until he married a beautiful actress by the name of Carol Nugent. Nugent helped pull Adams out of his funk and encouraged him to focus on his acting. Her inspiration energized Adams anew, and he cemented his place in the Hollywood pantheon with his role as Johnny Yuma in the television series, *The Rebel*.

The glow soon faded for Adams, however, as *The Rebel* was cancelled after only two

2126 El Roble Lane Beverly Hills

years. Soon thereafter, his marriage faded as well. A nasty divorce and child custody battle left Adams with majority custody of his two children. To support his kids, Adams began to appear in a slew of low-budget foreign films such as *Die, Monster, Die!* and *Godzilla vs. Monster Zero*. It was not high art, but at least he kept food on the table.

By 1968, Adams's career seemed to once again be on the upswing. He had just received a nice sized paycheck for a role in an Italian production and was in line for several other high paying, high profile acting gigs.

On February 7, 1968, Adams had a meeting scheduled with his friend and lawyer, Ervin Roeder. He never made the meeting. Roeder became nervous, because Adams was never late for anything. After waiting for more than an hour, Roeder decided to look for his friend. He retraced Adams's potential route to the restaurant, but did not find the actor on the road. Roeder decided to check in on him at his rented home.

Roeder knocked on the door to the home, but received no answer. He finally let himself inside, since the door was unlocked. What he found led to one of Hollywood's most enduring mysteries.

Adams was sitting on the floor, with his back against the wall. His eyes were wide open, but he was not breathing. Roeder realized that his friend was dead, but the scene made no sense. There was a phone only a few feet away from the body. There were absolutely no signs of struggle.

Adams's body was taken to the coroner's office. Assistant Coroner Herb McCoy claimed that Adams was filled with a drug known as paraldehyde, which was taken to combat the effects of alcoholism. Adams had received a prescription for the drug only a few months before from his doctor, but he was carefully informed about its potential dangers. McCoy reported that Adams had more than enough of the drug in his system to kill him instantly. Head Coroner Dr. Thomas Noguchi, however, insisted that there was not enough to kill the actor.

These analyses were further confused by other factors. Adams did not have an alcohol or drug abuse problem. Furthermore, there were no needle marks on his body or any evidence as to how the medicine could have been ingested. In addition, Adams left no suicide note, and he seemed upbeat over the new direction in which his career was headed. Not to mention that he was deeply in love with his two children.

Adams's death certificate listed the cause of death as "Accident-Suicide." Many people in Hollywood believed he died from something far more sinister.

2126 El Roble Lane Beverly Hills

ALBERT DEKKER

This highly respected stage and screen actor became more famous for his mystifying death than for his creative work. Albert Dekker, 63, an actor in several famous movies, such as *East of Eden*, *Suddenly, Last Summer*, and *The Wild Bunch*, met his unfortunate demise in a modest apartment complex around May 2, 1968.

After a date with his 45-year-old fiancée, Geraldine Saunders (they saw the play *The Latent Heterosexual)*, Dekker headed to his apartment for a night alone. When Saunders did not hear from him by the next afternoon, she popped over to speak with him. Dekker did not answer her knocks, so Saunders left him a note. Two days later, still with no word from her lover, Saunders returned to the complex. She convinced the manager to let her into Dekker's apartment, since she was sure something was wrong.

What the young landlord saw would be considered one of the most bizarre death scenes in Hollywood history.

Not an easy task.

Here is the basic description.

Dekker was found in his bathtub, kneeling down. Inserted into his mouth was a rubber gag ball that resembled a horse's bit. The ball was attached to a metal wire that was tied around his head. His eyes were covered with a silk scarf. He had handcuffs on each hand. A leather belt was cinched around his neck so tight that there were belt hole impressions on his throat. The leather belt was attached to a strap at his waist. This strap traveled down the length of his body and secured his two ankles together. A rope attached to these straps was

1731 N. Normandie Avenue Hollywood

connected to his wrists and secured rather tightly.

It got even more bizarre. A hypodermic syringe was found inserted into each of Dekker's arms. Profanity had been written on his body with dark red lipstick. On his left buttock, the word "whip" appeared, slightly above two needle puncture holes. His chest bore the words "slave" and "cocksucker." His nipples had been adorned with drawings of sunrays, and his throat had the phrase "make me suck." His stomach contained a drawing of a woman's vagina.

Dekker had apparently been dead since Friday, the same night he and Saunders returned from the playhouse. The lividity, or settling of the body's blood in the lowermost region after a person's dies, left Dekker's lower trunk portion a startling purple.

Speculations immediately began to leak out, and everyone wanted to know what the hell happened. Many believed Dekker had committed suicide. Just over ten years earlier, his 16-year-old son had committed suicide, and these people thought Dekker had never recovered from losing his own child.

Still others believed that Dekker fell prey to some form of kinky sexual act. Most theorists cited autoerotic asphyxiation, also known as AA. Considered the most dangerous of all sexual acts, AA is the act of self-hanging to increase sexual pleasure while masturbating. This act allowed the flow of oxygen to be cut off while the moment of climax approached, ratcheting up the intensity level of one's orgasm. In other words, squeezing off to get off. Dekker's son, Benjamin van Dekker, believed that his father probably got caught up in a crazy sex game with a partner when a major accident occurred. If his theory is correct, then someone was at least partially responsible and had never come forward.

Still others, such as Saunders, believed that Dekker was the victim of foul play. She commented that Dekker had several thousands of dollars in his apartment at the time of his death. She also noticed that all of Dekker's expensive audio and video recording equipment was missing.

Each theory had its supporters, but the official cause of Dekker's death on the coroner's report was listed as an accident.

1731 N. Normandie Avenue Hollywood

EDWARD DOHENY JR.

Edward Doheny Sr. was considered one of the "fathers" of Los Angeles. In 1892, he successfully drilled for oil in the Westlake area. Several thousand barrels were extracted from Doheny's

well over the next decade, leading to an oil boom in Southern California. Doheny's success also brought money, political influence, and power.

In 1910, Doheny Sr. bought 429 acres of ranch land in Beverly Hills. By 1928, he built an extravagant 55-room Tudor-style mansion for his only son, Edward "Ned" Jr. Before Ned moved into the home, however, the Dohenys became embroiled in a national disgrace known as the Teapot Dome scandal. Both Dohenys and Ned's male secretary, Hugh Plunkett, had bought access to federal oil reserves in the name of Doheny Sr.'s company. These reserves were earmarked for the military in the event of a disaster or war. The Dohenys were able to get their hands on the oil without other competitive biddings being given an equal chance. When Calvin Coolidge was named President in 1923, he exposed the schemes and the Dohenys with it. Both Ned and Plunkett were required to testify before the Senate Committee on Public Land and Surveys.

As the scandal continued, Ned finally moved into the mansion (known as the Greystone Mansion) with his wife in Sep-

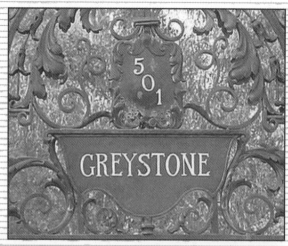

Public Entrance: 905 Loma Vista Drive Beverly Hills

tember 1928. Less than six months later and just days before he was to testify before the Senate, tragedy struck. On February 16, 1929, police were called to the Doheny estate late in the evening. When they arrived, they found the dead bodies of Ned and Plunkett in Ned's bedroom. Ned was clad only in underwear and a silk robe. He lay on his back and had a pool of blood around his body that had drained from a bullet hole in his head. Only 12 feet away

lay Plunkett's body, face down, also in a pool of blood.

This scene appeared to be your typical murder/suicide. This case, however, was anything but typical. Witnesses were comprised of the mansion's servants and one "socialite" physician, Dr. E.C. Fishbaugh. The servants claimed that they had heard a single shot and went to investigate. They supposedly came upon Plunkett who threatened to kill them, and then they heard a second shot. When they entered the room, they found Ned and Plunkett dead.

Dr. Fishbaugh was called to the scene less than one hour later. The Beverly Hills police were not summoned until two hours after the murder. Los Angeles homicide detectives were

not made aware of the bloody affair until four hours after the supposed time of death.

Upon his arrival at the scene, Detective Leslie White conducted a cursory investigation. He turned Plunkett over and found a pistol underneath his chest. It was still warm, but had no fingerprints. He also noticed a burned down cigarette that had singed the assistant's hand. Detective White subsequently examined Ned. He saw that the bullet had gone in one of his ears and out the other. He then saw something unusual—blood crisscrossed over Ned's face and seemed to flow up towards the hairline.

The other officers seemed to think this was an open and shut case. White, relatively new to the force, deferred to the more experienced investigators and got out of the way. Police Chief Wheeler, however, asked White to join him for a closer inspection of the bodies.

At the morgue, White took a second look at Ned Doheny. He noticed gunpowder burns

Public Entrance: 905 Loma Vista Drive Beverly Hills

around the entry wound. He then looked at Plunkett's wound. There were no such marks. Seeing this evidence, White concluded that Plunkett could not have killed Doheny and then turned the gun on himself. The burn marks were a good sign that it may have been the other way around. Furthermore, the detective reasoned that Plunkett could not have opened the door on the servants if he had a cigarette in his left hand and a gun in his right.

White returned to the mansion to continue his investigation. He heard from one servant that three shots were actually fired. All in succession—*Pop! Pop! Pop!* This report did not mesh with the story offered by the other servants. White then realized that the four-hour lapse between the crime and his arrival on the scene was more than enough time for the witnesses to corroborate their stories.

White also found Dr. Fishbaugh's participation suspicious. Dr. Fishbaugh claimed that Ned was dead when he arrived. He also stated that he had not touched the corpse. During the interrogation of the doctor, White only asked him one question. How could blood run *up* from the ears and crisscross the face of a man who was on his back? Dr. Fishbaugh stuttered and stammered. He had been caught in a lie. He admitted that Doheny had actually been alive when he arrived. He said that he found him on the floor and lifted him up to attempt to assist him. However, Doheny was dead 20 minutes later. Dr. Fishbaugh then placed the body back in the same position that he found it and concocted the ruse. White had no idea why Dr. Fishbaugh lied.

That, however, would be the end of the investigation. Allegedly, the Doheny money machine cranked up and had the murder buried. After a headline story in the *Los Angeles Times* Monday edition, the incident garnered scant coverage.

The lack of a continued investigation by the police and the media left the story open to multiple interpretations. Many claimed that Plunkett was mad at Ned for not giving him a raise and that he murdered his boss in a rage, then killed himself. Some suggested that Plunkett was about to be committed to an insane asylum and simply went ballistic. Still others claimed that Doheny Jr. and Plunkett were homosexual lovers and had blown up in a lover's quarrel. Some even pointed the finger at the world of big money, politics, and power. Were Ned Doheny Jr. and Hugh Plunkett killed because they were about to testify in the Teapot Dome scandal, and Mr. Doheny Sr. thought the younger men might crack under pressure?

We may never know.

Public Entrance: 905 Loma Vista Drive Beverly Hills

ERIK & LYLE MENENDEZ

August 20, 1989: Beverly Hills police responded to a 911 call from a frantic Lyle Menendez who screamed that his parents had been murdered. When police arrived at the palatial Beverly Hills mansion, they found a gruesome scene. Jose Menendez, 45, was missing his head and his brain was splattered across the family room. Kitty Menendez, 47, had her face blown in half with her nose and one eye missing. Her other eye remained open. Lyle, 21, and his brother, Erik, 19, were hysterical. They claimed that members of the Mafia probably killed their parents.

Jose Menendez was a successful immigrant from Cuba who got his start in the music business. As an executive for RCA, he signed such 80s hitmakers as Menudo, Duran Duran, and The Eurythmics. By 1986, Menendez had a falling out with the company and uprooted his family from New Jersey to Los Angeles. He soon landed a job at a company that became known as Live Entertainment, a subsidiary of Carolco, the company that created the *Rambo* film series with Sylvester Stallone.

Menendez was a tough, ruthless businessman who usually got what he wanted. He helped the struggling movie company turn a profit in less than two years and was rewarded handsomely for his endeavors with a $500,000 a year salary. His earnings allowed him to own a nice home in Calabasas, drive nice cars, and provide for his boys, Erik and Lyle.

Menendez's sons were treated like royalty. They attended the best private schools, drove the most expensive cars, and were given private tennis instructors to help them with their game. Anything they wanted, Jose and Kitty Menendez gave it to them.

Unfortunately, the boys wanted much more.

1988. Erik and Lyle were caught stealing from neighbors in Calabasas. They stole over $100,000 worth of money and jewelry. Jose cleaned up their mess by paying back the neighbors and forced younger brother Erik to take the fall for Lyle, who was 18 at the time. Jose's dream was for Lyle to attend an Ivy League school, however, he was afraid that an arrest would ruin his son's chances for admittance. Erik agreed and was sentenced to psychological counseling. The Menendez family relocated to Beverly Hills, because they were embarrassed by their sons' actions. Soon thereafter, Lyle enrolled at Princeton.

Winter, 1988. Lyle was kicked out of Princeton for cheating on a Psychology 101 exam. He returned home with his tail tucked between his legs. His father was furious. He began to believe that his sons would never amount to anything. The brothers worried that they might be kicked out of their Beverly Hills home and forced to actually work for a living. They also feared they would be dropped from their father's will. Jose Menendez was worth $14,000,000.

Three weeks before the murders. Erik watched an NBC rebroadcast of *Billionaire Boys*

722 North Elm Drive   Beverly Hills

Club. The movie revolved around young men, living in Beverly Hills, who decide to kill people for money. Erik allegedly told Lyle to watch this movie. The seed had been planted.

August 17, 1989. Lyle drove to San Diego and purchased two shotguns with cash. He used a stolen identification card to make the purchase.

August 20, 1989, 10:00 PM. Jose and Kitty Menendez were obliterated with shotguns in their Beverly Hills home.

Just days after the murders, the brothers Menendez went on a shopping spree. They bought new Rolex watches, a new Jeep for Erik and a Porsche for Lyle, and tennis lessons for the both of them. They stayed at $2,000-a-night hotels and claimed to be hiding from the Mafia. Lyle even bought a chicken wing restaurant in Princeton.

Lyle seemed nonplussed about the murders. He kept quiet. Erik, on the other hand, could not keep his mouth shut. He blabbed to a friend that he killed his parents. He also told his psychologist of the deed.

Big mistake.

The psychologist eventually told a girlfriend about the confession and she told the cops. Lyle Menendez was subsequently arrested at his home on March 8, 1990, almost seven months after the death of his parents. Erik, who was in Israel at the time, returned to Los Angeles and was arrested three days later.

Their trials were some of the most ridiculous fiascos in the history of our judicial system. Headed by firebrand defense attorney, Leslie Abramson, the Menendez brothers pled not guilty. They admitted that they killed their parents, but they did so out of self-defense. The brothers claimed that their father molested them since they were little boys and they feared for their lives. They claimed they killed their mother to spare her the agony of living with an infidel. The "Abuse Excuse" was given a national spotlight.

This first trial was a travesty. Gullible jurors fell for the boys' story, when they came back with a deadlocked vote that led to a mistrial. In 1997, more than seven years after the murders, a jury came back with a verdict of guilty against the brothers.

722 North Elm Drive   Beverly Hills

MARILYN MONROE

No death has raised more eyebrows than the supposed suicide of one of Hollywood's most beloved glamour girls, Marilyn Monroe. The sexpot starlet made a name for herself as the most alluring, seductive, and coquettish woman of the big screen in such films as *Niagara*, *Some Like It Hot*, and *Gentlemen Prefer Blondes*. By 1962, as Marilyn's career was faltering, she became romantically linked with some of the country's most powerful men. Namely the Kennedy brothers: President John F. Kennedy and U.S. Attorney General Robert F. Kennedy (see p. 121). Her association with the Boys from Camelot might have contributed to her early death at the age of 36.

On August 5, 1962, at approximately 4:45 AM, Sergeant Jack Clemmons received a phone call from Dr. Hyman Engelberg informing him that Marilyn Monroe had died from an overdose of pills. Clemmons took the call himself and drove out to Monroe's modest bungalow in Brentwood. He was not sure if this call was a prank, but his suspicions were doused when he arrived at the house.

Dr. Engelberg and Monroe's housekeeper, Eunice Murray, led Clemmons into Monroe's bedroom. He found the actress facedown on her bed and nude, her left hand sprawled across the bed touching the telephone on the nightstand. He noticed several prescription bottles on the stand as well. However, no glass for a liquid could be seen in the room. He asked Ms. Murray about the bathroom. The maid informed the detective that it had been out of service and had no running water. Clemmons also noticed that Ms. Murray had been cleaning laundry and questioned her about her odd behavior. She claimed that she knew the coroner would come to the house and seal it up for evidence and that she wanted to make sure everything was tidy.

Clemmons observed that Monroe's body seemed to be in an advanced state of rigor mortis, which usually indicated that a body had been dead for more than six hours. He asked

12305 Fifth Helena Drive Brentwood

Ms. Murray what time she found Monroe's corpse. According to the housekeeper, she noticed Monroe's locked door after midnight. When she knocked and Monroe did not answer, she got worried and called Dr. Engelberg. The doctor arrived and was also unsuccessful in waking Monroe. The two went to Monroe's window and saw the actress lying on the bed. Dr. Engelberg retrieved a fireplace poker and broke the glass window to gain entry. Monroe, however, was already dead.

Ms. Murray waited almost four hours to call the authorities after finding Monroe's body. She stated that she had contacted some of the studios first as well as some of Monroe's business associates. Clemmons knew that it would not take four hours to complete these calls. Despite all of the uncertainty surrounding Marilyn Monroe's death scene, Clemmons packed up his notepad, called the coroner's office, and headed back to the station to file his report. He was relatively new to the force and realized that a higher ranked detective would take over the case.

When Monroe's body arrived, the coroner's office became a zoo. Reporters, insurance company representatives, and curious onlookers flocked to the office that used to be located downtown in the old City Hall building. Monroe's body was put on display, like a freak in a traveling circus. Coroner staff, doctors, studio heads, politicians, and other actors viewed the actress's body. One enterprising paparazzi even snapped a picture of Monroe's corpse.

Head coroner, Dr. Theodore Curphey, helped create the aura of mystery surrounding Marilyn Monroe's death. He stated, unequivocally, that Monroe had died from taking an oral overdose of Nembutal and chloral hydrate. He estimated that she had swallowed at least 50 pills in "one gulp," despite the fact that there was no water present at the death scene. Also, Curphey was not dissuaded by the lack of some key evidence. Nembutal capsules, when digested, leave a yellow dye discoloration on the lining of the intestine. There was no such discoloration in Monroe. In fact, no evidence of partially or undissolved capsules even existed in her digestive tract. It seemed as if the coroner's office was determined to call Marilyn Monroe's death a suicide. At all costs.

The question is, "Why?" Why did the coroner fail to test her lower intestine for the tell-

12305 Fifth Helena Drive Brentwood

tale dye marks? If no apparent source of liquid with which to swallow the pills existed, why didn't the coroner's office look at other methods of introduction, such as an injection or colonically? Why did the "official" death certificate list the cause of death as "Probable Suicide," with the former word penciled in?

Theories abound to this day. Some believed it was suicide. Some believed Ms. Murray, Monroe's housekeeper, was angry for being fired that same day. Many more believed it had everything to do with the Kennedys.

In 1962, Monroe was coming off of two box office failures—*Let's Make Love* and *The Misfits*. She was working on a new film, *Something's Got To Give*, with Dean Martin. Monroe's troubled past with drugs and depression reared its ugly head on the set. She constantly missed days of filming, flubbed her lines, and seemed dazed and confused. For the first time in her illustrious career, someone did not want Marilyn Monroe. The studio fired her.

In that same year, her relationships with the Kennedy brothers heated up. On May 29, Monroe made her now legendary appearance at President Kennedy's birthday party at Madison Square Garden, where she sang "Happy Birthday" to the President. Monroe's skintight dress and seductive voice caught the attention of the President's brother Bobby, who became infatuated with the screen legend.

Allegedly, Monroe felt that Bobby was an even better lover than John and thought that Bobby would divorce his wife for her. She is also believed to have kept a diary of her late night pillow talk with the younger Kennedy. The diary supposedly contained conversations about several top-secret political matters.

As United States Attorney General, one of Robert Kennedy's goals was to crack down on Mafia-controlled unions and its leaders, especially Jimmy Hoffa. Hoffa was supposedly tipped off that Kennedy was sleeping with Monroe, despite being married, and he wanted to get the goods on the President's pesky little brother. Hoffa allegedly wiretapped Monroe's home, so he could record moments of intimacy between the couple. When Kennedy's handlers found out about Hoffa, they decided that he had to dump Monroe. He did.

What would Monroe do?

According to one of her former lovers and friend, Robert Slatzer, she had scheduled a press conference for Monday, August 7, 1962. She wanted to spill the beans on the Kennedy boys. She also had an appointment with her attorney before the scheduled press conference. She had planned to revise her will that day.

Reportedly, Robert Kennedy had been in Los Angeles on August 4, the day Monroe died. His staff claimed that he was in San Francisco all day and could not have made it down to Brentwood in time to kill Monroe. There are more inconsistencies, however, than assurances in that regard.

However Marilyn Monroe died, her legacy has only grown with time. Her legions of fans, from horny men to uber-feminists, find something positive in Monroe to this day. Her sexuality, charm, innocence, and wit have pulled in generation after generation of new fans. Her mysterious death only raises more questions and intrigues more people who want to find out what really happened to America's favorite screen Goddess.

12305 Fifth Helena Drive Brentwood

12305 Fifth Helena Drive Brentwood

JACK NANCE

Best known for his role as the fright-topped paranoiac in David Lynch's bizarre cult classic, *Eraserhead*, Jack Nance was a low-key actor who suffered from as many horrors in his real life as he did in his movies. Born Marvin John Nance on December 9, 1943, in Boston, Massachusetts, Nance grew up in Dallas, Texas. At the age of 20, he decided he wanted to become an actor. He packed up and moved to Pasadena, California, with every intention of joining the Pasadena Playhouse.

When he arrived, he was in for a big surprise. The Playhouse had been closed for a number of years. Nance scrambled for work, but he was basically less than motivated. Eventually, he hooked up with a young filmmaker who was working on a project through the American Film Institute. That young man's name was David Lynch, and his film was *Eraserhead*, the bizarre tale of a young man, Henry, who fathers a mutant child with his wife. The wife eventually left Henry alone to care for the baby. From that point, the movie metamorphosed into a hallucinatory nightmare where Henry was eventually sucked up into a radiator. Twisted, angry, and off-the-wall, *Eraserhead* became a cult favorite, and no one could think of the movie without seeing the blank stare of Nance and his uncontrolled mop of hair.

Nance would work on several more pictures with Lynch including *Dune*, *Wild At Heart*, *Blue Velvet*, and the ABC television series, *Twin Peaks*. It was Nance who spoke the first words on the show, "She's dead. Wrapped in plastic." Nance also appeared in other movies outside of the David Lynch world, but most were resounding failures: *Barfly*, *Johnny Dangerously*, *Colors*, and *Meatballs IV*, to name but a few.

Nance's personal life was also up and down. He had battled alcoholism for a number of years. In 1991, he sought out help from Dennis Hopper, his *Blue Velvet* co-star. Hopper rushed Nance into a rehab clinic, Studio 12, where he spent several months. While he was there, he

Nance's Apt: 505 S. Fair Oaks Ave. S. Pasadena

Winchell's Donuts: 438 S. Fair Oaks Ave. S. Pasadena

met and fell in love with Kelly Van Dyke, daughter of television actor Jerry Van Dyke, and niece of comedic legend, Dick Van Dyke. When Nance and Van Dyke were released from rehab, they immediately got married.

Marriage did not appear to solve the couple's individual problems. Nance discovered that Van Dyke had acted in several low-budget porno movies under the name of Nancee Kelly. Her films included *The Coaches* (sic) *Daughter, Rump Roast,* and *Anal Adventures 1, 2,* and *3.* Van Dyke apparently was not able to deal with the pressures of her porno career, as well as being a daughter in a celebrity family. She turned back to drugs to cope. In turn, she turned Nance off.

While working near Yosemite National Park for the filming of *Meatballs IV*, Nance received a phone call from his wife. He informed Van Dyke that their marriage was not working out; he was afraid that he might start drinking again if he stayed with her. She cried and begged and pleaded for him to come home. He said that he was going to hang up on her. Van Dyke said that if he did, she would kill herself. At that exact same moment, a thunderstorm struck the area where Nance was staying and disconnected the phone line. Van Dyke had indeed killed herself. She was found by her roommate, actress Lisa Loring (Wednesday of *The Addams Family* television series), hanging from a belt in her closet. She was only 36.

Nance stayed sober for two years after Van Dyke's death. When the work came in less frequently, he returned to the bottle. His relapse led to less work and more trouble. He was fired on the first day of filming of the movie *Joyride*. He was intoxicated from the moment the director picked him up at 11:00 AM.

Drunk, despondent, and desperate, Nance moved into an apartment in South Pasadena. He returned to where he had started in Hollywood. He kept to himself, just like Henry from *Eraserhead*, and worked infrequently. His old buddy David Lynch gave him another small role in the feature film, *Lost Highway*.

He would never see the finished product.

On December 29, 1996, 53-year-old Jack Nance went out for a late night/early morning snack. He popped into the Winchell's Donuts across the street. On his way out of the store, he reportedly bumped into two Latino teenagers. Nance was somewhat of a crotchety old fart and muttered something under his breath to the two

Nance's Apt: 505 S. Fair Oaks Ave. S. Pasadena

Winchell's Donuts: 438 S. Fair Oaks Ave. S. Pasadena

kids. The teen boys did not like what he had to say and confronted the grizzled old man. Then, one of the teenagers punched Nance in the face and he fell to the concrete. The kids

laughed and walked away. Nance, though bruised and embarrassed, seemed fine. He picked himself up, dusted off, and headed back to his apartment to eat his donuts.

Later that day, Nance had lunch with two friends, actress Catherine Case and her fiancée, screenwriter Leo Bulgarini. They noticed the bruise on Nance's face. He told them a blustery tale about being jumped by two punks, but he eventually told them that he "probably deserved it." They ended their meal, and Nance headed back to his apartment.

The following morning, Bulgarini stopped by to check on Nance. He knocked on the door, but Nance did not answer. He managed to get inside the apartment and looked around for his friend. It was not long before he found him. Nance's body was lying in the bathroom, stone cold dead.

The coroner's office ruled Nance's death a homicide, the result of a subdural hematoma caused by blunt force trauma to the head. Two detectives were assigned to the case, but no suspects emerged after one month of investigation. Five years later, his death remains unsolved.

Nance's Apt: 505 S. Fair Oaks Ave. S. Pasadena

Winchell's Donuts: 438 S. Fair Oaks Ave. S. Pasadena

GEORGE REEVES

"Faster than a speeding bullet." - *opening of* Superman *TV show.*

June 16, 1959. On this date, millions of little kids' dreams were shattered. In the early morning hours, George Reeves, who starred on television for five years as Superman, was found dead with a bullet to the temple, apparently self-inflicted.

George Reeves, a rugged yet genial man, spent his youth fighting. He was a Golden Gloves boxer with a spotless record of 31-0 by the age of 20. His mother, Helen Bessolo, wanted her son to preserve his handsome looks, so he could become the next Errol Flynn. Reeves granted his mother's wish and turned his attention to the stage. He soon began a fruitful career on stage, film, and television.

Reeves never quite attained Errol Flynn status, but he did make his way into some of the all-time film classics. *So Proudly We Hail!*, *From Here To Eternity*, and *Gone With The Wind* were some of his greatest success stories. By 1951, after returning from duty in World War II, Reeves was a bit down on his luck as far as his career was concerned. He kept losing roles to the bigger named stars of the time such as Humphrey Bogart, Tyrone Power, and Clark Gable. He was eventually relegated to playing small roles in B-movies.

Then he got his big break (some called it his biggest curse).

He was picked to play the lead role of the world's greatest comic book superhero, Superman. He reluctantly signed on for the television gig, but he needed the money and embraced the role with gusto.

Over time, Reeves came to love, as well as loathe, his famous role. He enjoyed the satisfaction that he brought to millions of kids who watched him leap out of windows and save the day on a weekly basis. On the other hand, he was embarrassed that he was reduced to

1579 Benedict Canyon Drive Benedict Canyon

acting in a pair of tights. He considered himself a serious actor and felt that the Superman role was demeaning. Nonetheless, he stuck it out for five years and 104 episodes. The show was cancelled in 1957, but George Reeves had left his mark on the American psyche.

He was Superman.

During his tenure as the world's greatest superhero, Reeves kept a less than All-American secret. He was involved in a relationship for several years with a woman by the name of Toni Mannix. Sounds innocent enough, except that Mannix was married. In fact, she was married to a high-powered executive at MGM Studios named Eddie Mannix. Reportedly, Mannix approved of his wife's infidelity and looked the other way.

Toni, eight years Reeves's senior, loved to pamper her lover. She set him up with a fancy car, a healthy bank account, and a cozy house in Benedict Canyon. She was, however, manipulative and controlling towards Reeves. After several years of this treatment, Reeves ended their relationship.

In no time, Reeves hooked up with a young looker from New York named Lenore Lemon. She reportedly had ties to the Mafia and was known as a "party girl." Lemon was also viciously jealous. If any other woman so much as looked at her new man, she would fly off in a rage. Reportedly, she even punched an unsuspecting flirt who made eyes at her Superman.

After a year of dating, Reeves and Lemon got engaged. They planned to marry on June 19, 1959. In the interim, there were reports that Reeves's life had been threatened. One night, a mysterious black truck appeared out of nowhere and almost ran over the actor. Another time, Reeves nearly drove into a tree when his brakes failed to work. When his car (which was a present from Mannix) was brought in for inspection, it was discovered to have absolutely no brake fluid. There was also no sign of a leak.

On the night of June 15, Reeves, Lemon, and a few friends were celebrating the couple's upcoming wedding with a small party in their home. Lemon and Reeves both liked to throw  back a few stiff ones, and this night, they did just that. After hours of loud conversation and drink after drink, Reeves decided to turn in. He climbed up the staircase to his bedroom and stripped down to his bare essence.

Half an hour later, he ran down the stairs and yelled at his friends to leave, because they were making too much noise. An argument ensued and Reeves angrily stormed off to his

1579 Benedict Canyon Drive Benedict Canyon

room. Stunned by Reeves's outburst, Lemon, out of the blue, shouted, "Oh no! He's going to shoot himself!" Suddenly, a loud pop resounded through the house. One of the male guests, Bill Bliss, went upstairs to check on Reeves. He found the actor on the bed with a Luger pistol between his feet and a hole in the side of his head.

The mighty superhero had been felled by a single bullet.

At least, that is the story that Lenore Lemon told the authorities.

Many people believed that Reeves was actually murdered. They pointed to the following facts: no fingerprints on the gun, no powder burn marks on Reeves's head, the location of his body on top of the spent shell casing, the angle of the body not matching with the bullet discovered in the ceiling, and finally, the two additional bullet holes in the floor below the body.

No one is quite sure what happened to George Reeves that early morning. Was he depressed? Some of his friends said that he was excited about having the *Superman* television show picked up for another year. Others said that he hated the role and was even more depressed, because he had to return to it to pay the bills. Was it an accident? Reeves's toxicological reports showed that he had a .27 blood alcohol level, well beyond the legal minimum for intoxication. Was he murdered? Did Toni Mannix put a hit on her former lover, because she was jealous of his impending marriage? Did Lenore Lemon have him killed?

The bottom line is, we may never know.

It may take a person of superhuman intelligence to figure this mystery out.

1579 Benedict Canyon Drive Benedict Can-

ELIZABETH SHORT AKA THE BLACK DAHLIA

In the early morning on January 15, 1947, a young mother was out on the city streets, pushing her baby around in a stroller. Enjoying the crisp, dewy morning air she came to a sudden stop. In an undeveloped field of weeds she spotted something unusual. At first, she thought it was a department store mannequin. Upon closer inspection, she realized that it was the naked dead body of a young woman. She became even more frightened when she saw that the woman's body had been cut into two pieces.

The dead woman's name was Elizabeth Short. The 22-year-old aspiring actress was born on July 29, 1924 in Hyde Park, Massachusetts. The beautiful dark-haired girl had dreamed of becoming a movie star and longed to move to California. By the age of 19 she did just that. She moved between the coasts over the next two years, but she eventually settled in Los Angeles. She began to make the nightclub circuit, hitting some of the most high profile scenes of the time, such as the Florentine Gardens, the Hollywood Canteen, and the Boogie Woogie Club, in an attempt to get noticed. Unfortunately, it seemed as if the wrong person paid attention to her.

Numerous theories have been written about the death of Elizabeth Short. She has been portrayed as everything from a slut to a virgin with a sexual deformity. The list of her potential killers have ranged from a nightclub owner to police officers to a famous film director. Over the years, the few known facts have mixed with the conjecture that surrounded this unusual crime.

One fact that is known for sure is that Short received her famous nickname before her murder. Short was fond of a feature film playing in her neighborhood, *The Blue Dahlia*. She also liked to wear her black hair up in a bouquet-like fashion. Somehow, these ideas were transposed into the "Black Dahlia" nickname that her friends adopted for her.

It is also known that Short was last seen alive, by someone other than her killer or killers, in the lobby of the Biltmore Hotel in downtown Los Angeles. She had just returned to Los Angeles from San Diego, where she met with a man by the name of "Red" Manley. Manley claimed that he could help break the young girl into films, but he was mainly interested in getting into her pants. After their meeting, Manley drove her to the hotel and waited with her in the lobby. She was supposed to meet some friends, but they had not appeared. Manley informed her that he had to leave. Short bid him farewell and walked out of the hotel onto Olive Street. It was the last time she was seen alive.

Near 3925 S. Norton Ave. Los Angeles

Whoever killed Short did so in a grim fashion. In addition to the severing of her body, there were serious signs of torture. Her mouth had been slit open from ear to ear, leaving a morbid death grin on her lovely face. She had bruises, cuts, and scratches on her face and arms. Her left breast had been mutilated and a hunk of flesh had been removed. The flesh was later found jammed into her vagina. To add to the bizarre picture, Short had been disemboweled and her entire body had been drained of all its blood. The killer had apparently washed her body to remove any trace evidence, even shampooing her hair. Indeed, when her body was discovered, her hair was dripping wet.

Police were sent into a tizzy over the butchering. More than 250 police officers pounded the pavement looking for clues. More than 50 people came to the police with confessions. They were all tossed out as delusional deviants with sick senses of humor. The only person arrested was Manley. The 26-year-old married man was placed under intense supervision and even paraded in front of the press while handcuffed. Alas, Manley passed every lie detector test and was cleared of all suspicion.

Throughout the years, many people have attempted to solve Elizabeth Short's murder. A detective summarized the murder best when he said, "the more you learn about this case, the less you know." Did a serial killer murder Elizabeth Short? Was it a surgeon with perfect cutting skills? Was it a famous Hollywood film director? Was it a drunk with a limp? All of these theories have been tossed about as the be-all, end-all solution to this crime. The bottom line to this tale of an aspiring actress who headed to Hollywood to become a movie star is twofold.

One. We may never know who killed "The Black Dahlia."

Two. She will always be remembered, but not in the way she hoped.

PICTURED LEFT: Several houses have been erected on the land where Short's body was discovered. This is the approximate location where police discovered her.

Near 3925 S. Norton Ave. Los Angeles

BENJAMIN "BUGSY" SIEGEL

When someone mentions the name "Bugsy," the first place most people think of is Las Vegas. Forever intertwined with the history and development of Sin City, Siegel is not instantly associated with Los Angeles. Beverly Hills, however, is where this gangster met an offer he could not refuse.

Benjamin Siegel was born on February 28, 1906 in the Williamsburg neighborhood of Brooklyn. Siegel was a rough and tumble Jewish kid who ran with the wrong crowd. His childhood buddy was none other than future gangster boss Meyer Lansky. The older Lansky recruited Siegel to help run a racket on the local food vendors in the neighborhood. This small time operation soon escalated into full-out mob action. By the age of 21, Siegel was involved in hotwiring cars, drug dealing, numbers, racketeering, bootlegging, rape, and murder. He also received the nickname "Bugsy" for his affinity to "go bugs" whenever confronted. He actually hated it when someone called him "Bugsy." Anyone who did, received a hard smack to the face and remembered to call him "Ben" or "Mr. Siegel."

Siegel became a member of the Mafia syndicate group Murder, Inc., along with Lansky and Charlie "Lucky" Luciano. Together, they ran the eastern seaboard and Philadelphia.

In the late 1930s, Luciano decided that they needed to get involved in Los Angeles. Mobster Jack Dragna loosely controlled L.A., but he was less than successful. By the time Siegel arrived, Dragna was answering to him. Siegel took over the local numbers rackets, the sports bookies, and even stuck his nose into the Hollywood unions.

A new man was in town.

And he wanted even more action.

Siegel was a good-looking man who liked the company of Hollywood's celebrities. When he got into town, he looked up his childhood buddy, actor George Raft. Raft, who made a career playing big screen gangsters, took Siegel under his wing. Soon, the thug was rubbing shoulders with the biggest names in showbiz: Clark Gable, Gary Cooper, Cary Grant, and

810 N. Linden Drive Beverly Hills

Jean Harlow.

Siegel, who was married and had two kids, also liked to rub more than shoulders with Hollywood's leading ladies. He was rumored to have dated Harlow and Ketti Gallian. He also wooed actress Marie MacDonald, Countess Dorothy Dendice Taylor DiFrasso, and bit actress Virginia "Flamingo" Hill.

Hill reportedly had a shady past. Some claimed that she was another mob boss's girl. Others claimed that she grew up around the mob and was interested in scaling the family hierarchy. Siegel and Hill had a fiery relationship that lasted over six years and hundreds of fights. Mostly verbal. Sometimes physical.

By 1945, Lansky wanted Siegel to check out a little desert oasis northwest of Los Angeles. He wished to set up a casino in a little dump called Las Vegas. When Siegel arrived, he was skeptical. Las Vegas was too remote, too hot, and deader than a doornail. While there, however, he hooked up with Billy Wilkerson of the industry trade magazine *The Hollywood Reporter*. Wilkerson was attempting to build a luxury hotel in Las Vegas, but had run out of money. Siegel became intrigued and was eventually able to raise $1.5 million to complete the project. He christened the new hotel, "The Flamingo," after his mistress.

"The Flamingo" costs began to spiral upward as construction continued. Siegel was repeatedly fleeced by unscrupulous construction workers who would sell him an item, bring it in the work area, take it out the back gate, and then sell him the same item the next day. Costs also rose for another reason. Lansky believed that Siegel was lifting money from the construction fund to line his own pockets. This wasn't any chump change either. Completed in 1946, the final bill for the construction of the Flamingo: $6 million.

Siegel's bosses were not happy. They became even more upset when the hotel opened on December 26, 1946. Despite appearances from Georgie Jessel, Xavier Cugat, and Jimmy Durante, the two-week Grand Opening was less than grand. It was a major flop. Siegel was forced to close the casino until all of the finishing touches were complete. In the meantime, Lansky and his boys decided enough was enough. Benjamin "Bugsy" Siegel had to go down.

Lansky, despite calling for his friend's death, postponed the inevitable for Siegel. He called off at least two hits in an effort to see if Siegel would pull himself out of the hole he had dug. Siegel seemingly redeemed himself when the hotel reopened in March of 1947. By the end of May, the hotel had taken off. Siegel cleared a $250,000 profit in just five months time.

But, it was not enough. On June 20, 1947 at 10:30 PM, Siegel sat on a couch in Virginia Hill's home in Beverly Hills, reading the next morning edition of the *Los Angeles Times*. His friend Alan Smiley sat across from him. Siegel felt good about "The Flamingo."

810 N. Linden Drive Beverly Hills

Everything was looking up.

Suddenly, eight rifle shots burst through the front window. Siegel was riddled with bullets. One ripped through the back of his head and came out his eye socket. So did his left eye. It ended up 15 feet away from him. His brains were splattered on the floor in front of him. He died instantly.

No one has ever solved the murder of "Bugsy" Siegel. Was it Lansky's boys who put a hit on one of their own? Did Virginia Hill off her lover to make a name for herself? Or was it Jack Dragna, the main L.A. mob boss before Siegel got into town?

Once again, we will probably never know. What is known is that Siegel was not a popular man when he died. The coroner even misspelled his name on the toe tag. A photo of his foot graced every paper in the country the next day. Furthermore, only five people attended his memorial service. Only three made it to his burial.

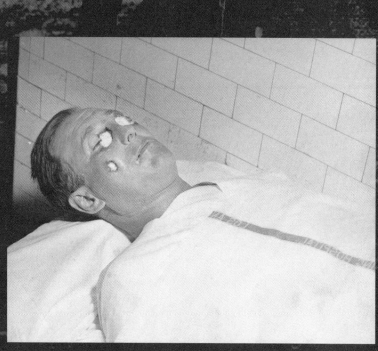

810 N. Linden Drive Beverly Hills

SILENT MOVIE MURDER

On January 17, 1997, several gunshots rang out in the lobby of Los Angeles's only silent movie theater lobby. A few seconds later, a young man ran through the partially filled theater and shot bullets into the ceiling. He escaped out the back door. The theater's organ player decided to check the lobby. As he pulled back the curtain separating the theater area from the lobby, he screamed, "Oh my God. Mr. Austin is dead!"

Laurence Austin, 74, proprietor of the Silent Movie Theater on Fairfax Avenue, lay in a pool of blood. He had been shot in the face and chest several times. A concession worker, 19-year-old Mary Giles, lay beside him. She had been shot in the chest, but somehow survived the attack.

The Silent Movie Theater had existed as a landmark theater that showcased old-time silent film classics. John and Dorothy Hampton, who had migrated west from Oklahoma, opened it in 1942. Their theater was considered a mecca for film purists during the 37 years that they operated it. The Hamptons shut the theater down in 1979, so that the couple could return to Oklahoma to tend to family matters. By the time they re-turned in 1982, John Hampton was in poor health, and they were unable to re-open the beloved movie house.

Laurence Austin befriended the Hamptons when he was 17. He attended Fairfax High School across the street and was a regular patron. He soon began to work for the Hamptons and simultaneously created the mirage that was his life. Austin was known to lie about himself. He created a faux biography that listed him as the son of the silent film actor William Austin; he claimed that his uncle was actor Albert Austin and that his mother was Cecil B. DeMille's personal seamstress. None of it was true. In reality, Austin was the son of a gardener and a seamstress who lived in modest means.

After John Hampton's death in 1990, Austin cozied up to Dorothy Hampton and convinced her to let him take over the theater. She agreed and Austin spiced up the dumpy little theater. He repainted everywhere, installed new comfortable seats, and even installed gold lamé curtains. By 1991, the theater was once again open for business.

611 N. Fairfax Avenue   West Hollywood

One of Austin's helpers who renovated the building was a 34-year-old man by the name of James Van Sickle. Van Sickle became the projectionist for the theater. He also became Austin's lover. He was also a crook. Van Sickle had been charged in the past with drug dealing and attempted murder. He also had a penchant for shacking up with older, wealthy gay men and using them for their money. In 1983, he was arrested for assaulting a Bel Air real estate tycoon.

James Van Sickle

Soon after Van Sickle hooked up with Laurence Austin, he began to take advantage of him. Austin bought all sorts of items for Van Sickle including a new Corvette. Apparently, this was not good enough for the young lover as he allegedly beat Austin up more than once. One report stated that Van Sickle even staged a robbery at the theater and had two guys hold him up and take his money.

Nice guy.

Van Sickle was involved with Austin in 1993 when Austin convinced Dorothy Hampton to turn over her possessions to him, including the theater and her extensive collection of rare films that were estimated to be worth more than $1 million. Some observers believed that Austin coerced the feeble old woman into signing everything over to him, in essence, leaving her penniless.

Dorothy Hampton developed Alzheimer's disease and was put up in the King Solomon rest home next door to the theater. Attendants to Hampton complained that Austin did not properly clothe the woman and that she had only one old, tattered cloth robe to wear.

Van Sickle wanted to get his hands on Austin's newfound wealth. He decided that he only had one way of getting the money. Laurence Austin had to be killed. He hired a 19-year-old man by the name of Christian Rodriguez to do the job for $25,000. Rodriguez, who had a wife and a child and no prior record, needed the cash. Rodriguez showed up at the theater and sat near the back. He nervously watched a Larry Semons short film, which was the lead-in for the full-length feature that night, *Sunrise*. No one would see the F.W. Murnau classic that night.

Christian Rodriguez

Rodriguez went to the lobby and asked Giles for all of the money in the cash register. He then told the girl he wanted to see the manager, Austin. The 74-year-old effeminate theater owner came out of his office, and Rodriguez immediately plugged him in the chest with a bullet. Austin fell hard to the floor. Rodriguez turned slightly and aimed at Giles. He shot her in the chest and she fell to the ground as well. Once again, he turned the pistol on Austin and fired the rest of the bullets into Austin's body. He bolted through the theater and made his escape.

He also left the money in the lobby.

James Van Sickle played the role of the mourning lover well. He fooled everyone for a while, including *America's Most Wanted* and *Hard Copy*. The police, however, had their suspicions from the beginning.

Those suspicions were confirmed seven weeks later when they brought Van Sickle in for questioning with regard to the matter of Austin's estate. Suddenly, Van Sickle pulled out a crumpled piece of paper, which he claimed he found the previous night while looking through Austin's belongings. It was a makeshift will, signed in 1994 by Laurence Austin, bequeathing all of his worldly possessions to James Van Sickle. Including the theater and all of its films.

The police were even more suspicious now and put a tail on him. They also tapped his telephone. That same day, they recorded a conversation between Van Sickle and Rodriguez. Van Sickle said that he had his $10,000 for the job. Rodriguez was grateful, but reminded Van Sickle that they agreed on $25,000. Van Sickle informed him that he would get the rest of the money very soon. Instead, Van Sickle decided to hire a new hit man to kill Rodriguez. The police set up a transaction with an officer acting as a hit man for hire. They wired the

officer, got a recording of Van Sickle seeking his services for murder, and nailed him.

Van Sickle and Rodriguez did not go to trial for almost two years. Both men were convicted of first-degree murder and given life sentences. Rodriguez also received 37 years for the attempted murder of Mary Giles.

The Silent Movie Theater shut its doors the day after Austin's murder. It remained quiet until songwriter Charlie Lustman bought and reopened the theater on November 5, 1999.

611 N. Fairfax Avenue   West Hollywood

WILLIAM DESMOND TAYLOR

In a town where illusion is law, William Desmond Taylor stood as the king. The façade that was Taylor, and Hollywood, was lifted on the morning of February 1, 1922, when Taylor's servant, Henry Peavey, ran down a courtyard sidewalk screaming that his master was dead.

The illusion that Taylor created for himself was quite grand. He was born on April 26, 1872 in Ireland. His real name was William Cunningham Deane-Tanner. He moved to New York City in 1890 and became an actor. By the age of 33, he was married and had a young daughter. Mysteriously, three years later, he disappeared, leaving behind his family.

No explanation was given for Deane-Tanner's disappearance. It was rumored that he went north to Alaska to prospect for gold. He eventually migrated south to Los Angeles and returned to acting. Deane-Tanner changed his name to William Desmond Taylor and began appearing in silent films. Though handsome, Taylor believed that he was better suited behind the camera. Even though he had never shot a single frame of film, he declared himself to be a director and was soon hired by Famous Players-Lasky, which would later become Paramount.

Taylor's first film was *The Criminal Code* (1914). He followed that movie with a string of successful box office hits including *Davy Crockett*, *Tom Sawyer*, *Huckleberry Finn*, and *Anne of Green Gables*. By 1922, William Desmond Taylor was the hottest director in town and everyone wanted to work with him. Apparently, everyone wanted to sleep with him as well.

Taylor was rumored to have bedded dozens of starlets. It was believed that he also had his share of male hustlers. Most of his intimate relations were kept quiet, since homosexuality and the bedding down with girls less than half his age was considered taboo.

Two young actresses vied for Taylor's attention during this time. One was 28-year-old Mabel Normand, who was second in popularity only to Mary Pickford. The other was a 17-year-old aspiring newcomer, Mary Miles Minter. Both women were beautiful, talented, and fetching. Each also had personal demons to deal with—Normand's was a $2,000-a-week cocaine habit; Minter's was her overbearing, dominant stage mother, Charlotte Shelby.

404 South Alvarado Street Los Angeles

Normand was the star of such films as *Mabel's Stormy Affair*, *Fatty's Wine Party*, and *Head Over Heels*. She was beloved by the filmgoing public for her numerous portrayals of a good woman who overcame evil. Normand, however, was rumored to have a slew of monsters to deal with in her real life. In addition to the coke, it was believed that she attended sex orgies and was also an alcoholic. Taylor reportedly confronted one of Normand's drug dealers and physically threatened and then assaulted the thug. Taylor feared that his actions may come back to haunt him.

Mabel Normand

Minter found success as the vestal virgin in such films as *The Eyes of Julia Deep*, *Periwinkle*, and *Anne of Green Gables*. Her popularity soared as she portrayed the innocent child, steeped with a hint of sexuality. Her mother made sure that Minter maintained her virginal image, which she knew was her daughter's key to financial success. It was Shelby's source of income as well, so she made damn sure that no one tarnished her daughter's name.

Mary Miles Minter

Most people believed that Normand and Taylor were just good friends. They also believed that Taylor had the hots for Minter. If that was the case, Minter's mother had plenty to be worried about. The movie-going public would not stand for their virgin-queen being boinked by a man more than 32 years her senior.

On the night of February 1, 1922, Normand paid a visit to Taylor's bungalow. He entertained her with the latest works of Freud and Nietzsche, but soon sent her on her way. What happened next was mere speculation.

When Peavey came screaming down the street, Taylor's neighbor, Faith McLean, made an emergency phone call. But, she did not call the police. Instead, she called Mabel Normand. She then made another phone call. This one was to Mary Miles Minter.

Normand, along with an executive from Paramount Studios, entered Taylor's bungalow. Taylor's dead body lay on the floor of his study. Still, no one had contacted the police. Normand and the executive began to search the place up and down. They were frantically looking for something.

Someone finally called the police, and they arrived to find the door to the bungalow wide open and various people wandering in and out of the house. Minter and her mother soon appeared on the scene, but they were not allowed to enter, even though Minter went ballistic and demanded to be let inside.

What was she afraid they would find?

The police wanted to know what Normand was looking for inside the bungalow. She stated that she had written several letters to Taylor and did not want them to be misconstrued by the press or the authorities. Her letters were later discovered tucked inside one of Taylor's boots. As she stated, they did not implicate a relationship of any sort between the actress and the director.

The police found more interesting information later that day. Stored away in a closet, police found several pornographic pictures of Taylor and various Hollywood concubines. They also found some rather childlike love letters written to Taylor and signed "Mary." They discovered a trunk that contained piles of women's fine lingerie. Among the camisoles and bras and panties was a silk nightie with the initials "MMM" emblazoned on the front.

The murder of William Desmond Taylor remains unsolved to this day. Some believe that Mabel Normand was responsible for his death due to jealousy. Some believe that it may have been Normand's drug dealer that killed Taylor. Most theories, however, point to Charlotte Shelby. Was she afraid that her daughter's relationship with Taylor would be discovered and exposed by the press, thereby ruining her paycheck? Or was Shelby involved with Taylor as well? Did she kill the director in a jealous rage, because he chose her daughter over her? Why did the studio representative show up at Taylor's bungalow? Did anyone ruin or steal evidence that may have led to the discovery of Taylor's murderer? Or, even more bizarre, did they plant evidence to make it seem as if Taylor were not a homosexual?

Charlotte Shelby and Minter

No one will probably ever know the answers to these questions.

The one certainty in this tragedy was the public became fed up with Hollywood and its shenanigans. The involvement of a top director and two leading Hollywood ladies turned the public off and lead to an increase in government attempts to censor motion pictures—a battle that continues to this day.

Some things will never change.

Taylor's apartment complex has been converted into a PIC 'n' SAVE parking lot.

404 South Alvarado Street Los Angeles

MICKEY THOMPSON

Race car guru and auto-parts magnate Mickey Thompson, 59, and his wife Trudy, 41, were gunned down in the driveway of their swanky home in the suburb of Bradbury, 20 miles northeast of Los Angeles, on March 16, 1988. The couple was up at 6:00 AM, ready for

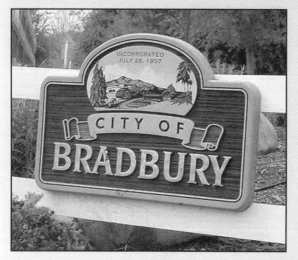

another hard day of work. Reports claimed that two men sped off on 10-speed bicycles after the murders. The couple had approximately $70,000 in cash and jewelry on their persons, but nothing was taken from them. It appeared to be a professional hit.

Mickey Thompson was a man full of gusto who tackled life headfirst on a daily basis. He began his career as a race car driver and eventually appeared in thousands of races and set over 500 speed and endurance records. He also set a land speed record in 1960 when he traveled 406.6 MPH in his Challenger I jet racer at the Bonneville Salt Flats. He also created many of the safety and competitive features in stock car and dragster racing, including wide oval tires, foul light systems, and the Hydro-Barricade, which is now used on many highways.

Despite all of Thompson's activity, he had just as much bad luck. He actually never won a single race during his career. He also killed six spectators in an off-road race in Mexico in 1953. His personal life was strained as well. In 1982, his nephew Scott Campbell was killed during a bad drug deal and tossed from an airplane over Catalina Island.

When Thompson's racing career ended, he parlayed his high-profile name into a successful auto parts and auto promotion venture known as Mickey Thompson Racing Enterprises. Thompson reportedly made lots of money. He also reputedly led a lavish lifestyle. He loved to throw parties and spend money. When he and Trudy were married, he flew 300 guests from Los Angeles to Las Vegas for an extravagant reception at Caesar's Palace.

Police believed that this cycle of making money and spending more than he had might have led to Thompson's murder. Reportedly, Thompson owed several creditors thousands of dollars. Some believed that he owed the wrong person money and had failed to pay up, the scenario for your basic contract hit.

A prime suspect in this case was Thompson's business partner in Long Beach, Michael

Goodwin. Goodwin promoted sprint-car races and had hooked up with Thompson to advance his business venture. In 1986, Thompson filed a lawsuit against Goodwin for more than $550,000 over a business dispute. He won a legal decision against Goodwin. Four months later, Goodwin filed for bankruptcy and never paid Thompson.

Thompson brought a follow-up lawsuit to collect his money. One month before his murder he received another favorable decision against Goodwin. Goodwin disappeared from the country in his yacht just days after the Thompson murders. When

he returned, he refused to answer questions about the murders, pleading the fifth in an attempt not to incriminate himself. In 1993, Goodwin was arrested in connection with the Thompson murders. Police, though they believed he was a suspect, could not pin the murders on him and Goodwin was released.

In 1997, Mickey Thompson's sister, Colleen Campbell, offered a reward of $1,000,000 for any information leading to the capture and conviction of the killer or killers of her brother. No arrests have been made as of this writing.

The Thompson home is located behind these gates in this private community.

53 Woodlyn Lane   Bradbury Estates

THELMA TODD

The death of Thelma Todd contains more Byzantine twists than a David Mamet screenplay. The famous actress from the 20s and 30s was found dead on December 16, 1935, slumped over the front seat of her car in her garage above her restaurant on the Pacific Coast Highway. Her death was ruled an accident due to carbon monoxide poisoning. The other theories, however, are much more sinister. They range from a mob hit to a jealous lover to suicide.

Thelma Todd was born on July 29, 1905 in Lawrence, Massachusetts. She grew up in the small town and was a good student who aspired to be a teacher. She also happened to be drop dead gorgeous. Todd, while contemplating a career as an educator, also appeared in several beauty contests. In 1925, she was awarded the "Miss Massachusetts" title and qualified for the "Miss America" pageant, where several talent scouts noticed her. Paramount Studios executive Jesse Lasky offered her a spot at an acting school in Astoria, New York. When she graduated, she headed for Hollywood and a short life of fame and respect.

Todd acted in over 100 films from 1926 to 1935. Many of these were comedy shorts, also known as "one reelers," in which she displayed an impeccable knack for comedy timing. She also had an adequate voice that allowed her to make the leap from silent movies to talkies, unlike many of her better-known peers who had less than appealing sounds emanating from their mouths.

Todd's looks, humor, and strong screen presence made her the number one choice as female lead in a comedy for some of the top names in the business, including Laurel and Hardy and The Marx Brothers. In fact, two of her most popular features were shot with the latter comedy troupe, *Monkey Business* (1931) and *Horse Feathers* (1932).

Her looks would not last forever, and Todd knew she had to plan for the future. In 1933,

Café: 17535 Pacific Coast Highway Pacific Palisades
Garage: 17531 Posetano Road Pacific Palisades

Todd created a partnership that would take her into the next phase of her career. It also may have led to her death.

Todd and film director Roland West partnered together to open Thelma Todd's Sidewalk Café at 17535 Pacific Coast Highway in Pacific Palisades, between Santa Monica and Malibu. The restaurant and nightclub catered to the Hollywood elite as well as the growing beach community. It may have also attracted the Mafia.

After Todd's death, rumors abounded that mob boss Lucky Luciano wanted to use Todd's establishment as a front for a gambling den. Allegedly, just days before she was discovered dead, Todd and Luciano met for lunch at the Brown Derby. Luciano supposedly informed Todd of his interests in her restaurant. She told him to kiss off and that he could have her locale over her dead body.

His retort: "That can be arranged."

She was dead in less than a week.

The night of Todd's death, she supposedly had a fight with her partner and lover, West, who also lived next to Todd in an apartment above the restaurant. Todd and West fought about her partying ways. Afterwards, she stormed off to a party at the Trocadero for debutante Ida Lupino. When she

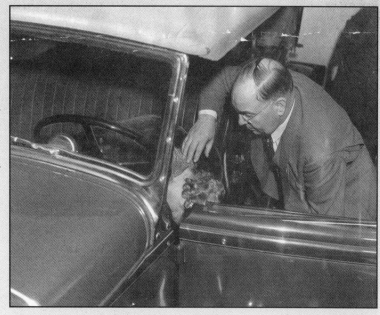

returned to the apartment, she discovered that West locked her out. She allegedly kicked on the door and screamed at him for ten minutes to open it up, but he ignored her pleas. Todd, in her cocktail dress, trudged up the 271 steps behind the restaurant to the garage on Posetano Road. She then got into her car and started the engine so she could warm up. Too drunk to stay awake, she passed out on the seat of the car and was overcome by the fumes.

Café: 17535 Pacific Coast Highway Pacific Palisades
Garage: 17531 Posetano Road Pacific Palisades

Some people believed that West followed Todd up the stairs and shut the garage door on her. Others wondered if it were really the fumes that did her in. Wildly varying descriptions

about the death scene also existed. Some claimed that blood was everywhere. Other officials claimed that Todd only had a slight trickle from her nose. The time of Todd's death was also disputed. The official report stated that she died in the early morning hours of Sunday, December 15, 1935. Other reports, however, claimed that Todd was spotted all over town, even as far as Hollywood, until late that same evening.

All in all, it seemed fishy. Luciano never said a word about his possible involvement. West's life changed instantly. He went from being a fairly high-profile director to never making another film again. The studios released at least three more of Todd's pictures posthumously. Her mother received her portion of Todd's estate and quietly accepted the police theory about the death of her daughter.

No one has been able to solve the mysterious death of Thelma Todd. With every new theory that is conjectured, the possibility of ever doing so decreases.

Café: 17535 Pacific Coast Highway Pacific Palisades
Garage: 17531 Posetano Road Pacific Palisades

LANA TURNER JOHNNY STOMPANATO and CHERYL CRANE

Famous Hollywood screen siren Lana Turner's love life seemed to resemble the old axiom: "Men, can't live with 'em, can't shoot 'em." In Turner's case, however, it was a knife rather than a gun that got her man. And it wasn't Turner who did the killing, but her 14-year-old daughter.

Lana Turner became known as the "Sweater Girl" for her penchant for wearing clingy clothes in some of her earliest films including *Love Finds Andy Hardy* (1938) and *Ziegfield Girl* (1941). She was best known for her role as the murderering adulteress in the original screen version of *The Postman Always Rings Twice* (1946). She later starred in other big pictures such as *The Bad and the Beautiful* (1952), *Imitation of Life* (1959), and *Peyton Place* (1957).

Turner was a male fantasy come to life. She was a favorite pin-up girl for the boys in World War II. Every man in the country seemed to want to get his hands on Turner. Many succeeded.

Turner was married seven different times. She had ten times as many boyfriends. Her friends claimed that once she landed her man she became bored and would begin searching out her newest conquest.

In addition to her man-hungry ways, Turner also became quite fond of booze. She worked in an overly dramatic business and that drama permeated her private life. The drama was evident in her relationship with a 33-year-old gangster bodyguard, Johnny Stompanato. He was a two-bit hoodlum bodyguard for notorious Hollywood gangster, Mickey Cohen. He also intended to woo Turner, marry her, and then use her name to establish a film production company as a front for the mob. Turner, unknowingly, would provide the cash and the cachet for the company's start.

Cohen used Stompanato to go after Turner for one reason and one reason only. The gangster had a huge "tommy gun." Stompanato was known by the nickname Oscar. Apparently, his phallus was the same size as the Academy Award golden statuette and every actress wanted to get her paws on it.

Lana Turner won the Golden prize.

Ironically, it was Turner's chance to get her hands on the real Oscar that may have led to Stompanato's death. In 1958, Turner was nominated for the Best Actress award for her role in the melodramatic big screen soap opera, *Peyton Place*. She was in London filming *Another*

Time, Another Place with newcomer Sean Connery when she received word of the nomination. She probably would have taken Stompanato to the ceremony, but an earlier fracas between him and Connery became the final straw. Allegedly, Stompanato was jealous of Connery and approached him on the set with a gun. The future James Bond whacked the gun out of the gangster's hand and decked him with a single punch.

Turner, Stompanato, and Crane

Stompanato also liked to punch things. Mainly Lana Turner. By the time the Oscars came around, Turner was sick of his antics and sick of his fists. She was ready to give him the boot. She started by snubbing her lover and taking her daughter, Cheryl Crane, 14, to the awards show.

Stompanato was pissed.

Turner did not care and went without him. She lost to Joanne Woodward and soon returned home to her angry boyfriend. Their relationship cooled off over the next two weeks and their fights escalated.

On April 4, 1958, Good Friday, Turner and Stompanato got into yet another argument. Crane was lying down in her bed and could overhear the heated discourse. She believed she heard Stompanato scream obscenities at her mother and then threaten her life. Though Crane liked Stompanato, she feared for her mother's safety. As the screaming escalated, Crane went down to the kitchen and grabbed an eight-inch knife. She then walked up the stairs to her mother's boudoir where the couple was still fighting.

Crane claimed that she walked into the room and held the knife, upside down, at her stomach level. She stated that she saw Stompanato raise his hand to strike her mother, so she hesitantly thrust the knife towards him. He immediately fell to the ground landing on his back. He was dead.

Several people were called to the scene of the crime, including Turner's doctor and lawyer. Oh yeah, and eventually the police were called. When they saw Stompanato's body, they noticed that the knife penetrated all the way through the man's stomach. One officer claimed "that you could see the carpet through the hole in his body."

Crane was arrested and taken to the juvenile detention center that night. The media jumped on the story, and the rumors began to spread. Many people believed that Turner, not her daughter, had killed Stompanato.

Crane was not held for long. The coroner's grand jury held a hearing in which Turner testified. The grand jury convened and, in less than 20 minutes, returned with the recommendation to not press charges. They considered Crane's actions to be justifiable. It was merely self-defense.

730 N. Bedford Drive Beverly Hills

WONDERLAND MURDERS

Police received a call from a worker who heard a woman moaning at a home in Laurel Canyon on July 1, 1981. Upon arrival, they discovered a gruesome scene. The moaning woman, Susan Lanius, was covered in blood, but still alive. She was lucky.

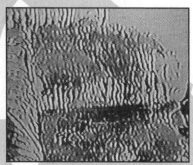

Four other people, Ronald Lanius, Joy Audrey Miller, William Ray Deveral, and Barbara Lee Richardson were all discovered bloodied and dead. Their blood was splattered around the house to such an extent that one officer said it appeared as if someone had thrown buckets of the grue on the walls. The four victims had been savagely beaten with what appeared to be either a baseball bat or a metal pipe. They were bludgeoned beyond recognition. One man had his face completely caved in.

The police realized that this house, just two blocks away from then-Governor Jerry Brown, was a known drug den. They soon discovered that the house had another notorious inhabitant—porno legend John Holmes.

Holmes, known for his prodigious physical enhancement, a 14-inch penis, was the first major star of the adult film industry. He claimed to have appeared in over 2,500 films and slept with at least 14,000 women. Many rich women of Los Angeles even paid for his services because they wanted him to sire their children.

Holmes reigned as the "King of Porn" for several years.

That is, until he got hooked on cocaine.

In the late 70s, Holmes met club owner Adel Nasrallah, also known as Eddie Nash. Nash was the "King of the Club Scene" in L.A., owning such famous spots as the Kit Kat and the Starwood, a rock club that showcased up and coming rock bands such as Quiet Riot and Van Halen. Nash was also a big-time drug dealer.

Holmes claimed that he never tried cocaine during the years he was on a porn set. Once he did, he was hooked. He turned to Nash, who made a small investment in the porno star. Nash gave Holmes $10,000 worth of free coke. Once Holmes was hooked, he made him pay. Holmes would spend up to $750,000 on cocaine in the next year. By the summer of 1980,

8763 Wonderland Avenue Laurel Canyon

Holmes was strung out, emaciated, and unable to sustain an erection. As a result, porno filmmakers blacklisted him.

He eventually stumbled into the den of drug dealers in the Wonderland house. The group made their mark by ripping off other dealers, posing as police officers, and confiscating their goods. They would turn around and sell the drugs to their own clientele. Holmes turned to them for his drugs. As a result, he became the delivery boy and house monkey. Most of the men did not care for Holmes as a person and constantly berated the screen legend. He was a party joke to them.

Holmes simultaneously sought out Nash for drugs. In the spring of 1981, he needed some cocaine. Nash charged him $1,000 for the score. Since he did not have that kind of cash, Holmes put up the Wonderland gang's gun collection as collateral. Holmes smoked the coke, but never paid Nash off. His Wonderland housemates were furious at Holmes for hocking their cherished weapons and demanded he do something to rectify his mistake.

Holmes informed his housemates that he would head over to Nash's home, get high with the club owner, and then take off through a sliding glass door in the back. He would leave the door unlocked and open for easy entry. The Wonderland crew could enter through the door and make their way into the house while Nash slept. Holmes knew where Nash kept his stash of jewelry, drugs, and money. He drew a diagram of the house for the gang, told them where to get the goods, and then headed for Nash's house.

When Holmes returned to the Wonderland house, he informed the crew that they should head out. Instead, they slept through the night, wiped out from too many drugs. They woke at 8:00 AM the next day and made their way to Nash's place.

Three men, Deveral, Lanius, and another guy by the name of Tracy McCourt slipped through the sliding glass door and into Nash's home. Nash's 300-pound bodyguard Gregory Diles confronted the men. They were able to place the large man in cuffs, but one of the robbers' guns went off and grazed Diles. Nash heard the gunfire and immediately dropped down to his knees and began to beg for his life. The crew found his reaction funny and, holding a gun to his head, made him continue the pleading. As Nash cried, they proceeded to clean him out. They stole over $100,000 in cash, several thousands of dollars worth of jewelry, and over eight pounds of cocaine, worth thousands of dollars. They returned to Wonderland and divvied up the drugs, giving Holmes a tiny amount of the supply.

Holmes took off to meet one of his girlfriends and snort the coke. Meanwhile, Nash immediately suspected the porn star. He had Diles track him down and bring him to Nash. Nash berated Holmes and then proceeded to torture him for hours. Eventually, Holmes squealed on the Wonderland gang.

The fun was just beginning.

Reports varied widely regarding what happened next. The most popular belief was that Diles and two other unnamed men took Holmes with them back to the Wonderland house. Holmes was sent to the buzzer to gain access. Diles and his men then grabbed the skinny actor and entered the domicile. From that point on, Diles and the two other men proceeded to beat Susan Lanius, who was only

8763 Wonderland Avenue Laurel Canyon

visiting, and Miller. They then went upstairs and killed Richardson, who was asleep in her bed. They found Ron Lanius and Deveral in another room and pummeled them.

In later years, Holmes revealed that he was forced to watch each of the murders up close. Reportedly, he was covered in blood and frightened out of his wits. Soon after the murders, however, Holmes would not talk. He went to Florida for over five months to escape the police and the wrath of Nash. When he returned, police quickly located him. They wanted Holmes to squeal on Nash, but he would not play their game. He claimed that he had no idea who killed the Wonderland gang. He acted as if he really did not care either, referring to the group as scum. Furthermore, it was believed that Nash had threatened Holmes's life should he rat Nash out.

The lawyers were furious with Holmes. They knew he was the key witness against Nash. He continued to refuse to speak, so they threw the book at him. Holmes's palm print was found above the headboard of the bed of one of the victims, so the district attorney used this evidence to charge Holmes with the murders. They did not seem to care that it was once the same bed where Holmes had slept. Holmes maintained his mute state and eventually won an acquittal in the murder case against him.

In 1988, John Holmes passed away. He died of AIDS at the age of 43. Police detectives were near his deathbed only two weeks before he died, trying to elicit information about the Wonderland case. They got nothing from him.

Eddie Nash was tried twice for the Wonderland murders. Each time he was let go. In 1990, the jurors deadlocked 11-1 for conviction. An 18-year-old female juror was the lone holdout and would not budge. The lawyers believed that Nash had bribed her, but no proof was ever offered. The charges were thrown out. In the second trial in 1991, the jury acquitted Nash of the murders.

In 2000, Eddie Nash was brought to Superior Court for racketeering, tax evasion, and drug charges. A charge for the Wonderland Murders also loomed under the guise of racketeering. Since it is in a different court and under a different charge, Nash could be tried again without the court violating the double jeopardy clause. On the day of his preliminary trial, jail doctors diagnosed him as suffering from tuberculosis. He also suffers from emphysema. Authorities are desperate to convict him of these murders before he dies.

Will they beat the clock?

8763 Wonderland Avenue Laurel Canyon

NATALIE WOOD

In the early morning hours of November 29, 1981, Hollywood's Princess perished in the chilly waters of Catalina Island. Authorities believed that Natalie Wood accidentally slipped into the water while attempting to board a small dinghy attached to her 55-foot yacht.

Natalie Wood was born Natasha Gurdin on July 20, 1938 to two Russian immigrants. She had appeared in her first movie at the age of four. Her most notable role in her early years was in the Christmas holiday standard *Miracle on 34th Street*. By the time she was 18 years old, she had already appeared in over 30 movies.

Her big break as an adult actress was in 1955's *Rebel Without A Cause*, alongside such other young, hot actors as James Dean, Sal Mineo (see p. 11), and Nick Adams (see p. 74). For her work in this film, she was nominated for a Best Supporting Actress Academy Award at the youthful age of 17.

Wood's success in Hollywood could not be stopped, on screen or off. She appeared in such major Hollywood productions as *West Side Story, The Searchers, Bob & Ted & Carol & Alice, Splendor In The Grass* (for which she received a Best Actress nod), and *Love With A Proper Stranger* (which garnered her second Best Actress nomination). During her explosive ascendancy to the top of the Hollywood throne she was said to have delved into the pleasures of the flesh off screen. She was rumored to have dated practically every leading man of that time, including Frank Sinatra, Warren Beatty, and Elvis Presley.

Despite her seemingly wild ways with Hollywood's leading men, most of her friends claimed that Wood was much more simple. She enjoyed working in movies, but preferred the

Blue Cavern Point, Isthmus Bay Catalina Island

low-key lifestyle of a married woman who wanted to raise children. So, in 1957, she married actor Robert Wagner. The young couple, however, felt pressured by outside influences, and eventually divorced in 1962.

Wood married again in the late 60s. She and her new husband, producer Richard Gregson, had a daughter, Natasha (herself an actress today who goes by the name of Natasha Gregson Wagner). Her marriage to Gregson, however, was ill-fated and they were soon divorced.

Subsequently, Wood and Wagner realized that they were meant for each other. They reunited and quickly married a second time in a small ceremony on a boat in Malibu in 1972. They had a seemingly peaceful marriage and even had another child, Courtney, in 1974.

By the early 80s, both actors' careers began to slowly quiet as they aged. Wood did land a role, however, in a sci-fi thriller called *Brainstorm*, which featured the hot young actor Christopher Walken. For whatever reason, rumors spread that Walken had a thing for Wood and that she had returned his interest. Walken denied that they were ever involved.

On November 29, 1981, just a few days after Thanksgiving, Wood, Wagner, and Walken headed out to Catalina Island to celebrate the success of the shooting of the movie. They decided to unwind at the Harbor Reef restaurant. Supposedly, this is when things started to unravel.

Waitresses at the restaurant claimed that the trio caused quite a ruckus. They had drunk numerous bottles of champagne and engaged in boisterous activities in front of the other patrons. One waitress stated that Wood seemed as if she wanted to be the center of attention. The staff complained later that the Wood/Wagner/Walken party was rude, messy, and miserable tippers. By the time they had left the table, all three were allegedly soused.

They returned via their dinghy to the yacht, *Splendour*, named after Wood's favorite film. From here, the story gets a bit murky.

Days after his wife's death, spokespeople for Wagner stated that his wife died from an accidental slip. He claimed that she went to her bed on the yacht and soon became annoyed by the insistent banging of the rubber dinghy against the boat. She went to do something about it, slipped over the side, and drowned in the chilly water.

The skipper, Dennis Davern, had a different tale. He claimed that Walken and Wagner were fighting. And, it was over Natalie Wood. Apparently, Wagner became incensed, because he knew that Walken wanted to sleep with his wife. Reportedly, Wagner smashed a wine bottle, held it up to Walken's face, and screamed at the actor, "Go ahead and fuck her if you want to so badly!" The altercation upset Wood so much that she hurriedly escaped to

Blue Cavern Point, Isthmus Bay Catalina Island

the dinghy to seek solace from the macho dick-swinging that was taking place.

Who knows if either of these stories was true?

Coroner to the stars, Dr. Thomas Noguchi, wasn't sure, but he definitely had a theory. According to his book, *Coroner*, he received a report from a colleague, who not only was a coroner, but also happened to be moored near Wood's yacht on the morning of her death. He concluded something far less sinister, but much more tragic.

He believed that the actress did indeed escape to the dinghy. She then slipped and fell into the water. Instead of being worried, however, Wood did not panic because she was only a couple of feet from the yacht. She attempted to crawl up the side of the rubber dinghy, but could not get in due to the watered-down coat that she had been wearing when she slipped off the yacht. By now, her coat weighed anywhere from 30-40 pounds--quite a burden for a 100-pound woman in icy cold water with a .14 (or higher) alcohol level.

As Wood attempted to get into the dinghy, she realized that the smaller boat was beginning to drift away from the yacht out into the open sea. This realization led to a more frightened state, as there were reports of a woman screaming for help. Simultaneously, a thoughtless band of revelers were cranking up their stereo on a party boat, drowning out her pleas for help.

According to Noguchi, Wood realized that no one was coming to save her. She decided she had to take action. She grabbed the 11-foot dinghy and steered it back toward the shore. She was aware of a windstream that could propel her and the boat to safety. Somehow, the diminutive woman did just that. Frightened, slightly intoxicated, shivering cold, and weighed down with soaked clothes, Natalie Wood was determined to live.

She almost made it.

The dinghy was found early the next morning on the shore of Blue Cavern on the northern Isthmus side of Catalina Island. Her body was found floating, in the red coat, less than 200 yards from shore. She was only minutes away from saving her own life.

No one knows for sure how Natalie Wood perished. No one is talking either. Walken and Wagner refuse to comment on that night. The skipper is not considered the most reliable source.

Was it an accident? Was there foul play?

The answers lie somewhere out in the open sea.

Blue Cavern Point, Isthmus Bay Catalina Island

CHAPTER 5
SEDITION

Hollywood tends to steer clear of national-level political chaos. Despite a low profile, there have been two cases that drew world-wide attention. Each story had a celebrity character as a victim and an antagonist with a desire to overthrow an entrenched system. In the end, the only statement made was that even the highest level of celebrity is not assured of his or her safety.

PATTY HEARST & THE SLA

On February 4, 1974, Patty Hearst, 19-year-old granddaughter of publishing magnate William Randolph Hearst, was kidnapped in Berkeley, California, by a radical group of political extremists known as the Symbionese Liberation Army (SLA). Over the next few months, the SLA forced Hearst to participate in their "revolutionary" cause against corporate capitalism. In the end, the group met its demise at the hands of the Los Angeles Police Department and SWAT team.

Hearst was held captive for several days in an apartment in San Francisco. She claimed that the SLA, led by former prison escapee Donald DeFreeze AKA Cinque Mtume, neglected, brainwashed, and raped her over a period of three months. Simultaneously, the group demanded a unique ransom from Hearst's parents. Mistakenly assuming that Patty's parents were rich beyond all measure, the SLA required that they give $70 worth of food to every poor person in California. By their calculations, the total ransom amounted to over $400 million. The Hearsts agreed to give $2 million dollars. The SLA scoffed at the counteroffer and continued their experimentation on Hearst.

The crux of Hearst's transformation occurred on April Fool's Day. The SLA informed the press that they had released Hearst, but she asked to join the group and help support their cause. She also changed her name to "Tania." The public sympathy for Hearst began to wane as they suspected she had rebelled against her family and sympathized with her captor's causes.

The SLA decided to show the world that "Tania" was now one of them. On April 15, 1974, Hearst and four other members of the group stormed the Hibernia Bank in the Sunset district of San Francisco. They held up the bank, took hostages, and posed for over 1,200 video surveillance photos.

The public was now solidly opposed to the SLA and especially Patty Hearst.

Mtume decided that the group needed to relocate to Los Angeles to go further underground. They first moved into a home at West 84th Street in Compton. They used it as a safehouse.

Meanwhile, on May 16, Hearst and two other members, Bill and Emily Harris AKA Teko and Yolanda, stopped in Mel's Sporting Goods Store at Crenshaw Boulevard to pick up some supplies. Teko and Yolanda went inside, while Hearst stayed in the car. She claimed that she did not escape, because she had been taught to defend her fellow members or else be

1974: 1446 E. 54th Street   South Central Los Angeles
Present: 1456 E. 54th Street South Central Los Angeles

Bill Harris

Emily Harris

killed. While in the store, Teko shoved some socks into his pants leg. This led to a confrontation between the SLA members and the security guards, who recognized them and called for backup. The cops surrounded Teko and Yolanda, when suddenly, Hearst/Tania ran out of the van and began to shoot a rifle over her head. The police took off, and Teko, Yolanda, and Hearst escaped to a motel in Orange County.

After arriving at the motel, the fugitives turned on the television. They saw a strange sight on every channel. The rest of their group had relocated the night before to 1446 East 54th Street in Compton. No one else in the neighborhood wanted to help the SLA in any way, so Mtume had to pay $100 to let his gang sleep there. The house was now on every television station with a live shot of police surrounding it.

In less than five minutes, shots rang out and a full-scale war erupted. Over 100 cops fired into the small stucco house that contained six members of the SLA, as well as the regular occupants of the house. The SLA members were decked out in full riot gear, including gas masks and armor, and had massive caches of weapons and ammunition. The cops were heavily armed as well with all manner of firearms and even hand grenades.

Gunfire was constant for over an hour. Two of the original occupants were released from the house, narrowly avoiding being killed by police. After their release, the house burst into flames. Within min-

utes, the entire house collapsed. Five SLA members, Mtume, William Wolfe, Angela Atwood, Patricia Soltysik, and Nancy Perry were found dead—two from gunshot wounds and the

1974: 1446 E. 54th Street   South Central Los Angeles
Present: 1456 E. 54th Street South Central Los Angeles

other three were burned beyond recognition. A sixth body, Camilla Hall, was found the following day. The police were not sure if Hearst was part of the destruction. It took a coroner's examination of all the bodies before everyone knew that she was not involved in the shootout.

A new house was built on the site and the address was changed to 1456 E. 54th Street.

Hearst, Teko, and Yolanda were soon on the run, but they would all be captured more than one-and-a-half years later. Hearst was convicted of armed robbery and sentenced to seven years hard time in 1976. President Jimmy Carter released her from prison on a recommendation for time served.

Former President Bill Clinton pardoned Hearst on his last day of office, January 20, 2001.

1974: 1446 E. 54th Street   South Central Los Angeles
Present: 1456 E. 54th Street South Central Los Angeles

ROBERT KENNEDY

"It is not enough to allow dissent. We must demand it." – Robert Kennedy

In 1968, Robert Kennedy, younger brother of former President John Kennedy, had just won the California Democratic primary. He was on his way to becoming the President of the United States. Many people, however, did not want to see him ascend to the highest level of power in the land.

The general consensus, indeed the official courtroom consensus, was that a deranged 24-year-old Palestinian immigrant, Sirhan Bishara Sirhan, was the lone gunman who took Robert Kennedy's life. It was reported that Sirhan, who remained loyal to his native Palestine, was upset by the younger Kennedy's support of Israel, the major religious and political enemy of Sirhan's homeland. Allegedly, Sirhan kept extensive journals that detailed his hatred for the potential Democratic nominee.

Other signs of Sirhan's mental instability surfaced during the trial. Charges were alleged that he was interested in the occult, self-hypnosis, and self-generated telekinesis. One report even stated that he willed a horse to be hurt by projecting his thoughts towards the animal before a race. The horse ran into a wall and finished last. According to the report, Sirhan believed he was responsible.

So the popular mainstream theory was sold as mental instability.

Similar to John Kennedy's assassination, however, severe doubts had been raised. Some believe that the acceptance of Sirhan as Kennedy's lone assassin may have been part of a vast cover-up. Allegations had been made that the real murderers were everyone from the FBI, to the CIA, to—you name it. No one knew for sure.

It was known that Kennedy had just given a celebratory speech in the main ballroom of the Ambassador Hotel, cheering on the troops over his recent victory in the Golden State. He left the room to a rousing ovation at approximately 12:15 AM on June 5, 1968. A last minute change of plans led Kennedy and his entourage  through the kitchen of the hotel. Kennedy slowly traversed the room, taking time to greet the

3400 Wilshire Boulevard   Los Angeles

employees.

At this point, things become fuzzy.

According to conventional wisdom, Sirhan approached the Senator and yelled either "Kennedy must die!" or "Kennedy, you son of a bitch!" He then plugged the Senator with four bullets. One bullet hit his jacket and did not enter the skin. Two bullets hit him in the back. A fourth bullet struck Kennedy in the back of the head. This last one was the fatal shot. Kennedy immediately slumped to the ground. He was rushed to Central Receiving Hospital, but fell into a coma and was dead by the next morning.

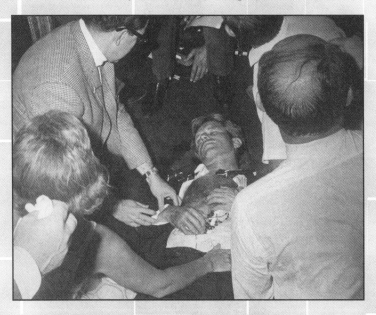

Some high-profile celebrities were present at the assassination. Football player (and later O.J. Simpson confidante) Roosevelt "Rosey" Grier, Olympic decathlon winner Rafer Johnson, and writer George Plimpton all rushed to the aid of the fallen Senator. Johnson even confiscated the gun from Sirhan's hand, took it home with him, and eventually returned it to the police—two hours later and not before he wrote down the serial number.

Bizarre!

Some people claimed that these facts did not tell the whole story. Witnesses present at the shooting believed that several more shots were fired. They claimed that more than one gun was used. They also believed that Sirhan's gun was not even a real gun, but a starter's gun that shot blanks. No official investigation agreed with these suspicions.

Several books have been written about the assassination of Robert Kennedy. The theories run a wide spectrum of ideas. The common theme, however, was that Bobby Kennedy posed a threat to the established government of the United States. After the death of his brother, Bobby became more of an activist who fought bitter battles against established powers and corrupt politicians. If he became President, he vowed to uncover the mystery that surrounded the death of his brother.

Robert Kennedy believed that every voice should be heard. Others, apparently, wanted to make sure his was silenced.

3400 Wilshire Boulevard   Los Angeles

CHAPTER 6
ORGANIZED GRIME

The Los Angeles Police Department and its surrounding forces are responsible for maintaining control in a county that consists of more than 18 million residents. The majority of the time, the police are able to work in conjunction with the citizens in a peaceful coexistence. Sometimes, they do not.

LORI GONZALEZ

Sometimes, no matter who you are, violent crime will rear its ugly head. Case in point, Lori Gonzalez, 20-year-old granddaughter of Los Angeles Police Department Chief Bernard Parks. She was murdered outside of a Popeye's Chicken & Biscuits fast food restaurant in Baldwin Village on Saturday, May 27, 2000, at approximately 10:15 PM. She was the victim of a possible gang retaliation hit. The intended victim was in the passenger side of her car.

The question everyone asked: What was Lori Gonzalez doing hanging out with a known gang member?

Gonzalez was the product of a biracial marriage: her mother black, her father Hispanic. They divorced when she was three, and her father remarried a white woman. Gonzalez would live with her father in the quiet upscale town of Mission Viejo in Orange County. She often returned to Los Angeles to visit her mother and other family members and friends. Some of these kids she grew up with became gang members. One was Ernest Thomas Gray.

Gonzalez and Gray were first loves for one another. Gonzalez, however, entered the "real" world of school and employment; Gray joined the Black P-Stones gang. Gonzalez worked two jobs, taught Sunday school classes, and attended cosmetology school. She was determined to make something of herself. Gray, on the other hand, was arrested several times for battery, robbery, and assault with a deadly weapon. But something about Gray attracted Gonzalez. Whether it was a fascination with a "Bad Boy," or merely Gonzalez's desire to help reform her friend, we will never know.

On that Saturday night, just one week before her 21st birthday, Gonzalez went out with Gray. She declined an offer to spend the Memorial Day weekend camping with her father. She also stayed away from her fiancée, who was looking forward to celebrating Gonzalez's birthday in Las Vegas the next weekend.

Unfortunately, Gonzalez did not know that the 19-year-old Gray, who had been in and out of juvenile correctional facilities and jail for several years of his life, was a wanted man that night. Not by the police, but by the local Crips gang. Just three weeks before, the Crips had shot at Gray. He had mistakenly been on their turf.

3050 S. La Brea Avenue Los Angeles

While driving around that night, Gonzalez and Gray pulled into the Popeye's drive-thru for a quick bite. They paid for their meals and headed out to LaBrea Avenue. Gonzalez pulled up to the street and waited to turn onto it. Suddenly, from nowhere, a young male walked up to the passenger side of her car, pulled out a gun, and squeezed the trigger. Gray saw the man approach and immediately ducked for cover. Instead of hitting Gray, the gunman's bullets hit Gonzalez. She was shot in the torso and head. The killer took off, running north on LaBrea Avenue and then east down an alleyway.

Gonzalez bled profusely. Gray attempted to staunch the flow of blood, but he was too late. Lori Gonzalez, granddaughter of the city's Chief of Police, was dead.

For a week-and-a-half, no one knew who killed Lori Gonzalez. Then, on June 8, 2000, the L.A.P.D. announced that they had arrested 18-year-old Samuel Sharad Shabazz, a member of the Crips. He had a laundry list of offenses that included robbery and assault. He also, allegedly, had a grudge against Gray. Sources claimed that Gray was the target that night, not Gonzalez. She was merely in the wrong place at the wrong time with the wrong guy.

Upon Shabazz's arraignment, it was discovered that he had only been released from custody 19 days before Gonzalez's murder. He had been held for the attempted murder of eight people during a drive-by shooting at the nearby Jeremiah's Pastrami restaurant. He was released, because the District Attorney's office was unable to track down any of the victims or witnesses who were needed to testify against the young gangbanger—an all too common occurrence. All charges were dropped, and Shabazz was never brought to trial. Nineteen days later, he allegedly shot and killed Lori Gonzalez. He is currently in jail awaiting his trial that may not take place until 2002.

3050 S. LaBrea Avenue Los Angeles

THE RODNEY KING BEATING AND THE 1992 L.A. RIOTS

In the early morning of March 3, 1991, California Highway Patrol husband and wife team T.J. and Melanie Singer received a call about a speeding motorist in a white Hyundai traveling at a high rate of speed down the 210 Freeway. The motorist, an African-American male, had two passengers with him in the car. He was traveling in excess of 110 MPH.

The driver's name was Rodney King.

King, 25, an unemployed construction worker, had been out on the town drinking malt liquor and smoking marijuana. He led the Singers on an eight-minute high-speed chase along the freeway. He exited Osborne Boulevard, where Foothill Division officers Laurence Powell and Timothy Wind took over. King stopped at a red light, but failed to yield to the officers' commands. King ended up in the Lake View Terrace neighborhood. After several minutes of pursuit, King finally pulled into an

empty lot across the street from the Mountainback Apartments at 11777 Foothill Boulevard.

By the time he stopped, several police cars arrived on the scene.

Bryant Allen and Freddie Helms, King's passengers, got out of the car without resistance. They had their hands raised high and got down on the ground when ordered by the police officers.

King, on the other side of the car, did not.

Officers on the scene claimed that King knocked over an officer and reached into his pocket, as if going for a gun. According to Sergeant Stacy Koon, he was forced to zap King with a Taser gun of 50,000 volts. Not once, but twice. Still, King would not go down. The officers claimed that they feared King was whacked out on PCP, a drug known to give its users superhuman strength. However, they seemingly had subdued the suspect.

At this time, 31-year old George Holliday, a manager of a plumbing store who lived in the Mountainback apartment complex pulled out his brand new video camera. He had a direct

King Beating: Across from the Mountainback Apts.
At 11777 Foothill Boulevard   Lake View Terrace

view of the scene unfolding before him, which was well lit by the headlights of the police cars and helicopters overhead.

What he recorded changed Los Angeles forever.

Over the course of the next 81 seconds, Holliday documented a scene of over-the-top police brutality. Officers Powell, Koon, Wind, and Theodore Briseno proceeded to pummel the doped up offender. King received 56 blows to the body with a metal baton, a foot on the neck, and a baton blow to the head, in addition to the electric jolts provided by Koon's Taser. King finally complied and was subsequently hog-tied by the officers. He was then taken away in an ambulance.

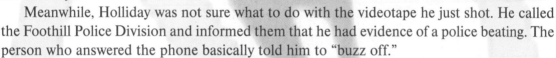

King was charged with evading arrest and held for four days.

Meanwhile, Holliday was not sure what to do with the videotape he just shot. He called the Foothill Police Division and informed them that he had evidence of a police beating. The person who answered the phone basically told him to "buzz off."

Holliday then contacted local television station KTLA. It was his favorite station. A representative from KTLA viewed the tape, confirmed its authenticity with the police department, and then broadcast it with one seemingly minor change. The first 13 seconds of the videotape was excised due to blurriness.

This edit changed everything.

Holliday's tape was immediately picked up by all of the major news networks and replayed ad nauseum. Almost everyone in the country witnessed the beating of Rodney King. Over and over and over again.

A huge uproar went out, and soon the four officers were placed on trial. Appellate Judge Joan Dempsey Klein decided to relocate the trial out of Los Angeles to avoid a potential disruption. Instead, the trial took place north of Los Angeles in Simi Valley, home to one of the most cop friendly areas in the country.

The KTLA edit factored into the trial immediately. The defense's first move was to play the unedited videotape, which contained the missing 13 seconds that no one else had seen. The all-white jury was shocked to see the beginning of the tape where an unrestrained Rodney King leapt from the ground and lunged towards Officer Powell. Powell, in defense mode, took a swing at King's neck, and then the tape went blurry for the next ten seconds. When the tape came back into focus, the beating of King commenced full throttle.

The Simi Valley jury believed that the media had lied to them. After numerous days of testimony, the jury deliberated on the fate of the police officers. They spent a total of ten days going over the charges. On April 29, 1992, they returned with a verdict of not guilty. Unfortunately, the Los Angeles Police Department and its Chief, Daryl Gates, were not

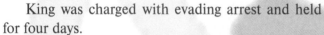

King Beating: Across from the Mountainback Apts.
At 11777 Foothill Boulevard   Lake View Terrace

ready for what would happen next.

Word of the verdict leaked out to the residents of South Central. Mayhem ensued. Several residents wandered in the streets and took potshots at motorists who were not black. Drivers were pulled from their cars and beaten into bloody pulps. One man, in particular, drew the attention of the entire nation.

His name was Reginald Denny.

Florence and Normandie is now a thriving business community.

Denny, a truck driver, was stuck in traffic at the corner of Florence Avenue and Normandie Avenue. A group of four young black males saw the driver and pulled him from the cab of his truck. They proceeded to beat the helpless driver, who was in the wrong place at the wrong time. News helicopters caught the assault on film and broadcast it to the entire nation. Damian Williams struck Denny in the head with a brick sending the large man to his knees, unconscious. Williams performed a celebratory dance, like an NFL player who had never been in the end zone. To add insult to injury, another man snuck up on Denny and pilfered his wallet.

From that point, it was on.

The riots lasted three days. People of all colors took part in the destruction. Blacks, Asians, Latinos, and whites looted stores from South Central to Long Beach, from Hollywood to Pomona. Nothing could stop the rage until the National Guard was brought in. By the third day, Rodney King surfaced to make an impassioned plea for everyone to "just get along."

It was too little too late. The results of the riots were the worst in modern American history: 53 people were dead, 1,100 buildings were burned, and over $900 million in damage was committed.

Then-President George Bush Sr. visited the city and declared that the Rodney King incident was not over. He demanded a federal investigation into the matter and a new trial was held in federal court. Officers Koon and Powell were convicted this time and sentenced to 30 months in prison for civil rights violations.

King sued the city of Los Angeles for $400 million. He was awarded $3.8 million. He took his money and started a rap label. However, he has still had trouble with the law, having been arrested more than five times with charges ranging from drug possession and drunk driving to spousal abuse.

Riot Epicenter: At the corner of 1400 W. Florence Ave. & 7100 S. Normandie Ave. South Central Los Angeles

ANTHONY DWAIN LEE

Nothing may seem harder than being a black man in Los Angeles. With racial barriers erected in business and suspicion alerted amongst police officers, it may seem impossible for many black males to live here.

One African-American male who overcame his early indiscretions was 39-year-old Anthony Dwain Lee. His personal ascent, however, was cut short at 12:15 AM on October 28, 2000 at a Halloween party in Benedict Canyon, when nine bullets were shot by an anxious police officer.

Lee grew up in the world of gangs in Northern California. He was a troubled youth who found an escape in the theater. He began his acting career in Ashland, Oregon and eventually did well enough to move to Los Angeles to follow his dream. Lee, while not a box office name, worked consistently. He landed a role as a lawyer in the 1997 Jim Carrey comedy, *Liar, Liar*. He also had a recurring role on the television series *Brooklyn South* and had recently completed a guest spot as a homeless man on the top-rated television show, *ER*.

Lee combined his success in the acting world with a sense of self-improvement in his real life. In 1985, he became a Buddhist as part of the Soka Gakkai International group. Lee gave inspirational speeches at the group's meeting places. He seemed at peace, and he was—except for one aspect. According to his friend Mary Lin, Lee told her his biggest fear "was getting killed by cops, because I'm a tall black man."

The 6'3" Lee attended a Halloween party in the tony Benedict Canyon neighborhood on Friday, October 28, 2000. It took place in an old blue mansion known as "The Castle." The party was attended by several L.A. scenesters, including actors, screenwriters, dot-commers, and more.

Lee arrived around 9:30 PM dressed in a devil costume. He also carried a prop revolver with him that resembled a .357 Magnum Desert Eagle semiautomatic handgun. Lee's friends begged him not to carry the gun, but he claimed he was not afraid. He was making a statement. The devil costume and gun represented his old gang lifestyle and the man he used to be. He was not that way anymore.

The party was a huge success. Everyone dressed up—there was the Al Gore and George W. Bush couple strolling around hand in hand, there was the *SNL* character "The Ladies' Man," and there were even a few people dressed up as cops. By midnight, the party was breaking up. The neighborhood had a strict noise policy, and the hosts of the party had leased out a nightclub for the party to relocate by 12:30 AM.

9701 *Yoakum Drive   Benedict Canyon*

At 12:15 AM, someone called the police. They were sick of the noise.

Around 1:00 AM, Officers Tarriel Hopper, a former USC football player, and his partner Natalie Humpherys approached the front door of The Castle. A security guard greeted them and escorted them into the kitchen. The guard asked them to wait while he located one of the hosts. When the guard left, Hopper decided to go around back and check things out. Humpherys stayed in the kitchen.

Hopper walked out to a sidewalk behind the house and in front of a small grotto pond. As he made his way to the end of the walkway, he noticed a man relieving himself. He then looked into a bedroom that belonged to Jeff Denton, one of the party's hosts.

Hopper allegedly shined his flashlight through the glass door. Lee, Denton, and another man turned towards the light. Hopper claimed that Lee brandished the gun directly at him. Others said that Lee turned around and said, "Hey, what's up?" Whatever really happened, one fact remained undisputed. Hopper unleashed a flurry of bullets, nine shots in all, into Lee's body. Lee fell forward against a stereo and then came to rest next to the bed. He was lying in a prone position as if taking a nap.

Several of the partygoers heard the commotion and thought it was a Halloween prank. When they looked at Lee's body, however, they knew it was no joke. The 39-year-old actor, who had turned his life around, lay in a pool of his own blood, in a fancy house in a fancy white neighborhood, and he was dead.

Killed by a cop—a black cop, no less.

9701 Yoakum Drive   Benedict Canyon

TYISHA MILLER

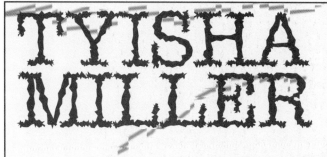

In the early morning hours of December 28, 1998, four Los Angeles police officers responded to a 911 call in Riverside, about an hour east of Los Angeles. The call came from a cousin of Tyisha Miller. Miller was asleep in her white Nissan Sentra in the parking lot of a 76 gas station on Brockton Avenue. Her stereo was blasting loudly, and her cousin was unable to rouse her out of her slumber. She also had a gun in her lap.

The officers arrived, drew their guns, and attempted to awaken the sleeping 19-year-old black woman by knocking on her car window. When they received no response, they smashed in the glass on the driver's side. The impact startled Miller who quickly jerked up. In a flash, a hail of bullets spewed from the police officers' guns. In total, 23 shots were fired. Twelve of them hit Miller in the back. She died instantly.

Was this a case of institutional racism? Was it merely officer inexperience? Or was it simply cops with itchy trigger fingers?

The biggest finger pointed in the direction of racism. Miller's cousins contended that the officers took several unflattering actions during the incident. First, the officers shouted racist remarks while trying to coax Miller awake. One was heard to have said, "Get your black ass out of the car." After they killed Miller, the officers reportedly slapped hands with one another and hugged. More racist remarks supposedly followed from the officers when mourners for Miller appeared on the scene. One witness claimed that an officer compared the mourners to animals and said that it looked like an impromptu "Kwanzaa celebration." When the family members began to cry, one officer dismissed their tears with the statement, "Here come the Watts death wails."

Some people believed Miller placed herself in the position to get shot. She had reportedly been hanging out and partying with several girlfriends all day. Indeed, her toxicological reports revealed that she had a .13 blood alcohol level, well over the legal limit for driving, and showed traces of marijuana in her blood stream.

Were these factors enough to warrant being pumped full of lead? And why was she at the gas station at that time of night anyway? And sleeping, no less? With a gun?

According to one of Miller's companions from that evening, the girls were on their way home when they got a flat tire. Miller pulled the Sentra into a convenience store parking lot where a white man helped them change the tire. After repairing the vehicle, Miller drove off, but realized that the spare was not holding air. She then drove less than a mile to a 76 gas station where she would call for help.

Miller called her cousin who said that he would contact a towing service. Meanwhile, her friend got a ride home from someone else. No one would know why Miller subsequently fell asleep in her car. Or why she had a gun in her lap.

6575 Brockton Avenue   Riverside

Were the officers justified in shooting Miller? A police board commission decided they were too quick on the draw. The four officers, Daniel Hotard, Paul Bugar, Mike Alagna, and Wayne Stewart, who had only a combined seven years on the force at the time of the shooting, were subsequently dismissed by the Riverside Police Department for acting in a manner that did not adhere to policy and putting other people and themselves at risk. The officers, however, were not charged with murder.

The officers lost many supporters when they rallied together to make a statement. All things considered, it was a stupid move. They shaved their heads in a show of solidarity. They ended up looking like a band of racist skinheads.

On the other side of the coin, the shooting drew national attention and sparked a rally and march against police brutality five months after Miller's death. National civil rights figures, such as Reverend Jesse Jackson, Reverend Al Sharpton, activist and actor Dick Gregory, actress Kim Fields, and Martin Luther King III, as well as 1,200 regular citizens, took to the streets of Riverside. The peaceful protest was set up to disrupt City Hall and demand that the officers be fired and prosecuted. They succeeded in getting 46 of the protest members arrested.

The family of Tyisha Miller filed a $10 million lawsuit against the city of Riverside and its police department. They settled for $3 million in November of 2000. The four officers were dismissed, with two officers claiming that the police department failed to accurately train them. The Reverends Sharpton and Jackson returned back home to the east. And Tyisha Miller is still dead.

All because she fell asleep.

6575 Brockton Avenue   Riverside

MARGARET MITCHELL

On May 21, 1999, at the corner of LaBrea Avenue and 4th Street, an L.A.P.D. officer gunned down a 55-year-old, frail homeless woman by the name of Margaret Mitchell. Her crime? She brandished a lethal screwdriver!

Mitchell was a known vagrant to the retailers in the area. They knew she was harmless and never bothered people on the sidewalks. Officers Edward Larrigan and Kathy Clark, however, were new to the beat. They had been recently assigned to the area and had never encountered Mitchell.

Mitchell had once been a successful and productive citizen. She received her bachelor's degree in business administration from Cal-State Los Angeles in 1977. She was gainfully employed for the next 17 years in various banks and accounting firms. Towards the end of her working career, however, Mitchell complained that she was hearing voices in her head. Apparently, the confusion was too much for her, and she stepped outside the real world. Mitchell, who refused to take medication for her condition, took to the streets.

On this warm May afternoon, Mitchell was pushing her shopping cart south on the LaBrea Avenue sidewalk. Larrigan and Clark were on bicycle patrol when they noticed the homeless woman. They presumed she had stolen the shopping cart. The officers approached her and told her to halt. Mitchell refused and continued walking. She then reached into her cart, grabbed a 12-inch screwdriver, and screamed at the officers.

A confrontation broke out between Mitchell and Larrigan and she threatened to kill him. The officers immediately pulled out their revolvers, choosing to ignore the mace and batons they carried. Suddenly, a 68-year-old homeless man intervened and attempted to dissuade Mitchell from further antagonizing the young officers. The intrusion distracted Officer Larrigan, who shooed the man away and again asked for Mitchell to stop.

She refused.

400 S. LaBrea Ave. & 5600 4th St.   Los Angeles

Larrigan asserted that he was calling for backup when Mitchell lunged at him with the screwdriver and aimed for his neck. He knelt down on one knee in a shooter's position and pumped a single bullet into Mitchell. The bullet entered the right side of her chest and exited out of her upper left back. In between, the bullet did serious damage. It fractured her clavicle, ripped open a jugular vein, destroyed a vertebra and sliced through her spinal cord.

Los Angeles Police Chief Bernard Parks claimed that the trajectory of the bullet was consistent with Larrigan's version of the events. Opponents claimed the evidence proved Mitchell was heading away from Larrigan and had turned back to look at him.

Unlike Tyisha Miller, there was little outrage over the police shooting of Margaret Mitchell. Less than two-dozen people showed up to protest against abusive police tactics, probably due to the fact that Larrigan is Latino and Clark is Latin/Asian-American.

Margaret Miller was laid to rest in a quiet ceremony. Singer Stevie Wonder paid for her funeral. Her son, Richard Mitchell, filed a multi-million dollar civil rights lawsuit against the City of Los Angeles and the L.A.P.D.

On November 23, 1999, Chief Parks issued a press release exonerating Larrigan. He claimed that the officer acted "in policy." He furthered proselytized that "police officers are not psychiatrists," and warned that "we will NEVER be able to turn police officers into professional mental health caregivers. It is not their job." On February 11, 2000, the Los Angeles Police Commission's Inspector General Jeff Eglash disagreed with Chief Parks and concluded that Larrigan had violated the L.A.P.D.'s standards on shootings.

As of this writing, no decision has been made on Larrigan's status.

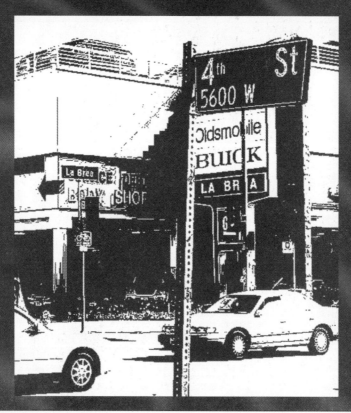

400 S. LaBrea Ave. & 5600 4th St.   Los Angeles

CHAPTER 7
MASS HYSTERIA

The recent spate of school shootings at the end of the 1990s sent the American public into a frenzy about the proliferation of violence in America. The phenomenon, however, is not recent, but rather endemic to the United States. From the Revolutionary War to the founding of the West, Americans have been known to snap and take several innocent individuals with them. The 20th century saw the instance of mass murder rise as far back as 1949 when Howard Unruh went on a shooting rampage in New Jersey. That was followed 17 years later by two massacres committed by Richard Speck in Chicago, Illinois and Charles Whitman in Austin, Texas in 1966.

Los Angeles's share of mass murders has covered a vast spectrum of explosive violence. With guns, fires, or automobiles used by both men and women from various ethnicities, some individuals are not immune to the pressure cooker environment the city has created. The reasons for the explosions range from hearing voices, to tortured personal relations, to the frustration of the workplace.

STEVEN ABRAMS

Steven Abrams felt he had been wronged. In 1994, a Costa Mesa judge ruled that Abrams had stalked his neighbor. Abrams was sentenced to jail time and ordered to stay away from the woman. Five years later, he sought revenge.

On May 3, 1999, at 5:00 PM, Abrams, 39, plowed his 5,000 pound 1967 Cadillac Coupe de Ville into the children's playground of the Southcoast Early Childhood Learning Center. The play area was filled with more than 40 exuberant children.

Abrams hit several kids and pinned four of them underneath his car. Abrams refused to get out of the car for more than 15 minutes after the wreck. As he sat in the Cadillac, several parents, who had arrived to pick up their children, lifted the car and freed the youngsters. Several of the children sustained critical injuries. A 24-year-old teacher's aide was also injured in the accident. Unfortunately, help arrived too late for two of the children. Sierra Soto, 4, died on impact. Brandon Wiener, 4, survived the collision, but died one hour later at nearby Hoag Memorial Hospital in Newport Beach.

When the police arrived, they noted that there were no skid marks at the scene. Witnesses told police that Abrams drove past the school, made a quick U-turn, accelerated his vehicle, and plowed directly through the playground's chain link fence. Police then removed Abrams from his car and handcuffed him. He began to sing to the cops. He informed them that his actions were deliberate. He calmly told them that he intended to "execute these children because they were innocent."

No one could have predicted the tragedy that occurred on May 3, 1999. Abrams was well liked, but he had no close friends. He worked at Ticket Shack with his brother-in-law and his daughter. He never seemed to cause problems. At least not until 1994.

Abrams reportedly fell in love with his married neighbor, Jennifer Brazer in 1993. She did not return his affections. In fact, she was creeped out by the man. He stalked her from September 1993 until May 1994, while they were both living in the same apartment complex near the Southcoast playground. She filed a restraining order against Abrams that he repeatedly violated. He was arrested and sentenced to three years probation.

On May 3, 1999, Abrams left work with his daughter and took her home. He subse-

300-1 Magnolia Street   Costa Mesa

quently rear-ended another car in the carpool lane, sending it forward 100 feet. Having split that scene, he drove to his old neighborhood and made the deadly U-turn.

Abrams was brought to court in August 2000. At his trial, he made some rather outrageous claims. He said that he heard voices commanding him to kill the children. He claimed also to have received messages from "the brain wave police." After a short trial, the jury convicted Abrams on all counts in less than two hours. In October 2000, a hearing went forward to determine if he was insane at the time of the homicides. Once again, the jury decided quickly; Abrams was not insane.

In November 2000, Abrams received a life sentence without parole.

PICTURED RIGHT:
Memorial plaque erected to honor the victims, Brandon Wiener and Sierra Soto.

300-1 *Magnolia Street   Costa Mesa*

EDWARD ALLAWAY

Cal-State Fullerton janitor Edward Charles Allaway committed the worst mass murder in Orange County history. He killed seven fellow college workers and injured two others on a shooting rampage that lasted only ten minutes. This mindless rampage would seem to fit in perfectly with the recent shooting massacres across the country. The biggest difference, however, was that this one took place over 25 years ago.

On July 12, 1976, around 8:30 AM, Allaway walked into the school library carrying a .22-caliber semiautomatic rifle. He entered the library from a side door and headed to the basement. He then walked down the basement hallway, methodically peeking into each office room and determining who would live or die. Some people were spared; others were not.

Allaway walked into one woman's office, looked at her and said, "Hi. How are you?" Then he moved on. He entered the next office and shot whoever was there. There seemed to be no rhyme or reason to his madness.

Allaway killed two of his fellow janitors with shots to the head and chest. One employee attempted to deter the gunman by striking him in the head with a metal pipe. Allaway took the glancing blow in stride, turned around and shot the man in the head, killing him instantly. No profession was spared in the murder spree; a professor, a photographer, a graphic artist, and a library assistant were also killed. Even the dean's son was gunned down.

When Allaway finished his business at the college, he jumped into his car and drove to the local Hilton hotel where his wife worked. He was covered in blood and gore. He calmly called the Anaheim police station and told them what he had just done. Then, he simply waited for them.

At his trial, evidence revealed that Allaway had been a strict Baptist. He became incensed when he learned that the college was showing allegedly pornographic movies to the kids on campus. According to Allaway, the employees at the school library taunted him about the movies and claimed that his wife had a starring role in the skin flicks. Apparently, these jibes were too much for Allaway.

The jury convicted Allaway of murder on all counts. His attorney, however, successfully

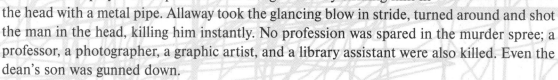

800 N. State College Blvd.   Fullerton

argued that Allaway was insane at the time of the devious act. He received a guilty by reason of insanity charge and was sentenced to a mental hospital. In 1992, Allaway was transferred to the Napa State Hospital, which declared him sane enough to re-enter society. Prosecuting attorneys, however, successfully argued that Allaway remained a serious threat and have barred his reintroduction into society.

A memorial for the victims at the Cal-State Fullerton campus was erected just north of the library. Seven trees, each representing a life lost on that day, and a rock commemorate the victims. An engraved plaque on the rock states: "This living memorial is dedicated in remembrance of the victims and their families and many other persons whose lives were touched by the tragedy of July 12, 1976."

800 N. State College Blvd.   Fullerton

The hallway where Allaway committed his killing spree.

800 N. State College Blvd.   Fullerton

DAVID ALVAREZ

September 29, 1996. David Alex "Spooky" Alvarez, 29, was inexplicably angry with his ex-wife. He decided to pay her a visit.

Alvarez, along with his girlfriend Trinia Aguirre, headed to his ex-wife's home in Baldwin Park. Aguirre knocked on the door and asked to borrow their phone. She claimed to have car trouble.

When Aguirre entered the home, she pulled a gun on the family and left the door open for Alvarez. Alvarez grabbed the family, led them to the living room, and tied them up. Alvarez was furious because his ex-wife was not in the house.

Instead, he took his frustration out on her relatives. They included two little girls, Evelyn, 8, and Massiel Torres, 12, the girls' uncle, Roberto Diaz, Pete

Torres, the father of the two girls, and Celia and Martha Diaz. Alvarez swept into a violent rampage of shooting and stabbing. As the victims screamed, Aguirre turned up the volume on the family television set to mask their pleas. By the time Alvarez was done, the two girls and their uncle were dead.

During the massacre, another unlucky soul came by the house. Jose Rojas, 33, a local gardener, knocked on the door to ask for a drink of water. He was parched from a hard day's work in the blistering sun. Alvarez dragged him into the house and killed him as well.

Miraculously, Peter Torres, Celia Diaz, and Martha Diaz survived the attack.

Alvarez and Aguirre fled the crime scene and evaded capture for more than a year. Alvarez was arrested in Tijuana by Mexican authorities.

Unfortunately for former Los Angeles District Attorney Gil Garcetti, Mexico would not extradite a criminal to the United States if that individual were subject to the death penalty. The Mexican authorities offered to send Alvarez back to California if the state lessened its penalties against him. If Garcetti refused, they threatened to let Alvarez go free. Garcetti did not back down, since he did not want to set a dangerous precedent concerning other criminals in California. He did not want future criminals to believe that they could commit a murder in Los Angeles and then flee to Mexico to avoid execution.

Mexico refused to release Alvarez to the United States, however they convicted him of the murders. This was a rarity. He was sentenced to 90 years for the killings. He was also suspected of killing another prisoner in Mexico while awaiting his trial.

Aguirre was also arrested and convicted as an accessory to murder. The previously clean Aguirre was sentenced to life in prison without parole.

Before the murders, Alvarez was convicted of battery and assault with a firearm in 1992. He received a five-year sentence, but was paroled in 1994. In August 1996, he was charged with kidnapping. One month later, he committed this crime.

4712 Stewart Avenue   Baldwin Park

JORJIK AVANESIAN

In October 1995, Jorjik Avanesian, his wife Turan, and their six children Roland, 4, Romik, 6, Rodric, 8, Ronika, 9, Rita, 16, and Robina, 17 immigrated to Glendale, California from Turkey. The Armenian father, who grew up in Iran, had been arrested for stabbing his wife in the early 90s. He argued to the immigration board that it was a case of wrongful persecution and that he loved his wife and family. He was allowed to come to America.

Once in Glendale, Avanesian attacked his wife by throwing a metal chair at her. During their argument, he brandished a knife and threatened to kill one of their children. He was not a happy man. The Glendale police took him in for questioning, but he was released and no charges were filed.

Big mistake.

Nine months after the family moved to America, the pressure became too much for Avanesian. On February 6, 1996, Avanesian seemed ready to end it all. He was upset with his

wife, because he believed she was cheating on him. He was angry that she would not divorce him. He felt that the only solution was a mass extermination. He was going to kill his wife, all six kids, and himself, so he could end the pain.

At a nearby gas station, Avanesian filled up several cans of gasoline. He also purchased a knife and an ax. He returned to his Glendale apartment. That night, as he went to sleep, he prayed to God to give him a sign. One that would tell him that what he was about to do was wrong. He claimed that he received no such sign.

Early the next morning, Avanesian laid the gas cans throughout the apartment. As he was preparing the conflagration, his youngest son awoke, startling the father. Could it have been the sign from God? Apparently Avanesian did not think so, since he told his son to go back to sleep.

Avanesian grabbed a couple of towels, doused them with gasoline, lit them on fire, and tossed them into the bedroom where his entire family slept. He was going to kill them all and take his own life. He had bought the knife and ax so he could use it on the little ones; he did not want them to feel the pain and misery brought on by the flames.

The apartment quickly caught on fire. Avanesian received burns on his hands and face. He began to have second thoughts—not about killing his family, but about his own death. He turned around and headed out of the apartment, while his entire family began to scream.

Several residents of the apartment heard the screams and attempted to assist. Avanesian brushed past them without turning back to help. The neighbors were too late; the entire

1319 Harvard Street #102   Glendale

room became engulfed in flames and thick smoke. Avanesian, meanwhile, observed his handi-work from the street. He then got into his car and began to drive.

Avanesian ended up at the office of a Persian-American newspaper in Encino. He confessed to a reporter that he set fire to his apartment. Wire reports alerted the reporter that the fire killed seven people. The reporter instantly contacted the police, and Avanesian was arrested.

When firefighters discovered the bodies, they saw a gruesome scene. Three of the bodies were piled on top of one another in the corner of a bed. According to one officer, they appeared to resemble a heap of clothes. Three more bodies were found in a bathtub filled with water. Turan Avanesian's body was found near her three smallest children. All seven family members died from smoke inhalation.

Avanesian, meanwhile, began to confess to the authorities. He spun a wild tale about his family. He claimed that his wife and two eldest daughters were drug users and under the influence of the Muslim Mafia. The Mafia, he believed, had also used his wife and two older daughters in pornographic movies. He claimed that his wife was also a prostitute. Avanesian could no longer bear the pain and embarrassment that his wife caused him and he flipped his lid.

Avanesian eventually faced a jury in Pasadena and was found guilty of the murders. His allegations fell on deaf ears as the jury took slightly more than one hour to convict him.

Although Avanesian did not agree, his attorneys argued that Avanesian was not sane at the time of the murders. The initial jury could not reach a consensus and split down the middle, 6-6, as to whether or not he should receive the death penalty. A second jury heard more evidence and elected to give the immigrant life in prison with no chance for parole.

Upon receiving his sentence, Avanesian made one last request. He asked to see a photograph of his family. Not an old photo of his family during happier times, but a picture from the coroner's office of their corpses.

1319 Harvard Street #102   Glendale

EDWARD CHARLES III

Sibling rivalry. A tale as old as man. As old as Cain and Abel.

Edward Charles III, 21, was living with his parents in Fullerton. He was a college dropout who was working as a mechanic. His brother Danny, 19, was attending college at the University of Southern California. Danny was an opera major with the voice of a saint. Danny was also a Resident Advisor in his dormitory and made perfect grades in school. Edward had been dating an actress, Tiffany Bowen, who appeared on the bikini-n-babes hit TV show, *Baywatch*. His parents did not approve of her. In Edward's mind, his parents loved Danny more than him. It drove him crazy.

Eddie was sick of his brother. He was sick of how his parents constantly doted on Danny. He was sick of being a mechanic, a failure, a loser.

On November 6, 1994, the family gathered together at the Charles household to celebrate Danny's singing success. The family dined on pasta and salad and spent the entire time praising the younger brother. Eddie was seething with anger.

Later that night, Eddie confronted Danny outside the house in the yard. He blew up and stabbed his little brother. He then smashed him over the head with an adjustable wrench.

The blow was so hard that Danny's skull was reduced to tiny little fragments of bone. To complete the job, Eddie broke his little brother's neck. He then placed Danny's lifeless body in the trunk of his car and headed inside.

It was a few more hours before he decided to take revenge on his parents. Eventually, he approached his father, Edward Charles Jr., and bashed him in the skull until it caved in. He then ap-

Charles Home: 3101 N. Terraza Place Fullerton

proached his mother, Dolores, and choked her to death. He stripped both of their bodies naked and placed them in the back seat of the car. He drove to the parking lot of the Los Coyotes Middle School in La Mirada and set the car on fire.

Eddie was immediately arrested, but his ordeal through the court system had only just begun. While in jail, he spoke with his grandfather, Edward Sr., on the phone. He asked his grandfather to take the fall for him, since "his life was over anyway." He even plotted an escape from jail by taking his defense attorneys hostage, but the plan never materialized. He had also been found with razors and hacksaws in his cell.

A year after the murder, Eddie attempted to hire a hit man to assassinate his grandfather. He wanted to show that the "real killer" had come back to finish the job and that he was an innocent man. Unfortunately for Eddie, he hired an undercover police officer.

Edward Charles III was quickly convicted, but his sentencing was anything but fast. Charles went through three sentencing phases, each resulting in either a hung jury or a mistrial. The first and third juries voted to sentence him to death by a count of 11-1. In the second trial, all 12 members of the jury requested death as his sentence. The verdict, however, was tossed out, because one juror sought counseling from his church on the day before the decision. Finally, on January 1, 1999, almost five years after the murders, during an unprecedented fourth death penalty hearing, a jury sentenced Edward Charles III to be executed.

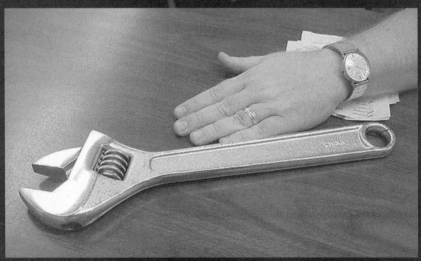

Wrench used by Eddie Charles to kill his brother and father.

Los Coyotes Middle School: 14700 Mercado Ave.
& 16000 Rosecrans Ave.   La Mirada

Danny, Dolores, and Edward Charles Jr. celebrate
Danny's success as a singer at another awards show.

Burnt out car which contained Eddie's family members' remains.

HUMBERTO de la TORRE

Twenty-one year-old Humberto de la Torre had a fight with his uncle that turned deadly for several people. On September 4, 1982, Humberto's uncle gave his nephew a lecture about gangs. Humberto did not take kindly to the criticism and decided to retaliate against his uncle.

Humberto's uncle was the manager of the Dorothy Mae Apartments in downtown Los Angeles. The apartment complex was a four-story building with a foyer and boiler room on the first floor. The top three floors housed 170 residents in 43 apartments.

Humberto decided to get his uncle where he would feel it the most, the Dorothy Mae Apartments. Humberto poured gasoline throughout the second floor, lit a match, and watched it burn. And burn it did.

This was one nasty fire. When the residents became aware of the flames, many rushed out into the hallway seeking safety. They were met with rushing walls of flames known as flashover or backdraft. These were caused by the configuration of the fireproof Ponet doors in the complex. The Ponet doors on the first floor stairwell had been closed, while the door for the second floor had been left open. This schematic allowed the fire to rush, unabated, through the second floor, killing 18 people on the second and third floors.

The other problem area was the fourth floor. The fire quickly spread through the second floor, up the stairwell, and into the fourth floor. This trapped several residents and forced many to evacuate by jumping out of their windows.

When firefighters arrived at the scene, the blaze had already died down. Most of the damage had been caused by the backdraft. The fire department's job at this point was mainly to pick up the bodies. Several victims had perished in the stairwell, their escape prevented by the backdraft working its way upstairs. Firefighters dealt with the gruesome task of removing charred corpses. They also assisted in helping catch the residents who jumped to safety.

In all, 18 residents died at the scene. Six more perished from their injuries within a week. An unborn child never saw the light of day as her mother passed away.

Humberto de la Torre was responsible for the worst mass murder in Los Angeles's history, because he was upset that his uncle had made fun of gangs. He was eventually captured, convicted, and sentenced to 690 years in prison.

821 W. Sunset Blvd. Los Angeles (now 900 block)

FLORES FAMILY MASSACRE

Pico Rivera is a quiet, tiny suburb of 65,000 middle class citizens looking for a sense of community in an overwhelming city like Los Angeles. It is comprised of 80% Hispanics. It is a peaceful town that more closely resembles a small rural town in Middle America than anything associated with L.A.

On July 21, 2000, that serenity was shattered.

In a small, single story home, the family of Richard Flores was nearly annihilated. Mr. Flores, 42, his son, Richard Jr., 17, his daughter, Sylvia, 13, and his youngest son, Matthew, 10, were all stabbed to death. It seemed as if a killer or killers had  come into their home and methodically massacred each of the Flores clan in their bedroom. It was a bloody scene.

Richard Flores was the patriarch of this close-knit, involved family that exemplified the city of Pico Rivera. He was a 23-year employee at Architectural Woodworking Company. He also coached Little League baseball and basketball teams. His wife, Sylvia, was a Eucharist priest who baked lasagna for the local softball teams. Their children were good, decent kids that excelled in sports, especially basketball. All of the kids seemed to be well behaved and never got into any trouble.

Three members of the house, Laura Reta, 18, Esperanza Flores, 18, and Monica Diaz, 16, survived the attack unscathed. Reta and Flores were adopted daughters of the Flores's. Sylvia Flores was stabbed by her intruder, but survived nonetheless. She gave police a description of her attacker as a clean-shaven, well-groomed 20-year-old Hispanic male.

When questioned, Diaz claimed that she awoke at 1:00 AM to use the restroom. As she made her way to the bathroom, she said that she heard "unfamiliar footsteps" in the house. She became nervous and hid in the bathroom. Supposedly, she had no idea that almost her entire family had been murdered.

Her story may have turned out to be a lie. Just six days after the killings, Diaz and her 17-year-old boyfriend, Michael Naranjo, were arrested for the murders of Diaz's family. Authorities claimed that Diaz and Naranjo were frustrated by Richard Flores's controlling manner. The two high school juniors began dating a year earlier and, according to fellow students, were intensely close. Almost inseparable. Reportedly, Diaz and Naranjo wanted to spend the weekend together away from the family, and Mr. Flores would have nothing to do with that idea. This decision was the alleged sparkplug that set the couple off.

Police believe that Diaz left the back door to the Flores home open for Naranjo. She then hid in the bathroom while Naranjo proceeded to stab the family. When he left, he reportedly tossed the bloody knife in the back yard. Police also speculate that the couple had spent quite a bit of time preparing this massacre.

Diaz and Naranjo have been charged with four counts of first-degree murder and one count of attempted murder against Diaz's adoptive mother, Sylvia Flores. Despite the special circumstances of the multiple killings, which is often enough to justify the charge of death, the couple can only receive a maximum sentence of life in prison, if found guilty, due to their young age.

When the couple was arraigned, they were seen laughing and hugging one another. Unfazed, showing no signs of remorse.

9650 Marjorie Street Pico Rivera

SANDI NIEVES

Los Angeles County firefighters were called out to another tragic scene on July 2, 1998. When they arrived at Cherry Creek Drive in Santa Clarita, they found 34-year-old mother Sandi Nieves, clad only in shorts and a T-shirt, standing beside her 14-year-old son, David. She was holding a cell phone and was covered in black soot. Small wisps of black smoke crept out of the front door of her rented home. The scene inside the house was much more traumatic.

Firefighters discovered the bodies of four young girls: Nikolet Nieves, 12; Rashel Nieves, 11; Kristi Folden, 7; and Jaqlene Folden, 5. All four girls were found lying on the floor of the kitchen, tucked inside sleeping bags. They died from smoke inhalation.

By the next day, police had arrested the girls' mother, Sandi, on suspicion that she deliberately murdered her four daughters. Several clues soon surfaced that pointed an accusatory finger at the single mother.

Sandi Nieves led a difficult life. She had been divorced twice and was recently dumped by her boyfriend. She was entangled in a potential legal battle with her first husband, David Folden, who also happened to be her stepfather. Folden, who fathered the two youngest girls with Nieves, sought custody of his children. The first court hearing about the matter was set for July 3, one day after the tragic fire occurred.

Nieves claimed that she was born into a dysfunctional family. Her brother was a drug addict who overdosed in 1991. Her mother, who was married six times, was an embalmer. Nieves claimed that her mother would often bring home photographs of her "handiwork," including one of her brother's dead body. She believed that her mother intentionally tried to traumatize her for some inexplicable reason.

Nieves also claimed that her former boyfriend, Scott Volk, traumatized her. He had recently ended their relationship. Nieves was unemployed and had to take care of five children. To compound matters, she was pregnant again. However, she aborted the fetus just five days before the murders. Nieves, a devout Catholic, claimed that the abortion caused her immense emotional pain. Her innards "were torn up inside." To deal with the pain she suffered after the abortion, Nieves took Zoloft.

On the night of the murders, she spoke with a friend on the phone. Her friend said that Nieves had been smoking marijuana, taking her prescription medicine, and drinking beer and wine. Nieves also composed two final letters that forecasted her homicidal demeanor. She first wrote to Folden and informed him, "Now you don't have to support any of us anymore....You are scum." She also wrote a letter to Volk that stated, "I'm sorry if my love wasn't good enough for you.... You just couldn't see it. Now you never will.... I can't live without you in my life."

27445 Cherry Creek Drive   Santa Clarita

Nieves mailed each letter just hours before she killed her daughters.

That night, she gathered her four daughters together in the kitchen. She told them to get their sleeping bags and to sleep on the kitchen floor. It was to be a slumber party. Reports after this point differ. Some said that she opened the oven door and turned the heat on to keep everyone from getting cold. Gas from the oven was strong enough to kill the girls, so she then decided to set the house on fire to cover up the crime.

Most other reports claimed that she made the girls sleep in the kitchen, then doused the carpet with gasoline, and lit a lighter to the accelerant. Although it was not a huge fire, it was strong enough to create a large amount of smoke. Nieves's son, David, reported that one of the daughters attempted to get up, but his mother told her to stay down. His mother would not let him help his sisters, assuring him that they would be fine. Eventually, all four girls perished.

Nieves's trial was a terse three-month battle in which her defense lawyer cast blame on everyone and everything, except his client. He claimed that she was on too many pills, that she was not in a legally conscious state, and that she was sleepwalking when the crime occurred. He even pointed a finger at 14-year-old David as the culprit.

The jury nixed these arguments. They convicted her in less than five hours. The jury reconvened a few months later and, in less than six hours, condemned her to die by lethal injection.

Sandi Nieves is currently one of only 12 women on California's death row.

27445 Cherry Creek Drive   Santa Clarita

RONALD TAYLOR

On the night of April 26, 1998, police were called to the scene of a suicide attempt. It was not, however, your usual case. A man had tried to kill himself by jumping off an overpass onto the 605 Freeway in Cerritos. He was discovered alive and rushed to St. Francis Medical Center in Lynwood. Approximately two hours after he leapt from the bridge, he died. Authorities learned from his driver's license that his name was Ronald Taylor of Artesia. They took down his home address, grabbed his house keys, and made an attempt to notify his relatives.

When police arrived at the man's home around 11:30 PM, the case took an even more bizarre turn. Everyone in the house was dead. Four people lay in crumpled heaps with blood coursing from their heads. A blunt instrument had been used to bash in their skulls. A fifth body was found almost six hours later. It too had been mutilated. Police had overlooked it in the initial crime scene investigation, because it was located in an enclosed patio at the back of the house.

Police soon determined that the suicidal leaper, Taylor, had murdered his entire family including his wife Ruthie, 40, his son Rick, 24, his sister-in-law, Mylissa Campbell, 29, her daughter, Jolissa Morales, 6, and Tomy Kang Jung, 24, a friend of Rick's. Based on interviews with acquaintances, police surmised that Taylor murdered the three females sometime during daylight hours with a hammer. The two women were killed in separate rooms at different ends of the house. The daughter was killed in the same room as her mother. A few hours later, around 7:00 PM, Rick Taylor and Jung showed up at the Taylor household for dinner after leaving Jung's mother's home. Taylor then attacked his son and his son's best friend. After the massacre, Taylor wandered to the freeway where he committed suicide.

Neighbors were shocked at the gruesome scene. No one in the neighborhood believed that Taylor could have killed his entire family. Likewise, his co-workers at Boeing, where Taylor worked for 16 years as a handformer in the aerospace division, doubted that he committed this crime.

The most likely reason for the Taylor family massacre was that Ronald Taylor was suffering from financial difficulties. Reportedly, Taylor was somewhat nervous about potential downsizing at Boeing. Also, he and his wife had recently filed for Chapter 7 bankruptcy. They had personal loan and credit card debts of $64,000.

The Taylor's real estate agent informed authorities that the sister-in-law and daughter were another source of tension for Taylor. The Taylors had taken in Campbell and her daughter after Campbell suffered a bitter divorce. She and her ex-husband were also fighting a nasty custody battle over Jolissa. Ronald and Ruthie Taylor were allowing the mother and daughter to live with them, while those situations were being resolved.

Despite these inconveniences, Taylor's neighbors could not predict such an explosion. They claimed that he was always friendly, liked to cook barbecues, and loved his family.

17345 Caine Drive   Artesia

ALAN WINTERBOURNE

Nothing seems more frustrating than hunting for a job. Every year, people find themselves out of work and on the prowl for something to help them pay the bills and put food on the table. The quest, which requires the perfect look, a snappy résumé, and the ability to impress people you have never met, can drive people batty. Sometimes, it can push a person over the edge.

On December 3, 1993, 33-year-old Alan Winterbourne walked into the *Ventura Star Free-Press* newspaper offices with an interesting package in hand. He asked for Timm Herdt in the paper's editorial department. He met Herdt, handed him a manila envelope, mentioned something about unemployment, and told him that they should talk in the future about the information. Winterbourne thanked Herdt for his time and walked out the front door. Herdt tossed the envelope onto a growing stack and resumed his duties.

Winterbourne then drove ten minutes south to the town of Oxnard, a small community about an hour north of Los Angeles. Winterbourne, nattily dressed in a suit, button-down shirt, and clip-on tie, arrived at the California Employment Development  Department and calmly walked through the main doors. Despite his proper attire, Winterbourne looked out of place, with ratty hair down to the middle of his back and a scraggly beard that lay flaccidly on his chest.

He walked directly to the service window, withdrew a .12 gauge shotgun, and proceeded to blast away. As state workers scrambled for safety, Winterbourne randomly shot in their direction. One of his shots hit a computer terminal, which exploded and caused 65-year-old Richard Bateman to fall to the floor in convulsions. The retired businessman was a volunteer for the Retarded Citizens of Ventura County. He was in the office volunteering his services to the unemployed mentally-impaired residents of Oxnard. Winterbourne had also shot clerk Phillip Villegas, 43, in the back as he attempted to hide. As Villegas fell to the floor, Winterbourne burst through the employee gate. He wanted to do more damage.

Winterbourne approached Bateman and shot him twice in the chest, killing the senior citizen. He turned around and spotted employee Anna Velasco. He aimed the gun at her hip and pulled the trigger; the impact knocked her to the ground. She scrambled to hide under a desk. He walked over to the desk, stood over her, and fired a second shot into her chest at point-blank range.

Massacre Location: 1960 North C Street Oxnard

Winterbourne calmly walked up and down the hallways of the state offices and selectively chose whom to shoot. He switched to a second weapon, a Smith & Wesson .44 Magnum revolver, and the shooting continued. Certain people were hit with multiple shots, while others were left unscathed.

The shooting spree did not last long. After Winterbourne made his walk-through, he jumped over the counter, leaving the employee section of the office. He casually walked to the side exit door and left the building.

Several police officers were waiting for him. But Winterbourne was not done yet. He pulled out his gun and returned fire. He managed to create enough time to get into his parked car and lead police on a deadly chase.

Winterbourne was forced to stop at the corner of Victoria Avenue and Olivas Park Drive between Oxnard and Ventura. He jumped out of his car and attempted to flee on foot, with a Browning .300 hunting rifle as his weapon of choice. Several police cars, filled with officers ready for a shootout, surrounded him, including Sergeant James O'Brien, 35, of the Oxnard Police Department. O'Brien had strategically positioned his car to point towards Winterbourne, providing himself protection from the madman's bullets. Or so he thought. Winterbourne, from 200 feet away, squeezed off several rounds at O'Brien. He eventually connected with the detective's head, killing the highly decorated officer instantly. It was the first on-duty death of an Oxnard police officer since 1981.

Police Shootout: Victoria Ave. & Olivas Park Dr. Ventura

Winterbourne turned back towards his car, jumped in, and hurriedly took off. Several more officers jumped into the fray and followed him to Ventura. Winterbourne made it all the way to the Ventura unemployment office. He exited his vehicle, this time carrying a Ruger Mini-14 rifle.

He did not get very far.

Police officers sprayed his body with a torrent of bullets. Alan Winterbourne was dead, along with four other individuals. The entire incident took less than 20 minutes.

Timm Herdt listened to the ordeal on the radio. When he heard the description of Winterbourne, he was reminded of the man who had just come to his office with the mysterious envelope. As he went to retrieve it, his assistant asked him about the box in the lobby that the strange man had left for him. Herdt looked puzzled. He went to the box, opened it up, and found a recorded history of sorts, of a man who had suffered the humiliation of being unemployed.

Through the documents found in the box and further interviews, the police discovered that Winterbourne had been fired over seven years earlier from his job as a computer systems analyst at an aerospace company in Newbury Park. He had been unable to get a new job—a full seven years without work.

His unemployment was definitely not from a lack of trying. Winterbourne had placed thousands of rejection letters in the box. He had clearly documented all of his futile efforts at obtaining a job. He also had made several claims that his former employer, Northrop, had blackballed him and made it impossible for him to get work anywhere.

Winterbourne enjoyed his first position at Northrop. The problems arose when he was transferred into a different department that focused on top-secret military issues. As soon as he was transferred, Winterbourne complained that he was being followed and threatened, and he feared for his life. The stress of the secrecy forced him to quit, making him ineligible for unemployment benefits.

Thus began the fruitless search for a new job and the eventual downfall of Alan Winterbourne, and the deaths of four innocent people.

Ventura Unemployment Office: 4839 Market St.

CHAPTER 8
So CAL
SERIAL
KILLERS

Do not let some FBI profiler try to sell you a bill of goods when it comes to serial killers. Especially, ones from Los Angeles. The elite officers will try to convince you that every crime scene left by a serial killer will help derive a set of clues that will lead to a specific determination of the person who could commit such atrocious crimes. Conveniently, the end result always comes together in a nice, tidy package with vague characteristics that are used to describe the killer. Usually, the killers are described to be white males, in their early 30s, with high intelligence, subpar social skills, and a general hatred of women. If these profiles are so accurate and perceptive, how come they have never been successfully utilized in catching one single serial killer?

A look at serial killers from Los Angeles and the surrounding areas will explain why. Each killer is different. Each has his or her own method of murder and their own reason for committing their crimes. A look at a few of the SoCal killers reveals how ludicrous it is to assume that a distinctive pattern can be uncovered amongst this unique breed. Indeed, the serial killers from here vary in many ways. They are men and women; they have white, black, and brown skin colors; highly intelligent or borderline retarded; sadistic in their violence and deluded in their belief that they are angels from above. In other words, no one common trait among all of these killers exists, and it is a mistake to assume that you can capture one based on an ill-conceived notion such as profiling.

LAWRENCE BITTAKER & ROY NORRIS

Lawrence Bittaker

These two guys make a strong case for the "three strikes" law in California. Lawrence Bittaker and Roy Norris met while they were both in the California Men's Colony in San Luis Obispo in 1978. When they were released, they went on a killing spree that stunned Southern California.

Roy Norris was born on February 2, 1948, in Greeley, Colorado. At the age of 17, he joined the Navy and relocated to San Diego, California. After a short stint in Vietnam, Norris was arrested in November of 1969 for rape and assault. He was released on bail in February of 1970, and attempted to break into a woman's home. She summoned the police before he could hurt her.

The Navy, meanwhile, discharged Norris based on a psychological report that stated he had a "schizoid personality." After his discharge, he was arrested for beating a female student at San Diego State College. Norris stalked the woman, confronted her, and then smashed her face into a concrete sidewalk. He was arrested again and charged with assault with a deadly weapon. He was sentenced to the Atascadero State Hospital for mental treatment.

Norris spent five years there. He was officially released and declared to be "no further harm to others." Three months after his release, Norris raped a young woman from Redondo Beach. He was captured a month later and sent to prison, where he met Lawrence Bittaker.

Bittaker was a real piece of work. He was born on September 27, 1940 in Pittsburgh, Pennsylvania, but his birth parents abandoned him. His adoptive parents moved around the country, so he never had a consistent cadre of friends. By the age of 17, he was your prototypical juvenile delinquent. He was first arrested in Long Beach, California for a hit-and-run, then for stealing cars, and finally, for evading arrest.

Thus, the life-long criminal career of Lawrence Bittaker had begun. Bittaker's rap sheet was unique. He served little prison time and was paroled often, no matter how bad his crime

Lawrence Bittaker & Roy Norris

nor how long his record became. In 1974, he was arrested for assault and attempted murder when he stole some meat from a grocery store and stabbed the clerk who confronted him. He was sent to prison again.

Bittaker was transferred to California Men's Colony in 1978 where he met Roy Norris. Norris claimed that Bittaker saved his life from a potential fight in the prison yard. He owed Bittaker and felt required to be compliant with him. While in prison, the duo hatched an evil plan. They were determined to kill one teenage girl for every age represented in the 13-19 range. They agreed to find each other and consummate their partnership of terror after they both got out of prison.

Bittaker was paroled in November of 1978. Norris was released two months later. By February 1979, the two men hooked up. They purchased a silver 1977 GMC van, dubbed it the "Murder Mac," and cruised the South Bay beaches for young girls.

Bittaker and Norris would usually spend the weekends getting high, walking up and down the beaches, and taking pictures of the young bikini-clad females. Soon, their escapades would involve trying to get the women into the "Murder Mac." They would ply the naïve girls with booze and marijuana. Most of the time, girls would not get in the van and party with these two convicts. Sometimes, they would.

On June 24, 1979, Bittaker and Norris were cruising up and down the streets of Redondo Beach. They spotted a cute blond girl, 16-year-old Cindy Schaeffer. She had just left Saint Andrews Presbyterian Church and was walking home. Norris pulled alongside the young girl and invited her into the van for a party. She declined. They followed her until she was almost home. Eventually, Bittaker jumped out of the van, grabbed her and threw her into the vehicle. They drove her to a remote area in the San Gabriel Mountains.

They took turns raping Schaeffer. Then, they decided to kill her. Norris attempted to strangle her. When he saw how hard it was for her to die, he panicked and threw up in

Murder Site: Glendora Ridge Motor Way San Gabriel Mountains

the van. Bittaker tried to strangle her as well but to no avail. He wrapped a wire coat hanger around her throat. She still would not die. Finally, the two men tightened the hanger with a pair of vise grip pliers until she died. The hanger was squeezed so tight; blood had dripped from the slice in her neck. After they were done with Schaeffer, they tossed her body over the edge of a steep cliff in the San Dimas Canyon.

The next killing occurred on July 8, 1979, when Bittaker and Norris picked up 18-year-old Andrea Joy Hall. The two men kidnapped Hall and took her to their mountaintop getaway. Once there, they raped and tortured her. Bittaker jammed an ice pick in her ear; it went into her brain, but did not kill her. He then jammed the ice pick into her other ear, but the girl still lived. Frustrated, Bittaker wrapped his hands around her throat and ended her life. He tossed Hall's limp body over another cliff.

On September 3, 1979, during the Labor Day holiday, the two killers decided to up the ante. They picked up two girls who were hitchhiking along the Pacific Coast Highway, 15-year-old Jackie Gilliam, and 13-year-old Leah Lamp. Once again, they took the girls to the mountains and had their way with them. They tortured and raped the girls for two full days. They allegedly tape-recorded the two girls' screams. Eventually, they tried to kill Gilliam with the ice pick, but it did not work. She too was strangled. Bittaker then attempted to strangle Lamp, but she refused to die. As Bittaker choked her, Norris smashed her in the head with a sledgehammer several times. After she finally died, they tossed both women over a cliff. Later, when police found their bodies, Gilliam still had the ice pick jammed into her skull.

The two killers decided to increase the stakes one more time. On Halloween, 1979, they located another victim, 16-year-old Shirley Ledford. Instead of taking her back to the mountains, they decided to have their way with her in the back of the van. As Norris drove, Bittaker turned on his tape recorder. On the audiocassette tape, Ledford's screams can be heard for over 18 minutes. Apparently, while the tape was running, Bittaker raped and mutilated Ledford her in various ways. If Ledford failed to do what Bittaker asked of her, he would squeeze her nipples with the pliers he used to strangle his previous victims. Norris joined in the torment and smacked her elbow with the hammer 25 times. Bittaker then allegedly wrapped a coat hanger around her throat, tightened it with his pliers, and choked the girl to death. Irritated that the media had not latched on to the other murders, Bittaker and Norris decided to rectify that situation. They tossed Ledford's body in someone's front yard at the corner of Stonehurst Avenue and Orcas Avenue in Shadow Hills.

1400 San Dimas Canyon Road San Dimas

Between the murders that took place on Labor Day and Halloween, Bittaker and Norris made a fatal error. They kidnapped and raped another girl, Robin Robeck, who was visiting

her father. Her captors released Robeck. Unfortunately, she was not able to track down the men who molested her.

Norris, feeling a bit cocky, began to brag about his murderous exploits to another former inmate, Joe Jackson. Jackson contacted his attorney, who in turn contacted L.A.P.D., who in turn contacted the Hermosa Beach Police department and Detective Paul Bynum. Bynum wanted to go after Bittaker and Norris, but he needed proof first. He had worked on the unsolved Robeck rape case and decided to show her a picture of the two ex-cons. She immediately fingered Bittaker and Norris.

On November 20, 1979, police moved in on Norris, who was selling marijuana out of his house. Once he was brought in for questioning, he began to squeal. He confessed to all of the murders, but he placed all of the blame on Bittaker. In exchange for his life, he agreed to rat out Bittaker. Norris received a 45 years-to-life sentence.

At first, Bittaker flatly denied the charges. He then laid all of the blame at Norris's feet. The authorities did not buy his claims. He went to trial, was found guilty of 26 charges, and sentenced to death. Bittaker is currently housed on Death Row in San Quentin. He used to play bridge with fellow serial killers William Bonin (see p. 163), Randy Kraft (see p. 175), and Douglas Clark (see p. 167). He has also filed numerous frivolous lawsuits against the prison system. In 1992, he even filed a lawsuit claiming that his civil rights were violated, because he had been served broken cookies and a soggy sandwich. The lawsuit cost the state almost $4,500 to settle.

Detective Paul Bynum committed suicide in 1986, because he was allegedly distraught over this case.

PICTURED LEFT:
Roy Norris's home and arrest site.

PICTURED RIGHT:
Bittaker lived in the Scott Motel at the time of his arrest.

Norris Home: 313 B Garnet Street Hermosa Beach
Scott Motel: 1635 N. San Fernando Blvd. Burbank

WILLIAM BONIN

Lawrence Bittaker's former bridge partner, William Bonin was executed on February 23, 1996. He had been on San Quentin's Death Row since 1982 for the murders of 14 teenage boys killed between May 1979 and June 1980 in Los Angeles and Orange Counties. The press nicknamed him "The Freeway Killer," because he had a penchant for dumping corpses alongside the freeways of Southern California.

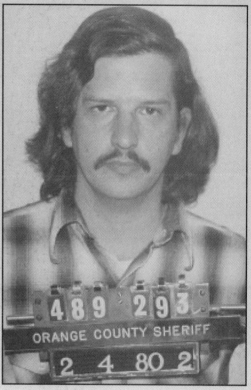

Bonin was born on January 8, 1947 in California. His father was an abusive alcoholic, and his mother, who did not much care for her son, dumped him off with his grandfather. Unfortunately, things did not improve for young Bonin. Gramps was a pedophile who sexually abused him. By the time Bonin turned eight years old, he was sent to reform school for stealing. Younger than the other boys, Bonin became their experimental plaything. He submitted because he feared the stronger, bigger juveniles would beat him.

When Bonin was released, he turned his sexual attentions to his little brother and other smaller kids in the neighborhood. He had learned the first rule of domination: pick on someone smaller than you.

Bonin kept his sexual predilections to himself for a number of years. When he turned 18, he joined the United States Air Force. He spent over 700 hours of combat time in Vietnam where he acted as an aerial gunner. He also forced soldiers to have sex with him at gunpoint, but he was never caught.

Bonin received an honorable discharge and relocated to the West Coast to the city of Downey. He moved in with his mother, who had abandoned him when he was a little boy, and soon got into serious trouble with the law. In 1969, he was arrested for sexually molesting five little boys. A psychiatrist who claimed that Bonin was a "mentally disordered sex offender" interviewed him. His analysis resulted in Bonin's incarceration in a mental institution rather than a prison.

That was Break #1 for William Bonin.

Five years later, Bonin was released. By the following summer, he was in trouble again.

William Bonin

He kidnapped and raped a 14-year-old boy, David McVicker. McVicker stated that Bonin had attempted to strangle him with his own T-shirt. Bonin could not complete the task and let McVicker go. The frightened boy reported the incident to the police. Bonin was captured and convicted of lewd and lascivious conduct. He was released from prison after only three years.

That was Break #2 for Bonin.

By 1979, one year after his release from prison, Bonin was at it again. He picked up a 17-year-old male hitchhiker in his van and attempted to rape and assault him. The boy escaped, reported the attack to the police, and identified Bonin as his attacker. Amazingly, a clerical error allowed Bonin to go free. He was never convicted of the attack.

That was Break #3 for Bonin. And a major turning point.

He was determined that none of his victims would pick him out of a line-up again. And no one ever did. From May 28, 1979 to June 10, 1980, William Bonin became one of the most feared serial killers in the entire country.

Bonin enlisted a group of lowlives to assist in his crimes. They included 22-year-old Vernon Butts, 19-year-old Gregory Miley, and 19-year-old James Munro. This group of young men, under the guidance of Bonin, executed at least 14 boys, all between the ages of 12 and 19. Most were raped and sodomized, then strangled to death. Others were stabbed—one more than 70 times. Bonin's gang inflicted other atrocities on their victims: near castration for one; a wire coat hanger shoved up the rectum of another; and chloral hydrate acid forced down the throat of another. The majority of the victims were innocent boys, including one 12-year-old who had been waiting at a bus stop to go to Disney Land. After each murder, Bonin and his murderous bunch dumped all of their victims alongside the various freeways that surrounded Orange and Los Angeles Counties, including the Artesia Freeway, the San Diego Freeway, and the 210 Freeway.

Bonin's last victim was 18-year-old Steven Wells. Wells was bisexual and liked to experiment. Bonin, along with Munro, picked him up and took him to Bonin's home on Angell Street in Downey, a quaint suburb about 20 minutes south of downtown Los Angeles. Bonin and Wells engaged in consensual sex while Munro left to pick up some food. When Munro

10282 Angell Street   Downey

returned, Bonin told him to get in on the action. He told Munro that he planned to kill Wells. Allegedly, Munro did not want to take part in the killing and told Bonin to do it himself. Munro claimed that Bonin strangled Wells to death, while he merely watched television.

After Bonin murdered Wells, he and Munro loaded Wells's body into a cardboard box, tossed it into Bonin's green van, and headed to Butts's house. Butts checked out the body, thought it was pretty cool, but informed

Couch in Bonin's home.

the men that they had to get rid of it. Bonin and Munro dumped the body behind a gas station in Huntington Beach and went home, stopping for burgers on the way.

After this last murder, police finally got their big break. During a routine traffic stop, 18-year-old William Pugh coughed up some "insider information" on Bonin. He claimed that Bonin had picked him up and bragged about being the "Freeway Killer." Bonin even showed Pugh a collection of newspaper clippings of the murders that he kept stashed in the van's glove compartment. Police checked out Bonin's arrest record, targeted him as a prime suspect, and put a surveillance team on him.

Interior of Bonin's van.

It took one week for the police to make a bust.

On June 11, 1980, police followed Bonin from his Downey residence up to Hollywood. They watched as Bonin tried to score with several young male boys. By the fifth pick-up attempt, Bonin was successful. He drove his prey, 15-year-old Harold T., to an empty parking lot at the corner of Santa Monica Boulevard and Normandie Avenue in Hollywood. By the time police approached the car, Bonin was sodomizing the unwilling boy. Police arrested him immediately.

10282 Angell Street   Downey

Bonin was arrested in this strip center parking lot.

Once in jail, Bonin denied everything. Some people claim that he implicated his little band of followers: Miley, Butts, and Munro. Others claim that Butts ratted out Bonin. Regardless, all four men were charged with killing 14 young boys, even though Bonin confessed to actually killing at least 22. While awaiting trial, Butts committed suicide by hanging himself in his cell with a sheet. It was his fifth suicide attempt. Both Munro and Miley were convicted of murder and sentenced to 15-years-to-life in prison. William Bonin was convicted of killing 14 boys, ten in Los Angeles County and four in Orange County, and received the death penalty.

As a resident of San Quentin, Bonin led an interesting life. He spent most of his time writing, painting, and playing bridge with three other well-known SoCal serial killers: Randy Kraft (see p. 175), Lawrence Bittaker (see p. 158), and Douglas Clark (see p. 167). The San Quentin Death Row gift shop even sells Bonin's book of short stories.

One week before his execution, a reporter interviewed Bonin. When asked if he had any regrets in his life, Bonin responded, "I wish I hadn't gone into the Air Force because I was at the peak of my bowling career. I had been averaging around 186 to 190 and I could have become a professional." Remorseless to the end, William Bonin was the first person in the state of California to be executed by lethal injection. For decades, the state had used the gas chamber, but its use was deemed to be cruel and unusual punishment.

Before his death, Bonin was granted his wish for a last meal. It consisted of a pepperoni pizza, an Italian sausage pizza, three pints of coffee ice cream, and three six-packs of Coca-Cola. After his meal, he was taken to the execution chamber, strapped in, and injected with a combination of sodium pentathol, pancuronium bromide, and potassium chloride. He said nothing to the people who gathered to witness his execution. He closed his eyes and looked asleep the entire time.

Arrest Site: 5101 Santa Monica Blvd. Hollywood

DOUGLAS CLARK & CAROL BUNDY

Serial killing teams are rare. One made up of a man and a woman is even more uncommon. In the summer of 1980, just such a killing couple terrorized the Sunset Strip in Hollywood. Several prostitutes were murdered. No one was sure who was responsible, but when they found out, they could not believe their eyes.

Carol Bundy was born Carol Mary Peters on August 26, 1942. She was the product of a broken home. Her mother died when she was a little girl. Upon her mother's death, her father demanded that she and her sister take their mother's place in his bed. He did not want them to sleep however.

Carol's abuse at the hands of her alcoholic father lasted until he remarried eight months later, but life was not any easier with the new wife at home. Carol was eventually sent to live in foster homes. After the constant berating by her father for being too fat or too stupid, she was grateful for the change.

Douglas Clark, on the other hand, grew up in a life of privilege. His father was a member of the Navy, so his family moved often, both in the United States and overseas. When Clark's father retired to Kwajalein, an island in the Western Pacific, he received a fancy home, servants, and many of the trappings of wealth.

Doug was not impressed. He was shipped off to the finest academy in Geneva, but the school failed to inspire or motivate him. He was lazy and unwilling to contribute. Though Clark was considered intelligent, he just did not seem to give a damn.

Clark eventually moved back to the United States. He also continued his indolent ways after settling in Southern California. He went through a variety of jobs as well as a variety of women. For female companionship, he preferred a woman who was heavy, unattractive, and lacking in self-confidence.

Enter Carol Bundy.

Clark wooed the chubby woman with coke-bottle sized glasses. He made her feel special. He made her feel wanted. He also used her like a dog.

Bundy seemed to want that.

Shortly after their relationship began, however, Clark informed Bundy that he was already tired of having sex with her. He started bringing prostitutes into the picture. Bundy willingly complied, thinking that a handsome man like Clark would not stick around otherwise.

Douglas Clark & Carol Bundy

The unusual sexual partnerings soon escalated to bizarre fantasies. Clark told Bundy that he wanted a young girl as a sex slave. He also told her that he had fantasies of necrophilia. Although Bundy wanted to be Clark's only fantasy, the unusual suggestions actually aroused her. So she agreed to help Clark fulfill his fantasies.

Clark began the killing spree on his own. On June 11, 1980, he murdered two young girls, Cindy Chandler, 15, and her stepsister, Gina Marano, 16. Clark picked the two girls up at a bus station on the Sunset Strip in Hollywood. While he forced Chandler to perform oral sex on him, he ordered Marano to look the other way. When Marano failed to comply, Clark shot her in the back of the head. Clark also shot Chandler in the head while she still had her mouth on his penis. Neither girl died with these first bullets, so he shot each girl one more time.

Clark was not finished with Chandler and Marano. He took the dead girls to a garage in Burbank. Clark positioned their bodies on an old dusty mattress and began to defile their corpses. He posed the girls' bodies, so they appeared to be pleasuring one another. Then, he raped the two corpses.

After he was done, Clark put the girls' bodies in his car and drove towards Disney Studios, where he decided to leave a morbid gift for the neighbors. He dumped the girls' bodies on the Forest Lawn on-ramp of the Ventura Freeway, right next to Disney Studios and near the Forest Lawn Hollywood Hills Cemetery (see p. 280).

Clark reported his misdeeds to Bundy. Instead of being repulsed, she was electrified. She wanted to take part. On June 20, 1980, Clark and Bundy drove to Hollywood to pick up a hooker. They found one at the Hughes Market parking lot on Highland Avenue. The young prostitute, who called herself "Cathy," agreed to give Clark a blowjob while Bundy watched from the back seat. The trio drove to a gas station at the corner of Franklin Avenue and Highland Avenue to get busy.

When Clark was unable to sustain an erection, he reached for Bundy's gun and shot Cathy in the back of the head.

The murder did not freak Bundy out. Instead, it excited her. She helped Clark cover up the bloody hooker to prevent other motorists from seeing her dead body. She then gladly went with Clark to dump the body near the Magic Mountain Amusement Park.

After Cathy's murder, Clark went cruising for more hookers on the Sunset Strip, when he encountered Exxie Wilson. Wilson

Girls: Westbound 134 Freeway On-ramp   Burbank
Gas Station: 6800 Franklin Ave. & 1800 Highland Ave. Hollywood

moved to Los Angeles from Little Rock, Arkansas only one week earlier. Clark picked her up and drove her to the Studio City Sizzler restaurant parking lot on Ventura Boulevard. He convinced Wilson to give him a blowjob. As she began her business, he stuck the gun to the back of her head and pulled the trigger. The violent act caused Wilson to bite down on Clark's manhood.

Parking lot where The Sizzler used to be located.

Clark was furious, but Wilson was already dead. He dragged her out of the car and retrieved his "kill bag" from the trunk. Bundy had put together this bag that consisted of knives, liquid cleaners, paper towels, gloves, and trash bags. Clark, still furious from the bite, took out his frustrations on the young girl. He cut off her head, placed it in one of the trash bags, and took it home to Bundy.

Bundy, once again, was not horrified by Clark's actions. Instead, she and Clark used Wilson's head as a sex toy. When they were done, they placed it in a refrigerator to keep it from rotting. They would later take it out and play with it in the shower. Clark enjoyed sticking his penis inside the decapitated head's mouth.

After a few days of fun and frivolity with the noggin, Clark decided to get rid of it. Bundy bought a special chest for its storage. Before placing the head in the chest, Bundy proceeded to give it a makeover. She applied blush, mascara, and lipstick, before Clark worried that they might leave fingerprints. They put the head into the chest and dumped it in an alley behind Hoffman Street in Studio City. An unfortunate passerby who thought he had found a treasure chest unveiled it.

The pair continued their killing spree for weeks. Bundy, however, wanted to secure Clark's love, so she decided to kill someone on her own. Her chosen victim was Australian singing cowboy John "Jack" Murray. Murray and Bundy had an affair before she met Clark. Murray, who was married, only used Bundy for sex, so she decided he deserved to die.

Bundy went to the Little Nashville Club in North Hollywood, where Murray performed. She told Murray that she wanted to have sex with him in his van. He readily agreed. They got into the van, located around the block from the club on Barbara Ann Street.

A furniture store eixsts on Little Nashivlle's former location.

Once in the van, Bundy had Murray lie on his stomach. She then took a gun out and shot him in the head. Since he was still alive, she took a knife out and stabbed him in the back, on his buttocks, and near his anus. Fearing that the bullet would lead police to her, Bundy used her knife to remove Murray's head. She placed it in a trash bag and drove off.

Street where Jack Murray's headless body was found.

A few days later, Murray's van, along with his headless body, was found. All fingers pointed at Bundy as the last person seen with Murray. She denied any involvement with his murder. Bundy, however, had trouble keeping a secret.

Only two days after the discovery, Bundy told her coworkers that she had killed Murray. She also told them of her exploits with Clark. Both were soon arrested.

Bundy blamed everything on Clark. She claimed that he was insane and had overpowered her. Clark, on the other hand, claimed ignorance and innocence. He said that Bundy was a lunatic, and he had nothing to do with any of the crimes.

Clark's trial took place more than two years after his arrest. He unsuccessfully defended himself. The chief witness against him was Carol Bundy. The jury found Clark guilty and sentenced him to execution. He is currently on death row in San Quentin.

Bundy originally wanted to plead not guilty by reason of insanity. Upon the date of her trial, however, she pleaded guilty and received a lesser sentence. She was sentenced for two terms of 25-years-to-life. She is currently serving her time at the California Women's Colony. She will be eligible for parole in 2010.

Club Present: 13550 Sherman Way N. Hollywood
Murray Site: 13400 Block of W. Barbara Ann St. N. Hollywood

ROBERT DIAZ JR.

Whenever you feel sick, you want someone you can turn to for medical help. Unfortunately, for 11 souls who were treated at the Community Hospital of the Valleys near Perris, California, they did not receive proper medical care. Instead, they came face to face with the "Grim Reaper."

His name was Robert Diaz Jr.

Diaz, 42, had always wanted to be a doctor. Unfortunately, he was not very bright. He did, however, attend Purdue University where he received his degree in nursing. He also received strange looks from his fellow classmates due to his unusual occupation. To pay his way through school, Diaz proffered up astrological readings for his classmates.

More unusual, however, were the outrageous claims Diaz made. He claimed that he was an Egyptian mystic who once lived in King Tut's body. He also claimed that he was a long-lost descendant of the conqueror El Cid, who won the battle at Valencia in 1064.

After college, Diaz worked as a nurse in Southern California. He rotated between various hospitals in the area, including the Perris hospital, the San Gorgonio Pass Memorial Hospital in nearby Banning, and the Centinela Hospital in Inglewood.

From March through April of 1981, Diaz worked the graveyard shift at the Perris hospital. Strangely, several elderly patients passed away during his shift. All died at 1:00 AM, 4:00 AM, or 7:00 AM. Most of the patients were never autopsied, which was usually the procedure when it was believed a person died from natural causes. One worker, however, became suspicious.

This anonymous person called police and pointed out the unusual number of patients' deaths during the time period. Authorities conducted autopsies on the bodies that had not been cremated or buried. What they found startled the Southern California medical community. Unusually high doses of Lidocaine were found in each victim's body. Lidocaine is a drug used to stabilize erratic heartbeats and is used in very small doses.

Simultaneously, Diaz was being investigated as a possible thief of a doctor's notes from an intensive care unit. Police raided Diaz's home looking for the notes. Instead, they found something much more damaging. Diaz had several syringes in his home, heart medicine, and numerous vials of morphine. He also had two vials of Lidocaine.

Diaz was arrested five months later for the murders of 27 patients at the Perris and Banning hospitals. He was tried in 1984, more than two years after his arrest. His charges were lowered from 27 counts of murder to 12, representing 11 victims from the Perris hospital and one from the Banning hospital. Diaz was found guilty on all counts and sentenced to die.

Community Hospital of the Valleys is now known as Valley Plaza Doctors Hospital.

2224 Medical Center Drive   Perris

HARVEY GLATMAN

Don't let anyone try and fool you by claiming that serial killers are a new phenomenon. Even ignoring the earliest infamous killers, such as Vlad The Impaler, Elizabeth Bathory, and H.H. Holmes, these predators existed even in what was considered more peaceful American times. Try the *Happy Days* era of the 1950s, when everything was supposedly about carhops, school dances, and apple pie. Underneath this polished exterior, lived one person who could not repress his rampant sexuality. His name was Harvey Glatman.

Glatman was born on December 10, 1927 in the Bronx, New York. He was the son of a milliner who worked in a women's undergarment factory. Glatman was a quiet child who kept to himself. He also liked to sexually abuse himself. At the age of four, his parents found a naked Harvey with a string tied around his penis and the other end attached to a dresser. He was leaning back with the string taut on his little Glatman. His parents, though shocked, did nothing to help him out.

By the time he was a prepubescent boy, Glatman developed into an unattractive nebbish. He had big floppy ears and greasy hair. He also smelled funny. His classmates, including the girls, liked to tease him about his looks. Glatman thought he would never touch a female.

To compensate, he began to experiment in some serious ways. By the age of 11, Glatman was prone towards autoerotic asphyxiation. It is a sexual masturbation method whereby the engager hangs himself while masturbating. At the point of climax, the air supply that is cut off from the hanging supposedly lends an extra level of excitement to the masturbator. It has also led to several accidental deaths. Glatman continued his unique form of self-pleasuring for a number of years.

Although he was a good student in school with a high IQ, Glatman still could not make friends or meet girls. He resorted to breaking into young women's homes, stealing their money, and tying them up with a rope. He then fondled the women. It was his first experience with the female flesh.

Eventually, his misdeeds led to incarceration while he lived in Denver, Colorado. He spent less than eight months in jail on a charge of kidnapping and rape in 1945. He was released and moved back to New York. While there, he embarked on a crime spree of robbery with the intent to rape women. He was captured and sent to Sing Sing Prison where he spent five years.

Upon his release in 1956, he headed out to Los Angeles. He found a small apartment on Melrose Avenue in West Hollywood and bought himself a beat-up used car. He also made one more important purchase—a Rolleicord camera.

Glatman possessed an artistic streak in school and endeavored to fulfill his sexual needs through his camera lens. He posed as a professional photographer and lined up appointments with young women from Hollywood modeling agencies. He photographed them in cheesecake poses and various states of undress, and afterward, would go home and masturbate to the developed photos.

But, he wanted more.

Harvey Glatman

On August 1, 1957, he answered a want ad in the paper. The ad led to a 19-year-old model, Judith Dull, who lived with two other models. Glatman was especially attracted to the buxom beauty and agreed to meet her at her apartment on Sweetzer Avenue. Once he arrived, he informed her that his friend had rented him a studio for the photo shoot. The "studio" was Glatman's apartment.

He took Dull there and proceeded to shoot what he called "true detective" photos. These photos consisted of Dull tied up in ropes and restrained. They were made to look as if the woman's captor was just off screen, threatening her life. While Dull posed for the photos, Glatman found the nerve to make a move on the young girl. Since she was tied up, he raped her for more than an hour. After he was done, he made her sit by him on the couch, lean her head on his shoulder, and watch television with him. He then informed her that he would take her out of town and dump her off. He didn't.

Instead, he drove her to the desert near Indio, about 120 miles east of Los Angeles. He took her to a secluded spot in the desert and wrapped a rope around her throat. He pulled tight until he squeezed the life out of the young model.

But Glatman wasn't done yet. He used his camera to document the dead woman. He took several photographs after placing her in lurid death poses.

Glatman continued his killing spree over the next year, killing Shirley Ann Bridgeford and Ruth Mercado. He followed a similar pattern in both murders. He picked the women up at their homes under the guise of a blind date or photographic session. He tied the women up, tortured them, and drove them to the Vallecito Mountains near San Diego. He then killed the women and photographed them for his unusual photo album.

On October 27, 1958, Glatman picked up the wrong woman. He had hired Lorraine Vigil from the Diana Studio on Sunset Boulevard. It was Vigil's first assignment, and her boss had her suspicions about the smelly photographer. As a result, Vigil was on her guard. When Glatman picked her up, he told her they were going to his studio. Instead, Glatman headed down the freeway towards the desert. Once they passed Anaheim, Vigil got worried and yelled at Glatman. He eventually pulled off the freeway and attempted to confine Vigil. She resisted, so he pulled out his gun. She attempted to grab it, but the gun went off and shot right through her skirt. The bullet only nicked the young woman. She eventually wrestled the gun away from Glatman and got out of the car. Seemingly out of nowhere, the police appeared and arrested Glatman.

Glatman confessed to the murders of the three women. He told police about his special photo collection stashed in a toolbox in his new home on Norton Avenue. Police returned to the home and found numerous photographs of frightened women, tied up and tortured. Many of the photographs also show these women dead.

Glatman was convicted and sent to a cell in San Quentin's Death Row. He was the original inhabitant of the same cell used by Charles Manson (see p. 183) and Richard Ramirez (see p. 232).

Glatman was executed on September 18, 1959. He wanted to die. He got his wish.

1011 S. Norton Avenue Los Angeles

PATRICK KEARNEY

During the late 1970s, three sadistic serial killers were traipsing around Los Angeles, terrorizing the homosexual community. William Bonin, Randy Kraft, and Patrick Kearney did not know one another, but they were all on the same wavelength. Each man picked up young homosexuals and raped and killed them. Police were not aware of Kearney until July 5, 1977, when he walked into a Riverside Police Department with his lover David Hill, saw a "Wanted" poster with their pictures on it, and proudly stated, "That's us."

Kearney became known as the "Trash Bag Murderer" due to his penchant for cutting up men's bodies and neatly packaging them in industrial strength garbage bags. Under interrogation, Kearney confessed that he alone was responsible for several deaths of young men over the previous eight years. He claimed that he often fought with his lover, Hill, and when Hill would leave, Kearney would kill.

Kearney was a small man with large ears who was teased his entire life. As a child, the kids in school constantly picked on him. His parents were no help and expected him to stand up for himself. He began to daydream about how he would take care of his various nemeses. He fantasized about killing the mean boys and skinning their bodies.

Kearney's fantasies became reality in 1968. His first victim was simply known as "George." Kearney murdered George, cut him up into small pieces, and skinned his body. He then buried the dead man behind his duplex in Culver City, where he lived from 1968 to 1970.

Kearney always employed a routine that was simple and efficient. He picked up some young gay man and drove down the freeway. As his passenger looked out the car window, he

stuck a tiny gun behind his ear and pulled the trigger. He then drove to a secluded area and had sex with the dead body. After he was done, he took the corpse to his home in Redondo Beach. Once inside, he carried the corpse to the bathroom and removed all of the limbs with a hacksaw. He also disemboweled the bodies. Afterwards, he neatly bagged the remains, put them in the back seat of his car, and went for a drive. He usually dumped the bags in remote areas, so no one would readily discover them. Kearney claimed that he had been doing this for almost nine years.

Kearney was charged and convicted of 21 murders and sentenced to life in prison, rather than death, in exchange for his cooperation. He was also a suspect in many of the other murders that occurred during the same time period. Police, however, determined that he was not responsible for these other murders, because his method was too clean and efficient. And, these other murders were not done that way. They were the work of an even more sadistic individual, Randy Kraft.

1906 Robinson Street Redondo Beach

RANDY KRAFT

Randy Kraft should have become the prototypical All-American computer geek. He was born on March 19, 1945 in Long Beach, California. He was a precocious child who seemed intelligent beyond his youthful years.

Kraft attended college at Claremont Men's College. He received a scholarship, studied Economics, and was also the dorm President of Green Hall. He lived in the dorm his entire four years of school and stayed in rooms 13, 8, 31, and 7. During his junior year in 1966, he was arrested in Huntington Beach for "lewd conduct." Despite this blemish on his record, Kraft graduated in 1967 with a degree in Economics and seemed to be on his way.

Kraft enlisted in the Air Force upon graduation and was released in a year for "homosexual misconduct." Disgusted by the subpar treatment he received from the military for his sexual preference, Kraft moved back to Long Beach to seek out his homosexual identity.

In 1972, only five years after his graduation from college, Kraft would murder his first human being. By 1983, Kraft was suspected of killing more than 60 men.

On May 14, 1983 Kraft was pulled over for suspected drunk driving on the San Diego Freeway. Kraft hopped out of his car and walked to the police cruiser that pulled him over. Suspicious, police officers walked back to Kraft's brown Toyota Celica and made a startling discovery. A 25-year-old Marine, Terry Lee Gambrel, was found slumped over in the passenger seat, seemingly passed out. Upon closer inspection, the

Randy Kraft

Terry Gambrel

officers realized that the half-naked Gambrel was dead.

Kraft was arrested for murder. A search of his car was conducted that led to another chilling find. Kraft had photographs of several males, all either unconscious or dead. When they searched the trunk of his car, they also found a cryptic sheet of paper that appeared to be a list of some kind. It contained phrases such as "2-in-1 Beach," "Carson Marine," and "Portland Head." Approximately 61 entries were listed on the paper, which many later considered to be a tally sheet for the total number of Kraft's victims. He had kept score.

Another search was conducted at Kraft's home in Long Beach. Police found more photographs of potentially dead males, including three men who had been reported missing. There was also a large amount of blood found at Kraft's residence.

Police now believed that Kraft was responsible for several murders.

Kraft was vicious. His victims were found with numerous sadistic wounds. They often had a burn mark on their left nipple. Many were strangled, shot, and sliced. Some men had their testicles removed. Every one of Kraft's victims was tossed haphazardly from his moving vehicle. They were also found with relative ease, since many were simply lying on the side of the road.

Kraft was egotistical in his murders. He would pick 'em up, slice 'em, torture them, and fling them to the side like an unwanted hamburger wrapper.

Kraft was finally brought to trial in 1989 on 16 murder charges. He was convicted on all counts despite claiming his innocence throughout the trial. He was sentenced to death and shipped off to San Quentin. In prison, he played bridge with fellow serial killers William Bonin, Douglas Clark, and Lawrence Bittaker. Kraft, the most intelligent of the foursome, was known to win most times.

824 Roswell Avenue Long Beach

GERALD PARKER

On the night of September 30, 1979, United States Marine Corporal Kevin Green stepped out of his Tustin apartment for a late-night snack. When he returned 40 minutes later, his life changed forever. His wife, Dianne, was lying on their bed in a coma. She had been beaten and bloodied. She had also been raped. Kevin feared the worse, as his young

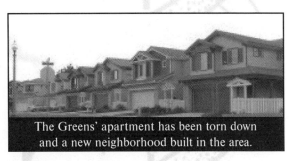

The Greens' apartment has been torn down and a new neighborhood built in the area.

bride was an overdue nine-and-a-half months pregnant.

One month later, Dianne emerged from her coma. She claimed that she had no memory of the attack. Kevin was crushed because he had to pass along the sad news to his wife that their unborn daughter, Chantel Marie Green, had died as a result of the attack. The couple was devastated.

Another month passed before Dianne made a claim that shattered everything. She believed that it was her husband who had attacked her. She stated that they had fought over sex. She claimed that Kevin became angry when she refused to have sex with him and had hit her with his keys. Then, he allegedly raped her.

Green was arrested, quickly tried, and sent to San Quentin for second-degree murder. He was handed a 15-years-to-life sentence. Green steadfastly proclaimed his innocence, even during his parole hearings. The board wanted Kevin to show remorse for his crime, but he refused. As a result, his parole was denied.

In 1996, the world spun sideways yet again for Green. Officials at the California Department of Justice lab made a startling discovery. Another Marine from Orange County, Gerald Parker, a 43-year-old African-American who was in prison in for sex crimes during the 80s, had consented to a DNA test. The lab researchers matched Parker's semen to DNA found on five victims that were murdered in Orange County from 1978 to 1979. Parker's DNA also appeared at another crime scene in the area during that same time: the one involving Dianne Green.

When confronted with the DNA test results, Parker quietly confessed to being the infamous "Bedroom Basher." He described his modus operandi to the police. He would get

Formerly 230 W. 6th Street   Tustin

drunk, follow a cute woman without her knowledge, and then enter her home. Once inside, he bashed the unsuspecting victim with either a piece of wood, a mallet, or a hammer. Usually, he raped his victims while they were still alive and sometimes even after they were dead.

Parker also confessed to the attack on Dianne Green. He admitted that it was he, not Kevin Green, who beat, raped, and caused Dianne to lose her unborn child. Based on Parker's confession, authorities allowed Kevin Green to leave prison, 16 years after he was wrongly convicted.

Not much is known about Parker. He, allegedly, had been stationed all over the country, from Mississippi to Alaska. In Orange County, he was stationed at the El Toro Marine base. All six murders occurred within miles of the base.

Parker had been arrested in 1980 for the rape of a 13-year-old girl. He spent over ten years in prison for that crime. He was released, but sent back to prison when he violated his parole. In 1996, his second release date was almost set when his DNA sample was received. At his trial in 1999, Parker claimed remorse and agreed that he deserved to die. The Orange County jurors honored his request and recommended the death penalty.

PICTURED RIGHT:
DNA chart used in court to convict Gerald Parker.

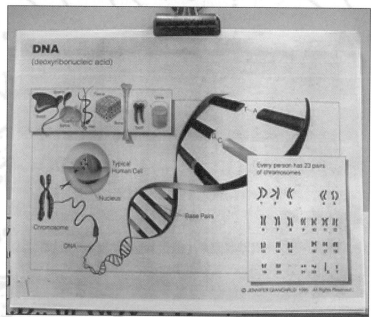

Gerald Parker

EFREN SALDIVAR

On March 11, 1998, 29-year-old respiratory therapist Efren Saldivar walked into the Glendale police station and began to unspool an amazing story. For four hours, he confessed to killing 40 to 50 elderly patients over the previous decade at the Glendale Adventist Medical Center. He called himself the "Angel of Death."

Saldivar claimed that he had suffocated the patients by cutting off their air supply through a respiratory tube. This method of murder was almost impossible to detect in a corpse. His other method of murder was to poison the patients with a muscle relaxant known as Pavulon and another known as succinylcholine chloride. These drugs were supposed to be used to relax patients enough to place a respiratory tube down their throat. Only nurses or doctors, not respiratory therapists, were allowed to administer these drugs.

After his confession, police held Saldivar for two days, but were forced to let him go due to lack of evidence. He was released on March 13, a free man.

One month later, Saldivar went on national television to recant his claims. He told reporters from *Extra* and *20/20* that he had made the confessions up, because he was depressed and wanted to die. He believed that if he claimed to have killed more than one person he could get the death penalty. He insisted that he was too afraid to commit suicide, and he wanted the state to kill him.

Despite Saldivar's retraction of his detailed confession, the police continued to investigate him, but it was a slow moving machine. Authorities set up shop outside the hospital and began the arduous task of searching through both Saldivar's files and the hospital records. They first had to determine how many deaths had occurred on Saldivar's watch. They focused on the years 1996-1997 and discovered that 171 patients had died while Saldivar was at work. Out of these deaths, 54 were immediately eliminated, because their bodies had been cremated. They whittled the choices down to 20 to determine if traces of Pavulon or succinylcholine chloride were in their systems.

The process of exhuming the bodies of these chosen few began in the summer of 1999, almost 16 months after Saldivar's confession. Many medical experts claimed that the police had waited too long, and the drugs may no longer be detectable. This was true for the chloride, but not the Pavulon.

The investigation was lead by Brian Kelberg, who had given medical testimony at the O.J. Simpson trial (see p. 259). Cognizant of the recent criticism heaped on the L.A.P.D. and the Los Angeles Coroner's Office, Kelberg appeared to take the cautious route, possibly too cautious.

By November 7, 2000, Kelberg had still not pressed charges against Saldivar. On that day, the citizens of Los Angeles overwhelmingly voted out District Attorney Gil Garcetti and elected Republican candidate Steve Cooley. Cooley was inducted into office in December 2000 and made an immediate impact.

Cooley replaced Kelberg with Al McKenzie, a District Attorney with a medical background. McKenzie wasted no time. On Tuesday, January 9, 2001, McKenzie announced that Efren Saldivar had been arrested on six charges of murder. Of the 20 bodies that had been exhumed, six had shown definite traces of Pavulon, a drug that had not been prescribed for them.

Police arrested Saldivar at 5:45 AM outside of Tujunga, where he still lived with his parents, as he drove to work. Saldivar did not resist.

Saldivar had kept a low profile since his recantation of the confession, but his career as a respiratory therapist had ended. He was fired the day the police released him. He lost his respiratory therapist license in 1998. He also worked a series of odd jobs as a security guard and as a phone sex worker.

No trial date has been set for Saldivar as of this writing.

1509 East Wilson Terrace   Glendale

BRANDON THOLMER

This Jimi Hendrix/Phil Lynott look-alike terrorized elderly women in the East Hollywood-Silverlake area during the early 1980s. He was once believed to have been responsible for more than 30 murders. Brandon Tholmer's case is relatively unknown, but fascinating nonetheless.

Tholmer, 29 at the time of his arrest, was a struggling musician who tried to make it big in Hollywood. He was a drummer for a new garage band known as "The Hostages." His band mates fondly described him as a nice guy who dressed like a rock 'n' roller. His girlfriend felt like her life was better with Tholmer by her side. She also pointed out his love for rock music. She informed police that his favorite song was "Killer on the Loose," by Thin Lizzy.

How could a seemingly decent kid be accused of over 30 murders of old, fragile women? Tholmer grew up in New Orleans in a broken home. He went to a psychiatrist at an early age and was diagnosed as "borderline retarded." Furthermore, he seemed to spend more time in juvenile institutions than in school, because he constantly committed petty crimes. He never got his act together.

Indeed, in 1975, Tholmer was arrested for sexually molesting an 80-year-old woman. He was not sent to prison. Instead, he was turned over to a psychiatric facility for treatment. He showed progress, but continued to seek treatment for several more years.

By 1981, Tholmer was living in a Hollywood apartment, at 611 ½ North Alexandria Avenue, with a fellow band member. He had found a girlfriend, had a good job, and was seeking help at the Gateways Satellite mental health facility.

Tholmer, however, also liked to wear a knife sheathed to his leg and go for late night walks to "clear his head." Part of clearing his head was killing defenseless old women. He began his murder spree, on August 16, 1981, at the home of 80-year-old Rose Lederman at 3464 Plata Street in East Hollywood. Tholmer broke into her home and strangled the woman to death. When her body was discovered, she was covered with bruises over her head, thighs, arms, neck, chest, and eyes.

Tholmer's brutality increased with every new victim. His next victim, Woolloomooloo Woodcock, who was 66 and resided at 151 North Normandie Avenue, had been strangled, beaten, and raped on August 19, 1982, one year after the murder of Lederman.

He increased his murder toll the following year:
   –5/10/83: Lorraine Wells (5529 Fernwood Avenue), 82, was beaten, raped, and smothered to death with a pillow. Her left ear was torn, her teeth loosened, her fingernails broken, and she had a bite mark on her chin.
   –8/31/83: Dorothy Fain (6142 ½ Romaine Street), 72, was beaten, raped, and

sodomized. Tholmer burned down her home, while Fain was still inside.

−9/12/83: Mary Paquette (4005 Monroe Street), 72, was beaten, stabbed, raped, sodomized, and strangled before Tholmer burned her and her trash-cluttered home.

Tholmer became a suspect after Paquette's murder. The police put him under surveillance and arrested him two months later when he was caught entering another elderly woman's home in his neighborhood.

When he was originally arrested, police believed he was responsible for a slew of elderly lady murders: 34 of them to be exact. However, they knew it would be difficult to pin enough evidence on him to convict him of each of the murders. The charges, therefore, were reduced from 34 to 12 and eventually to the five ladies listed here.

Assistant District Attorney Lance Ito (see O.J. Simpson p. 259) prosecuted Tholmer's case. Ito secured convictions in four of the cases. The jury deadlocked on the murder of Lorraine Wells. Ito, who believed that Tholmer was responsible for many more murders, made a curious move during Tholmer's sentencing. He suggested to the defense counsel that they put Tholmer's brother on the stand in effort to get a more lenient sentence. The jury, citing Tholmer's tough upbringing, gave the killer four life sentences.

611 1/2 N. Alexandria Ave. Los Angeles

CHAPTER 9
CHARLES MANSON

The name conjures up fear and dread more than 30 years later. But the story of Charles Manson and "Helter Skelter" is much more complex than the screaming headlines he inspired.

Charles Manson was a habitual tenant in America's penal institutions even before he became a household name. He moved to the West Coast in the 1960s, at the height of the era of free love. When Manson settled down, he gathered a group of seemingly directionless youths and formed what has come to be known as his "Family." Comprised of disenfranchised middle-class suburban kids, the "Family" followed Manson's philosophy of free love and no rules.

At first, it all seemed so perfect. So serene. So right.

But bad drugs, bad deals, and bad thoughts distorted Manson's utopian view. The hope of peace and love irrevocably turned into bigotry and bloodshed.

It all culminated in a succession of cold-blooded murders in the summer of 1969, the same summer that the United States sent a man to the moon, the same summer of Woodstock, the same summer of Ted Kennedy's incident at Chappaquiddick.

The gruesome killing of Sharon Tate and her friends, and the subsequent murder of a suburban couple, stunned Los Angeles and the world and overshadowed everything else that happened that year.

The Helter Skelter murders brought to an end the peace, love, and understanding decade of the 60s. A lone figure rose out of the atrocities and became the symbol for all that was wrong and evil in American society. That figure was Charles Manson.

NO NAME MADDOX

Charles Manson's birth certificate reads "No Name Maddox." He was born on November 12, 1934 in Cincinnati, Ohio. Manson's mother, Kathleen Maddox, lived with numerous men and took her little boy in tow wherever she went. She eventually married a William Manson, and thus Charles was given his surname. The identity of Manson's biological father is unknown.

Unwanted, Manson was bounced back and forth between his promiscuous mother and a God-fearing aunt, but he eventually ended up in a boys' reform school. He soon turned to a life of petty crime. At the age of 16, he stole a car and attempted to drive to California. He made it as far as the Indiana border before he was caught. Such actions escalated to more serious offenses, including robbery, assault, and even homosexual rape.

He would spend the majority of his youth and early adulthood in and out of reform schools and jail. By 1967, at the age of 32, Manson had spent more than half of his life incarcerated in some form of correctional institution.

Charles Manson

CHARLIE DON'T SURF?

After serving a ten-year stint at Terminal Island prison, Manson headed for the hippie mecca of San Francisco's Haight-Ashbury. On March 21, 1967, Manson's whirlwind journey began as he amassed a motley crew of dropouts, misfits, and hippies known as his "Family."

After months in San Francisco, the Family packed up and moved to Los Angeles, where they found themselves on the perpetual couch circuit. This was a common practice among the free spirits of the day, and Manson's clan was certainly no exception. All of that changed, however, when two of Manson's girls, Patricia Krenwinkel and Ella Jo Bailey, were hitchhiking. A charismatic longhaired driver offered them a ride and a place to crash. This was not your typical surfer dude. It was Dennis Wilson of the Beach Boys (see p. 71).

When most people think of the Beach Boys, the image is a clean-cut, wholesome one. But towards the end of the 60s, the group was prone to their fair share of life in the fast lane. Wilson, in particular, had a fondness for young girls, and Manson had them in abundance. Thus, the odd, albeit brief crossing of paths was consummated. As Manson and his girls moved into Wilson's spartanesque residence, they blended in well: drugs, orgies, the works.

Eventually, Wilson got sick of Manson and his legion, so he moved out before his lease was up. Manson was forced to pack up once again before the next rent check was due. Upon leaving, one of the items Manson took with him was a Beach Boys Gold Album plaque.

Speaking of gold records, perhaps the oddest legacy of the Manson/Wilson experience was that Wilson bought a song written by Manson that was eventually recorded by the Beach Boys.

14400 Sunset Boulevard   Pacific Palisades

YELLOW SUBMARINE

January 1969. The cold winter forced Manson and his gang inside a ramshackle two-story house in Canoga Park. Former Family member Paul Watkins claimed that the name "Yellow Submarine" was inspired by one of the house rules: once inside you were not allowed

Capitol Records released the Beach Boys' single, *Bluebirds Over The Mountain*. The B-side was a song entitled *Never Learn Not To Love*. The song, co-written by Charles Manson, hit #61 on the pop music charts.

to leave and could only look out the windows. The claustrophobia that was present in submarines was comparable to the environment here during the Family's stay.

This location is where Manson allegedly conjured up the theory of Helter Skelter. Manson and his followers were arguably major Beatles fans. They made phone calls and wrote letters to England with the intent of getting in touch with the influential rock band. The Beatles self-titled album, also referred to as the *White Album*, supposedly was a major influence on Manson. With songs like "Blackbird," "Happiness is a Warm Gun," and the acidic "Revolution 9," Manson believed the Beatles were attempting to speak directly to him. Specifically, he believed the band was telling him that he would lead a new uprising. The key song from the *White Album* that would become Manson's mantra was "Helter Skelter."

Watkins claimed that Manson created specific escape routes from the Yellow Submarine that would lead the Family to the safe haven of Death Valley. Charlie also spoke of a series of murders that would ignite a race war. Watkins lamented, "Before Helter Skelter came along, all Charlie cared about were orgies." Oh, the times they were a-changing. Quickly.

The Yellow Submarine house no longer exists. Just this empty lot.

Formerly 20910 Gresham St. Canoga Park

SPAHN RANCH

Before their stay in the Yellow Submarine, Manson and his Family lived at this old Chatsworth movie set. Spahn Ranch was located only 20 minutes from Beverly Hills but could not be more different. Its beautiful pastures and rugged looking mountains provided a scenic backdrop for numerous western movies in the 50s and 60s. By 1968, the ranch had lost its usefulness as a movie set and was converted into horse stables.

Spahn Ranch got its name from its owner and caretaker, 80-year-old George Spahn. The semi-blind rancher enthusiastically welcomed Manson and his crew, as Manson instructed some of his female followers to take care of Spahn's sexual needs. As the grinning recipient of oral gratification, the docile Spahn granted the Family full reign of the grounds.

1969: 12000 Santa Susanna Pass   Chatsworth
Present: 23000 Santa Susanna Pass   Chatsworth

According to former members, the Family's stay at Spahn Ranch in the summer of 1968 began romantically enough. They would waste away days at a time: communing with nature, playing dress up, and partaking of numerous chemicals. Drugs, carefree orgies, and loss of time were the rules of the day. Biker gangs occasionally stopped by to get high and have their way with the flock.

Terry Melcher

After leaving the Yellow Submarine in 1969, Manson and his family returned to Spahn Ranch. However, the idyllic lifestyle of the year before began to fall apart. The musical career that Manson wanted so desperately was going nowhere. During this time, music producer Terry Melcher disrespected Charlie. Manson believed Melcher, the son of Doris Day and friend of Beach Boy Dennis Wilson, could open the doors to a successful life in the music industry. Melcher's rejection of Manson was a critical signpost in the downslide of life at the ranch. Negative, violent thoughts seeped into Manson's subconscious and were further fueled by the drugs.

The carefree days of sex and drugs were jolted into a new order. Manson began to conduct life on the ranch as if he was the head of a militia group and the Family was his group of personal soldiers. Members, armed with rifles, patrolled the grounds around the clock.

Drug use continued, but it took on a whole new dimension. It became a tool for mind-control, not for pleasure. Manson would get his followers high on several hits of LSD, while he himself would take much smaller doses. Here, the recurring theme of Helter Skelter was preached and reinforced in his followers.

Manson would also use ritual tirades to reinforce his domination over his Family. Members spoke of one bizarre ritual. Across the street from the ranch, Manson led his followers through a mock crucifixion, with himself in the leading role. The symbolism of Charlie as Christ took root in the minds of these seemingly young lost souls, and his complete control over them as their leader had begun.

The end results would stun an entire nation.

In an effort to turn a negative into a positive, Spahn Ranch was purchased in 1999 and will be converted into a church.

1969: 12000 Santa Susanna Pass   Chatsworth

Present: 23000 Santa Susanna Pass   Chatsworth

HELTER SKELTER

Charles Manson's theory of Helter Skelter came from two disparate sources: the Bible and the Beatles. The Bible provided Manson with Revelations, Chapter 9. The Beatles' *White Album* gave him "Revolution 9." According to former Family members, Manson became obsessed with the *White Album* and believed the record was a living, breathing, modern-day roadmap of the doom prophesied in Revelations 9.

Manson's interpretation of the Bible was as follows: five long-haired angels (John, Paul, George, Ringo, and Charlie) with shields of fire (electric guitars) and brimstone voices (Charlie's and the Beatles) would descend into a bottomless pit (the desert—Death Valley) while the black race would destroy a "third of man" (the white race), also known as "pigs" (the establishment). Manson theorized that once the black race's domination was complete, they would be incapable of running the new world order. And who better to show them how than the man who considered himself to be the new Jesus Christ.

Charles Manson.

Manson believed that various lyrics on the *White Album* showed the way to facilitate the black man's ascension. "Revolution 1" spoke of the need for a new regime. He saw "Happiness is a Warm Gun" as a call to arms for the black man. "Revolution 9" was the soundtrack to war, with its cacophonous nightmare screams, the use of the word "RISE," and the ominous repetition of the phrase "Number 9." Finally, "Helter Skelter" was decoded to mean that while the war raged on, Manson and his band of marauders would hide out below the Earth and one day rise to see the blacks again. Manson would become their messiah and lead the way (a belief that was rooted in a racist notion of black incompetence).

The Helter Skelter theory has been decried by critics who believe this ploy was Prosecutor Vincent Bugliosi's grasp for the golden ring. They contend it was a way to generate some far-out publicity from an already far-out case. Manson always claimed that he was never a Beatles fan, because they were too "teeny bopper." Regardless of the veracity of the Helter Skelter theory, it has become a part of the collective consciousness and widely perceived to be the undeniable truth.

Charles Manson

LOTSAPOPPA

Bernard Crowe, AKA Lotsapoppa, played a pivotal role in setting off the Manson powder keg. Manson and his clan hung out with the Black Panther and indulged in crazy drug and group sex parties.

On July 1, 1969, however, things took a turn for the worse. Manson sent Family member Charles "Tex" Watson out with Crowe to El Monte to make a drug buy. Crowe gave Watson $2,400 to make a sizable purchase of marijuana. Instead of doing the deal, however, Watson went into a building and snuck out the back. While Crowe waited, Watson hightailed it to Spahn Ranch with his money.

Crowe was furious. He headed over to the apartment of Watson's girlfriend. A pissed-off Crowe called Manson and sought revenge for Watson's scam. He warned Manson that he would come to the ranch and kill all of his Family. Manson convinced Crowe that the two should meet at the apartment. Many versions have been spun about what happened next. One of the most popular had Manson begging for his own life and then sweet-talking Crowe. Crowe supposedly claimed that he only wanted Watson and not Manson. Taking Crowe by surprise, Manson pulled out his .22 Longhorn revolver, aimed it at Crowe, and squeezed the trigger.

Click.

Nothing happened!

Manson burst into laughter and said, "How could I kill you with an empty gun?" Catching Crowe off guard again, Manson pulled the trigger a second time. This time the gun fired

a bullet into Crowe's belly. As Crowe collapsed to the floor, Manson believed he was dead and walked out of the apartment. Crowe, however, did not die.

1900-02 N. Sycamore Avenue Hollywood

GARY HINMAN

UCLA music professor Gary Hinman got tangled in the Family's web on a sweltering late July weekend in 1969. He made the mistake of getting crossways with Charlie and paid for it with his life. Manson accused Hinman of ripping him off of $20,000 in a drug deal gone wrong.

Manson said Hinman had sold him a bad batch of LSD and wanted his money back. Manson sent Family members Bobby Beausoleil and Susan Atkins to Hinman's home to square up. The two were not impressed by his denials or his lack of funds. After receiving a phone call from Beausoleil, Manson made an angry visit, demanding repayment from Hinman. Again, the 30-year-old Hinman denied everything.

Reportedly, Manson brandished his trusty bayonet and proceeded to slice off Hinman's ear. The peaceful Buddhist bled profusely as Manson and company kept him bound for more than a day. Beausoleil would later end Hinman's life with several fatal stab wounds.

Bobby Beausoleil

To throw off the authorities and make them think the murder was the handiwork of the Black Panthers, Atkins wrote the words "political piggy" on the wall with Hinman's blood and left a bloody paw print, the Black Panther symbol.

On August 6, Bobby Beausoleil was arrested while driving Hinman's car.

964 Old Topanga Canyon Rd Topanga Canyon

AUGUST 9, 1969

Late in the evening of August 8th, four of Manson's followers headed to the Benedict Canyon residence of actress Sharon Tate, the former home of producer Terry Melcher. Tripping on LSD, Charles "Tex" Watson, Patricia Krenwinkel, Susan Atkins, and Linda Kasabian made the winding, treacherous drive from Spahn Ranch and arrived at Tate's house shortly after midnight. Tate, wife of notorious film director Roman Polanski, was eight-and-a-half months pregnant and had a handful of guests staying over.

1969: 10050 Cielo Drive Benedict Canyon
Present: 10066 Cielo Drive Benedict Canyon

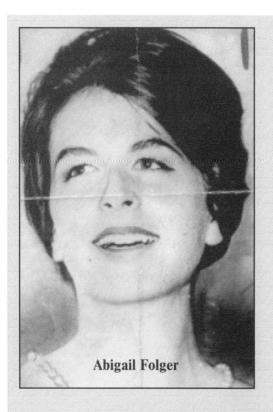

Abigail Folger

Jay Sebring

Tate's guests that fateful night included Abigail Folger, heiress to the Folger coffee empire, Jay Sebring, hairdresser to the stars and Tate's former lover, and Polish playboy Voytek Frykowski. The fateful gathering of the Tate party and the Manson clan would forever change the face of an innocent nation.

Watson scaled the embankment to get past the gate. He then climbed up a telephone pole to cut the phone wires. The remaining three Family members followed Watson onto the premises. Watson, Krenwinkel, and Atkins proceeded to the beautiful ranch-style home while Kasabian stood guard at the gate.

Patricia Krenwinkel

1969: 10050 Cielo Drive Benedict Canyon
Present: 10066 Cielo Drive Benedict Canyon

THE MURDERS

Manson's minions first encountered recent high school graduate Steven Parent as he was driving away in his car. Parent, 18, was visiting the housekeeper and had tried to sell him a clock. Watson slashed Parent with a knife then shot him in the face four times just as he was leaving the estate. He was the first to die.

Voytek Frykowski, 33, was shot twice, brutally stabbed 51 times, and beaten over the head 13 times with the butt of a gun.

Abigail Folger, 25, was stabbed 28 times. Her white dress appeared red due to the heavy saturation of her own blood.

Jay Sebring, 35, was shot in the face and stabbed seven times. He bled to death.

Sharon Tate, 26, was stabbed repeatedly in the chest and back, a total of 16 times. She was found with a bloody towel covering her face and a noose around her neck. The other end of the rope was attached to Sebring. Tate reportedly begged for her killers to spare the life of her unborn child. Instead, Atkins screamed at her, "I don't care about you or your baby" and proceeded to scrawl the word "PIG" on the front door in Tate's blood.

1969: 10050 Cielo Drive Benedict Canyon
Present: 10066 Cielo Drive Benedict Canyon

This telephone pole is the only remaining original structure on the property. The address has changed from 10050 to 10066 Cielo Drive.

A new 12,000 square foot Mediterranean style mansion was built on the property. It was originally priced at $12 million and sold in 2000 to Hollywood producer Jeff Franklin (*Full House*, *Casper*, and *Stuart Little*). The cost: $6,000,000.

CIELO CELEBS

The "Tate" house on Cielo Drive has a celebrated history. Many high-profile residents set up digs there before and after the 1969 murders.

Cary Grant—star of *Notorious* and *North by Northwest* once owned the house in the 50s.

 Henry Fonda—star of *On Golden Pond* and father to Peter and Jane Fonda once rented the house from Grant.

Candice Bergen—Terry Melcher's lover in the mid-60s. They rented the house prior to the Polanskis and were potential targets of Manson. She starred in the television sitcom *Murphy Brown*.

 Trent Reznor—In 1993/1994, the Nine Inch Nails leader rented the house and recorded his smash album *The Downward Spiral* there. "March of the Pigs," "Piggy," and "Big Man With A Gun" are among the songs on the CD. The house was torn down after Reznor moved out.

1969: 10050 Cielo Drive Benedict Canyon
Present: 10066 Cielo Drive Benedict Canyon

AUGUST 10, 1969

The second night of terror occurred at the Los Feliz home of Leno and Rosemary LaBianca. Leno, 44, owner of a neighborhood grocery store, and Rosemary, 38, owner of a dress boutique, returned home late Sunday night from a water-skiing vacation. Shortly thereafter, Charles Manson and his followers paid them a visit.

Manson strolled into the LaBianca home, smiled at Leno, and proceeded to tie the couple up with a pair of buckskin thongs. Manson left the house and allegedly ordered his cohorts to take care of business. Patricia Krenwinkel and former high school prom queen Leslie Van Houten joined Tex Watson. The acts they committed on the LaBiancas were as gruesome as the murders at Cielo Drive.

Leno received 12 knife wounds and an additional 14 wounds from a doubled-tined fork. The word "WAR" had been carved in his torso. The fork was left protruding from his throat.

Rosemary was found in her bedroom with a pillowcase over her head and a lamp cord tied around her throat. She was viciously stabbed 41 times in the back and buttocks.

Once again, blood smeared messages were left at the scene of the crime. The words "RISE" and "DEATH TO PIGS" decorated the LaBianca's walls. Krenwinkel misspelled a cryptic "HEALTER SKELTER" on the refrigerator door in Leno's blood. After the trio slaughtered the LaBiancas, they relaxed with a refreshing snack of milk and sandwiches from the same 'fridge.

1969: 3301 Waverly Drive Los Feliz
Present: 3311 Waverly Drive Los Feliz

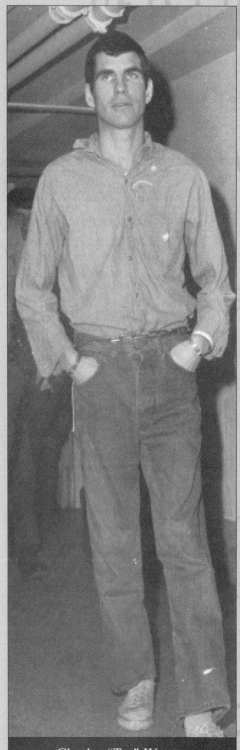

Charles "Tex" Watson

Patricia Krenwinkel & Leslie Van Houten

1969: 3301 Waverly Drive Los Feliz
Present: 3311 Waverly Drive Los Feliz

BARKER RANCH

One week after the murders, Manson and his bunch were arrested during a pre-dawn raid at Spahn Ranch. Authorities had been conducting a sting operation of car thieves and the Family got snagged in its web. A judge later threw out the charges, due to an incorrect date on the search warrant.

Fearing that the authorities were closing in on him, Manson prepared to move the Family again. The move was part of his plan to prepare for the beginning of Helter Skelter. Consistent with Manson's interpretation of *Revelations*, he was to seek refuge in a "bottomless pit." Once he assembled his Family, they would descend into the underground haven while the race war would rage aboveground. Manson believed the gate was located at Barker Ranch in Death Valley, about 200 miles northeast of Los Angeles.

Barker Ranch was a rugged, rocky enclave that could best be accessed with an all-terrain vehicle. Once Manson and approximately 40 of his members settled in at the ranch in September, they began to prepare for war. Guns, knives, and dune buggies were stockpiled. Manson also decided that hand-to-hand combat training was in order. He even taught each of the girls the best way to slit a person's throat. As the drugs heightened his sense of paranoia and reinforced his fear of being arrested, Manson's behavior became even more erratic and violent. He would often slap the women around to intimidate them and keep them in line.

The authorities eventually caught up with the Family. On October 10, 1969, officials raided Barker Ranch and arrested several of the members on charges of arson, theft, and receiving stolen property.

One key person was missing: Charles Manson. He was out of town on "business," but surprisingly, he would return to the ranch. He had no idea that his followers were in custody. Upon his return on October 12, Manson was arrested.

Death Valley

CONFESSION

4500 E. City Terrace Drive Los Angeles

In late October, Susan Atkins was moved from the Inyo County Jail in the desert to the Sybil Brand Institute in Los Angeles to face a charge of murder in the Gary Hinman case. The exuberant Atkins spent most of her time at her new residence running around screaming, singing, and dancing. She also had a penchant for flashing her privates at her fellow inmates. Fearing that her odd behavior may cause the young woman harm, older inmate Virginia Graham befriended Atkins.

Atkins quickly warmed up to Graham and immediately began to spill the beans on Charlie and the Family. She blabbed about her involvement in numerous crimes and her participation in the murder of Hinman. When Atkins and Graham were watching a television news broadcast on the unsolved murder mystery of Sharon Tate, Atkins became uncontrollably giddy. She told Graham about how she had dealt the fatal blow to the spoiled actress and how they had also killed the LaBiancas.

Graham, of course, thought Atkins was lying. Prisons were full of cons that spun stories to bolster their reputations, and Graham believed that this was the case with Atkins. But as Atkins excitedly went on about her merciless killing of Tate and her unborn baby, Graham began to believe that this innocent looking girl was indeed a cold-blooded sadist.

Graham approached fellow inmate and friend Ronnie Howard and told her about Atkins's claims. Howard immediately realized this bit of information could provide a great bargaining chip for both her and Graham to get their own sentences reduced, so they concocted a plan. They wanted to make sure Atkins was speaking the truth and not just engaging in braggadocio. Howard had actually visited the Cielo Drive residence earlier in the year and knew specific details about the property that someone would not know unless they had been there. Atkins answered every question that Howard threw at her. She also seemed to know several details about the case that were not aired on television. Howard was convinced that Atkins was indeed the killer.

On November 17, 1969, Ronnie Howard ratted out Susan Atkins. In the process, the flimsy house of cards that surrounded the Manson Family finally began to tumble over.

4500 E. City Terrace Drive Los Angeles

4500 E. City Terrace Drive Los Angeles

THE TRIAL

The trial of Charles Manson and his followers was among the most fevered legal spectacles in America's history. It came long after the Charles Lindbergh baby kidnapping trial (the original "Trial of the Century") and long before the O.J. Simpson murder trial. Regardless, for total shock value and sheer hysteria, the Charles Manson conspiracy and murder trial remains one of the most publicized and chaotic legal events ever.

On June 15, 1970, Charles Manson, Patricia Krenwinkel, Leslie Van Houten, and Susan Atkins were paraded into court. They were all charged with several counts of first-degree murder. Additionally, Manson was charged with conspiracy to commit murder. Since Manson did not directly participate in the murders, Prosecutor Vincent Bugliosi employed the "vicarious liability" rule of conspiracy. This concept

111 N. Hill Street   Los Angeles

basically stated, "each conspirator is criminally responsible for all of the crimes committed by his co-conspirator if said crimes were committed to further the object of the conspiracy. This rule applies even if the conspirator was not present at the scene of the crime."

The defendants gathered in Judge Charles Older's courtroom on the eighth floor of the

Los Angeles Superior District Court for a trial that would last six months. The trial began with Van Houten firing her attorney for alleged incompetence. In reality, her attorney attempted to separate Van Houten from Manson, arguing that she had only stabbed Rosemary LaBianca after she was already dead. When word of this strategy got back to Manson, he sent Van Houten a message that demanded she dump her attorney and let Manson take over her defense. Manson's motive for such a move was less than honorable—he wanted Van Houten, Krenwinkel, and Atkins to take the fall.

As the trial got underway, Manson's influence over the girls was evident. On the first day of the trial, Manson carved an "X" in his forehead. The next day, the three girls followed suit. Their self-mutilation reflected their beliefs that they were outcasts from society and that they should be crossed out. The three young, middle-class killers constantly disrupted the pro-

111 N. Hill Street   Los Angeles

proceedings by singing, yelling, or refusing to speak when required to do so.

Manson's influence even seemed to carry outside the courthouse building. On the court sidewalk, several Family members, including Lynette "Squeaky" Fromme, set up a daily camp to pray for their fallen leader and vehemently proclaim his innocence. When Manson shaved his head bald, they followed suit. The Family also threatened the media and warned of impending doom if Manson was convicted.

One Manson follower, however, would not act as Manson's patsy. Linda Kasabian, who had been present at both murders but did not participate in the acts, became the key witness for the prosecution. She gave detailed descriptions of the two nights of terror and how Manson orchestrated the whole scenario to ignite a race war.

Such testimony infuriated Manson. He once pointed at Kasabian and followed with a "slit throat" motion. Another time, he leaped at Judge Older and threatened to kill him. Yet another time, Manson got a hold of the *Los Angeles Times* newspaper with the headline glaring his predetermined guilt and flashed it at the jury with glee.

111 N. Hill Street   Los Angeles

Susan Atkins in the courtroom.

Manson's courtroom histrionics, however, would not get him off the hook. On January 25, 1971, after almost seven long months of gruesome testimony and aggravating legal maneuvers, the jury returned with a verdict of guilty for all four defendants. They were later sentenced to death in the gas chamber for their incredible atrocities. In a separate trial, Charles "Tex" Watson was also convicted and sentenced to die.

On February 18, 1972, the California State Supreme Court abolished the death penalty as a means of punishment, because it was considered to be "cruel and unusual." As a result, Manson and his followers had their death sentences commuted to life in prison. In 1975, the United States Supreme Court overruled the California decision and reinstated the death penalty. However, any prisoner whose sentence was commuted, by law, could not be executed by the state. Susan Atkins, Patricia Krenwinkel, Leslie Van Houten, Charles "Tex" Watson, and Charles Manson had their lives spared and remain eligible for parole.

111 N. Hill Street   Los Angeles

CHAPTER 10

THE HILLSIDE STRANGLERS

Kenneth Bianchi

Angelo Buono

The city of Los Angeles was caught off guard during November of 1977. Over a period of three weeks, three women were found nude and strangled along the hillsides of the city. Most people did not give a damn since the girls were just prostitutes. Seemingly, no one paid attention.

That would all change over the Thanksgiving holiday.

Five more women were found dead upon the green hillsides of the city. They had been strangled. They were nude. Their bodies were displayed in morbid positions, in a sense, mocking the residents of the city. One victim's body was found naked, her legs splayed towards City Hall. The police believed the killers were also mocking them.

What finally caught the attention of the residents of Los Angeles? These other girls were not hookers. They were fine, upstanding citizens. They were college students. They were innocent little girls. The city was outraged.

Finally.

And then, as soon as it all started, it stopped. There were no more "Hillside Stranglings." Los Angeles forgot about the killings and settled in for Christmas.

One year later, everything erupted. A young man was arrested for a double murder in Bellingham, Washington. His name was Kenneth Bianchi. Investigators up north gave the Los Angeles Police Department a call regarding their strangling homicides from the prior year. As it turned out, Bianchi was their man. Bianchi also had a cousin who still lived in Southern California. His name was Angelo Buono.

KEN BIANCHI

Ken Bianchi was born in Rochester, New York, the home of Kodak and Bausch & Lomb. He was born to an alcoholic hooker on May 22, 1951. She gave him up for adoption when he was only three months old. His adoptive parents christened him Kenneth Alessio Bianchi.

Despite his tainted lineage, Bianchi was a smart child, maybe too smart for his own good. Unfortunately, he was also a pathological liar, lazy, and quick to anger. Ken's adoptive father died when he was only 13. His adoptive mother loved young Ken dearly, but felt he was out of control. She worked two jobs, so she could send him to Catholic School to help keep him in line. It appeared to work. Ken did well in school and steered clear of any trouble.

In 1970, Ken married, but the marriage failed almost immediately. Apparently, Ken had created a near-impossible high standard for his women, and no one could ever measure up. Women always disappointed Ken.

Ken was also disappointed in his career ambitions. From a young age, police work fascinated him. In fact, he wanted to become a cop. He took several courses with this goal in mind. His favorite classes involved psychology. This interest would play an important role later in his life. Despite his fascination, Ken never had the right stuff to become a cop. He repeatedly failed in his attempts to secure a position in any police force.

Ken eventually obtained a job as a security guard, the next best thing to being a cop in his mind. He liked the feeling of power. He liked the authority a badge gave him. He also liked to use his position to steal things. His stealing caused him a bit of trouble with the "real" authorities.

In 1972, Ken also became a suspect in a series of murders of little girls known as The Alphabet Murders, because each victim had a first and last name that began with the same letter. Nothing came of it and the cops left him alone.

Three-and-a-half years later, Ken decided it was time to move. He was wearing out his welcome in Rochester. He decided to head west.

His first stop was the home of his cousin, Angelo Buono.

The Hillside Stranglers

ANGELO BUONO

Angelo Buono, Jr., the self-proclaimed "Italian Stallion," was also born in Rochester, New York, on October 5, 1934. By 1939, Angelo's parents had divorced, and his mother uprooted the family and moved west to Glendale, California. They moved into a little house on LaClede Avenue.

Angelo was a trouble-maker from day one. He hated school. He did not care for religion. He could never learn right from wrong. He had no moral compunction and only cared about himself.

By the age of 14, he delighted in calling his mother a "cunt." It infuriated her to no end. As he got older, he brought home black girls and told his mother that they were to be engaged. His mother was a racist and would cringe in disgust at his "fiancées." Angelo loved to torment her.

As a teenager, Angelo was the typical rebellious loser. He smoked, drank, ran with the wrong crowd, and got in trouble with the law. So, it was off to reform school. Of course, this did nothing to help him either. As an adult, Buono never seemed to grow up. He plowed through numerous marriages and fathered several children, possibly as many as nine or ten. Buono never respected any women, including the ones he dated and married.

Buono did respect an infamous L.A. criminal, Caryl Chessman. Chessman gained infamy in the 1940s with a series of rapes that he committed on lovers who were making out in their cars in the hills of Hollywood. His modus operandi was to place a red police light on top of his car and pose as a police officer. When he pounced upon the lovers' lane kids, he proclaimed that he was a policeman and demanded that they get out of their cars. He then raped and terrorized the women.

Carryl Chessman was Angelo Buono's idol.

Nice.

3113 LaClede Avenue   Glendale

THE BUILD-UP

Buono became an auto upholster. He was fairly successful at it. More importantly, he had his own workshop and home at the same location. He also did not have any employees. He had all of the space and privacy he needed to do whatever he wanted without anyone ever knowing.

Bianchi arrived on Buono's doorstep in January 1976. Angelo was not thrilled about having his cousin stay with him, but he was family. Ken was only going to stay for a few weeks, until he found his own place. A few weeks turned into a couple of months before Angelo had enough. He forced Ken to find his own pad, which he did, in Glendale.

Buono's auto trim shop is now an A&M Auto Repair Shop.

Angelo's trim shop was located at 703 East Colorado Avenue in the heart of Glendale. Ken found a modest-sized apartment at 809 East Garfield Avenue, just a few blocks away. The close proximity allowed the cousins to work together on their latest venture: pimping.

Angelo had turned Ken on to luring girls with a badge. It was his homage to Carryl Chessman. Furthermore, since both men were not doing well financially, they decided to recruit some hookers and start a business. They eventually "recruited" two teenage girls, Sabra Hannan and Becky Spears, and sold them for sex. Both men had a predilection for

Buono's Trim Shop: 703 E. Colorado Street   Glendale

Bianchi's Apartment: 809 E. Garfield Avenue   Glendale

unusual, brutal sex and often took out their frustrations on Hannan and Spears.

Their pimping lasted for more than a year. A client, attorney David Wood, was appalled at the treatment the girls received. He encouraged Spears to leave the clutches of the cousins. Spears's departure convinced Hannan to leave as well. Ken and Angelo were shit out of luck, whores, and money and they were pissed.

Buono's house was located in the back corner of this alley.

Scrambling to save their pimping racket, Buono approached a black prostitute by the name of Yolanda Washington. She worked with Deborah Noble, a fairly well-to-do prostitute, on Sunset Boulevard. Washington had once told Buono that Noble kept a trick list and that she could get her hands on it for them. Buono knew that the client list would be useful for when they found some new girls. Buono paid Washington $100 for the list.

The list turned out to be bogus. When Buono found out about the fraud, he was furious. He was going to do something about it.

Something terrible.

Courtyard of Bianchi's apartment.

Buono's Trim Shop: 703 E. Colorado Street   Glendale
Bianchi's Apartment: 809 E. Garfield Avenue   Glendale

YOLANDA WASHINGTON

After Sabra Hannan and Becky Spears took off, Buono and Bianchi needed to fill their whore quota. They took in 17-year-old Jennifer Snider. She was pretty, but would not perform anal sex. On her third night with the guys, Bianchi attempted to sodomize her. She would have nothing to do with that. Bianchi was furious and wanted to kill the girl. Buono talked him out of it. He argued that if they killed Snider, she could be traced back to them. He suggested a new plan.

Their first victim was Yolanda Washington. The cousins drove down to Sunset Boulevard near Highland Avenue in Hollywood to seek out her services. As Angelo drove back up the Hollywood Freeway and over to Glendale, Ken sat next to Yolanda in the back seat. Without provocation, Ken raped her.

Washington lay in the back seat, naked, handcuffed, and pleading for her life. Instead of showing mercy, Ken began to choke her. At first, he got her into a headlock, but he could not kill her. Angelo handed him a rag. Ken wrapped it around her throat and tightened it. She fought desperately. She kicked Angelo in the head over the back of the driver's seat. Infuriated, he grabbed her legs and held them still. She was completely restrained. Ken pulled the rag tighter.

She was dead.

Angelo then drove over to the Forest Lawn Hollywood Hills Cemetery (see p. 280) in Burbank, across the street from Warner Brothers Studios. Having once lived at the Oakwood Apartments, he was familiar with the area. They dumped Washington's body next to some rocks at the entrance of the cemetery.

Their first morbid calling card.

ONE CALL OR VISIT ARRANGES ALL.
Undertaking, Cemetery, Church and Flowers,
FOREST LAWN—HOLLYWOOD HILLS

GLENDALE ➡
⬅ HOLLYWOOD

Dump: 6300 Forest Lawn Drive   Burbank

JUDITH MILLER

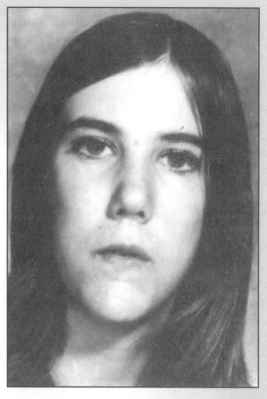

Bianchi and Buono's second victim was also a prostitute. Not much is known about Judith Miller or the specifics of her murder. It is known that she was only 15 years old at the time of her death.

Miller's body was actually the first one discovered, even before Washington's. She lay on the ground, naked, and covered with ant bites. She was placed in a flowerbed. Her legs were bent in such a way that they resembled a diamond. Her hands were underneath her bottom, clutching her flesh.

The police tracked down Miller's parents, who lived in a beaten up motel room. They had the eyes of zombies. When asked of their daughter's whereabouts, they shrugged. They had not seen her for nearly a month. When police showed her parents a coroner's photo of Judith, they acknowledged that it was their daughter. That was all they did. No tears. No "How did this happen?" Nothing.

2844 Alta Terrace Drive   LaCrescenta

LISSA KASTIN

Lissa Kastin was a struggling waitress at the Healthfaire Restaurant near Hollywood Boulevard and Vine Street in Hollywood. The 21-year-old was having a hard time in her life. The night before her murder, she confided a terrible secret to her mother. Kastin was considering prostitution. She felt that she could no longer survive in Hollywood without turning some tricks. The next day, she was dead.

Her body was discovered near the Chevy Chase Country Club golf course in Glendale. It was located less than seven miles from where Judith Miller's body was found. She was naked and had the same ligature marks around her throat as Miller. The similarities were unavoidable.

Her body was dumped over a three-foot high guardrail, down the embankment, and rolled onto the golf course. Her body showed no signs of abrasions due to dragging. Detective

3067 E. Chevy Chase Drive   Glendale

Frank Salerno concluded that she was carried to the side of the road and tossed over the guardrail. He also believed that one man could not have done this. He was certain that two people were involved.

Two very sick people.

Bianchi and Buono had tired of picking up prostitutes. Their police scam was a sure-fire method for luring innocent girls. Ken wanted to try it on someone other than a hooker. Lissa Kastin was just the person.

Bianchi and Buono were cruising Hollywood around Dix Street and Argyle Avenue when they spotted the waitress. She was less than a block away from her apartment. As soon as she got out of her car, the cousins were in her face. They claimed that a robbery had taken place nearby and Kastin was considered a suspect. She laughed, thinking that this was some kind of joke.

It wasn't.

Buono and Bianchi tossed her into their car, handcuffed her, and headed out to Buono's trim shop. Once inside the building, Buono cut off her clothes. Kastin's unshaven legs repulsed the killers. She appeared somewhat mannish to the pig cousins and did not fit their idea of the perfect woman. Neither man wanted to touch her. Angelo begged out, but Ken was willing to give it a try. Angelo decided to watch. Sensing his cousin was not up to the task, Angelo decided to lend some artificial assistance. He tossed Ken a root beer bottle that was used to rape Kastin. She started to bleed, which pissed Angelo off. He did not want his pristine carpet messed up, so he placed a coat underneath her.

The men's twisted style of killing reached a new level this time. Angelo looped a cord around her neck and squeezed. This time, however, he decided to play with his victim. He tightened the cord around her throat until she could no longer breathe. Just when he thought she was about to die, he released the cord. He let her regain consciousness. Then, he did it again. And again. And again.

Angelo turned the duties over to his cousin. As Ken completed the task, he laughed at her and screamed "Die, cunt, die!"

3067 E. Chevy Chase Drive   Glendale

KRISTINA WECKLER

Kristina Weckler was the brightest student in her art class at the Pasadena Art Center of Design. She was a lovely 20-year-old woman who took her studies seriously. She enjoyed staying up at night, working on her drawings. She also had the misfortune of living at 809 East Garfield Avenue in Glendale. Next door to Ken Bianchi.

Weckler's body was found just west of Glendale. She had been dumped on the corner of Ranons Avenue and Wawona Street beneath a tree. Detective Bob Grogan spotted the familiar ligature marks around her wrists, ankles, and throat. When he rolled her body over, blood leaked out of her rectum. Another brutal rape and murder.

Upon closer inspection, Grogan noticed two needle puncture wounds in her arm. He assumed she was a junkie. However, she did not have the telltale signs of a hardened smack user. No bruises or track marks lined her arms, only the two puncture wounds.

As with Lissa Kastin, Grogan noticed that Kristina Weckler had not been dragged to this site. More than one person had probably placed her there. And they probably knew the area very well.

He was right.

Kristina Weckler had once been the object of Ken Bianchi's lust. In the Garfield Avenue apartments, Ken had made a move on the young student. She spurned his advances. Something about the huckster did not sit right with her. By August of 1977, Ken had moved out.

In late November, he returned. He knocked on Kristina's door and flashed his badge to her. He lied that he was a member of the L.A.P.D. Reserves and that he noticed her car had been hit. He offered to help her write up the problem so that she could get her insurance to deal with the situation. She left her apartment and followed Ken.

Angelo was waiting.

4100 N. Ranons Ave. & 3800 E. Wawona St. Los Angeles

The men repeated their torturous ways with Kristina. But now, they wanted to mess with the police. Angelo produced a needle. He filled it with Windex and inserted it into Kristina's neck. She convulsed violently, but did not die.

Determined to end her life, they thought up a different method. They dragged Kristina, kicking and screaming, into the kitchen. Angelo had a new stove that had not been assembled yet. He hooked it up and devised his newest torture. He grabbed Kristina and forced her head next to the stovepipe. He then placed a plastic bag over her head and the pipe and sealed it with a rope. Angelo turned the gas on and off. At the same time he periodically untied the paper bag and allowed her to breathe. Just as she would regain consciousness, he placed the bag back over her head and resumed the gassing treatment.

JANE KING

Jane King was a young, leggy blond who could have easily passed as a fashion model. She was waiting for a bus one day, at the Mayfair Market on the corner of Franklin Avenue and Bronson Avenue in Hollywood. Unfortunately, Ken and Angelo noticed her as they drove by the store.

Both men were hot for her and were determined to pick her up. They knew it would be difficult. A pretty woman by herself in L.A. would not trust two guys, they thought. Ken planned to smooth talk her into the car, so he got out around the corner. Ken approached King at the bus stop. He asked if a bus was coming and then struck up a conversation with the beauty. She had just returned from an acting class at the Scientology Manor across the street. Ken politely quizzed her on her beliefs in the Southern California based religion, and she found him somewhat charming, even non-threatening.

Angelo pulled up in the car and acted as if Ken were a long lost friend. He offered Ken a ride. Ken, in turn, asked Jane if she needed a lift. She declined his offer. Ken, however, flashed her his police badge, lying that he was part of the L.A.P.D. Reserves and would be glad to help her out. Jane accepted and jumped in. Ken told Jane that Angelo had to run home and take care of some business. He inquired whether she would mind if he took her home instead. She had no problem with that arrangement.

They headed off to Angelo's trim shop.

When they arrived, the two men grabbed King and handcuffed her. While Ken held her, Angelo retrieved his tools: a sponge, a rag, and some rope. Once tied up, King began to struggle. Angelo responded by cutting off her shirt and bra. Then, Ken removed her jeans. She stood, clad only in her pantyhose, alone and frightened.

They flipped a coin for her. Angelo won. Ken decided to watch before he took his turn. Jane King fought valiantly. When Ken was done, he tied her up like a pig. She lay on her belly. He pulled her legs up to her neck and tied them to the handcuffs around her wrists. Aroused, he resumed his violation of the young woman. Angelo headed to the kitchen for more supplies.

He returned with a plastic bag. As Ken raped her, Angelo placed the bag over the poor girl's head. He tied the rope around her throat. As with Lissa Kastin, Angelo played games with King, closing off her access to air and then releasing the bag over and over again. Once she was dead, Ken continued the desecration.

They later put her dead body in the car and drove towards Dodger Stadium. Nothing was discussed between the cousins. They simply headed out on the Golden State Freeway. Before reaching the stadium, they decided to exit the freeway at the Los Feliz ramp and dumped Jane King alongside the road.

The cousins thoroughly enjoyed themselves with Ms. King. They were awestruck by her beauty, but they wanted something else. Something young.

Westbound I-5, Los Feliz Exit Offramp Los Feliz

DOLORES CEPEDA & SONJA JOHNSON

Kristina Weckler's body was discovered on November 20, 1977. That same day, another gruesome discovery was made. Little nine-year-old Armando Guerrero was playing out in the trash dumps near Dodger Stadium, down the hill from 1500 Landa Street. While he was picking through the debris, he noticed what he thought were two small mannequins. He retrieved his brother, who also thought they were mannequins until he noticed the blood on one of them.

When the police arrived, they realized the young boys had found two missing girls, 12-year-old Dolores Cepeda and 14-year-old Sonja Johnson. Both girls stood less than five feet tall and weighed less than 100 pounds. They had been missing for several days.

After Ken and Angelo's sexually charged encounter with Jane King occurred, they decided they wanted something young. They headed out in Angelo's sedan and drove by the Eagle Rock Plaza bus stop on Colorado Boulevard. The two men noticed the little girls and the light bulbs flashed. A double dosage of pubescent girls would be the appropriate fix after King. They followed the bus.

When the girls got off the bus at York Street and North Avenue 46, the killers immediately approached them. Ken flashed his badge and warned the girls that a burglar was on the loose in the neighborhood. The men claimed they were there to protect the girls. Dolores and Sonja got into their car. Apparently, the girls had just stolen some jewelry from a local store and thought they had been busted. Little did they realize.

Once again, Angelo drove to the trim shop. He ordered the young girls to take off their clothes. The girls still thought they were in trouble with the police, so they complied. They figured a strip search was part of the routine. Ken and Angelo then raped and sodomized

each of the little girls. They eventually took Sonja into the bedroom and choked her to death. Later, they killed 12-year-old Dolores.

After the murders, the two men tossed the girls' bodies from Landa Street over the hillside. The bodies then rolled fifty feet down into a trash heap.

1977: 1500 Landa Street Los Angeles
Present: 1600 Landa Street Los Angeles

LAUREN WAGNER

With several murders under their belts, Angelo and Ken decided it was time to expand their abduction area. They drove to Lemona Avenue, roughly 25 miles from their home base of operations. Angelo was driving the Cadillac when he spied the lovely 18-year-old redhead, Lauren Wagner.

Wagner had just pulled up to the house where she lived with her family. Angelo parked beside her and flashed his badge. He informed her that she was under arrest and had to go with the two men. She immediately argued with them and was grabbed by Ken. She kicked at him and screamed that he would never get away with it. She knew that the "Hillside Stranglers" had abducted her.

After a 35-minute drive back to the trim shop, Wagner decided the only way to survive was to do what the men wanted. She informed Angelo that she enjoyed sex; as a matter of fact, she had made love with her boyfriend earlier that day. She would do whatever Angelo and Ken wanted. Both men had their way with her and she eagerly complied. She thought this was her only way to escape alive. However, these two never let anyone go.

Ken was ready for something new and twisted. He grabbed some electrical cord, sheared off the plastic covering, and tied it around Lauren's wrists. He then plugged in the cord and electrocuted the young girl. She screamed, but did not die. Ken tried again, repeatedly. Still, she would not die. So they resorted to their tried and true method: strangulation.

Ken and Angelo seemed to be getting sloppy. They dumped Lauren's body on Cliff Drive in Glendale near Mt. Washington. They made no effort to properly hide her body. Half of it lay in the bushes, while her legs flopped onto the street. She was nude and had the same ligature marks as Kristina Weckler. One difference with Lauren was the strange marks on her wrists. The marks were abrasions caused by the failed electrocution attempt.

Detective Grogan realized something awful. Lauren Wagner had been tortured in a new manner by these psychopaths. They were no longer excited by simple rape and murder. Mutilation now seemed to factor into their bloodlust. The killers were hungry and would probably want more.

Near 1217 Cliff Drive Glendale

KIM MARTIN

Ken and Angelo were looking for a new way to get off. Ken had the perfect plan. They used one of his old apartments on Tamarind Avenue as their luring point. They wanted to throw the cops off their trail by redirecting them back into Hollywood.

Hollywood Public Library

Ken and Angelo made a beeline for the Hollywood Public Library on Ivar Street. Ken called an "escort service" from the library pay phone. He put in his request for a girl and was assured one would be at his Tamarind address in 30 minutes. When the girl-for-hire showed up, she told Ken her name was "Donna." Ken apologized to Donna for the lack of lights in his apartment. He mentioned that he forgot to pay the electricity bill. They continued to chitchat for a few minutes until Ken whipped out his trusty police badge. Angelo descended from the shadows and told her that she would have to go with them.

Kim Martin may have been turning tricks, but she was no idiot. She knew that the Hillside Stranglers were using the old cop ruse to lure their victims. She knew these two slimy looking dudes were not cops. She screamed, which brought out the neighbors. Ken and Angelo corralled her back into the empty apartment and threatened her life if she made a sound.

After the commotion died down and the tenants returned to their dens, Ken and Angelo cuffed Martin, threw her into a car, and headed for the trim shop. Angelo was pissed at Martin for screaming and even more pissed at Ken. His idiotic idea almost got them busted. They were getting sloppy, Angelo thought. Especially Ken.

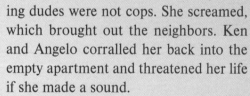

Hollywood Public Library: 1623 Ivar Ave. Hollywood

Apartment: 1950 Tamarind Ave. #114   Hollywood

Angelo had his way with Martin and then told Ken he could have sloppy seconds. This time, however, they did not try any new methods of torture. They simply strangled the young woman.

Though the killing may have been routine, Kim Martin's dumping was not. They dumped her over a hillside off of Alvarado Street. When she was discovered the next day, police noted

that she was naked and displayed in a spread-eagled pose. From the vantage point of the body dump site, one could clearly see the City Hall building. This infuriated the authorities. They took the display of Martin's body as a personal affront to their efforts. A big "Fuck You" from the killers. The cops would not take much more of this.

PICTURED RIGHT:
The Alvarado Street
hillside as it looks today.

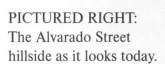

2006 N. Alvarado Street Los Angeles

CINDY HUDSPETH

Cindy Hudspeth was another young, struggling waitress trying to improve her life. She worked at the Robin Hood Inn in Glendale and was sweet, articulate, and friendly. She had aspirations of attending college and was working extra hard to improve her financial situation.

On February 16, 1978, Hudspeth was driving from her apartment at 800 East Garfield Avenue to work. As she drove, she noticed a business card that a man had given her in the restaurant. It was for an auto upholstery shop. She remembered that she wanted some new floor mats for her car and decided she would pop in.

Angelo Buono greeted her with enthusiasm. He found her attractive and began chatting her up. Ken showed up and also noticed the attractive brunette. Angelo motioned Ken into the back room. He was ready for another scam.

Cindy sat in Buono's chair and talked about how hard the job market had been. Angelo, thinking he had the perfect con, informed the girl that he had to close his shop for the night. However, if she wanted to come into his adjacent home, he could set her up with some job opportunities. Cindy eagerly agreed. She entered Angelo's house, but not long after, she realized she had entered a nightmare.

The men tied her to Angelo's bedposts with nylon in a spread-eagled position. They had their way with her for over two hours. Upon completion, Ken strangled Cindy. This time, they wanted a new dumping site. After stuffing Cindy into the trunk of her car, Ken drove north to the Angeles National Forest. Angelo followed. Ken also donned a beard to make the

adventure more exciting. When they arrived at a secluded spot, Ken began to brag about a recent sexual conquest he had at this location. Angelo told Ken to keep quiet and get to work. Ken obeyed and pushed Cindy's car over the cliff, with her in it.

Cindy Hudspeth was found on February 17, 1978 by helicopters that routinely check the forest for cars that may have plunged over the treacherous cliffs.

Apartment: 800 E. Garfield Ave. Glendale

Dump Site: Mile Marker 28.86 of the Angeles Crest Highway

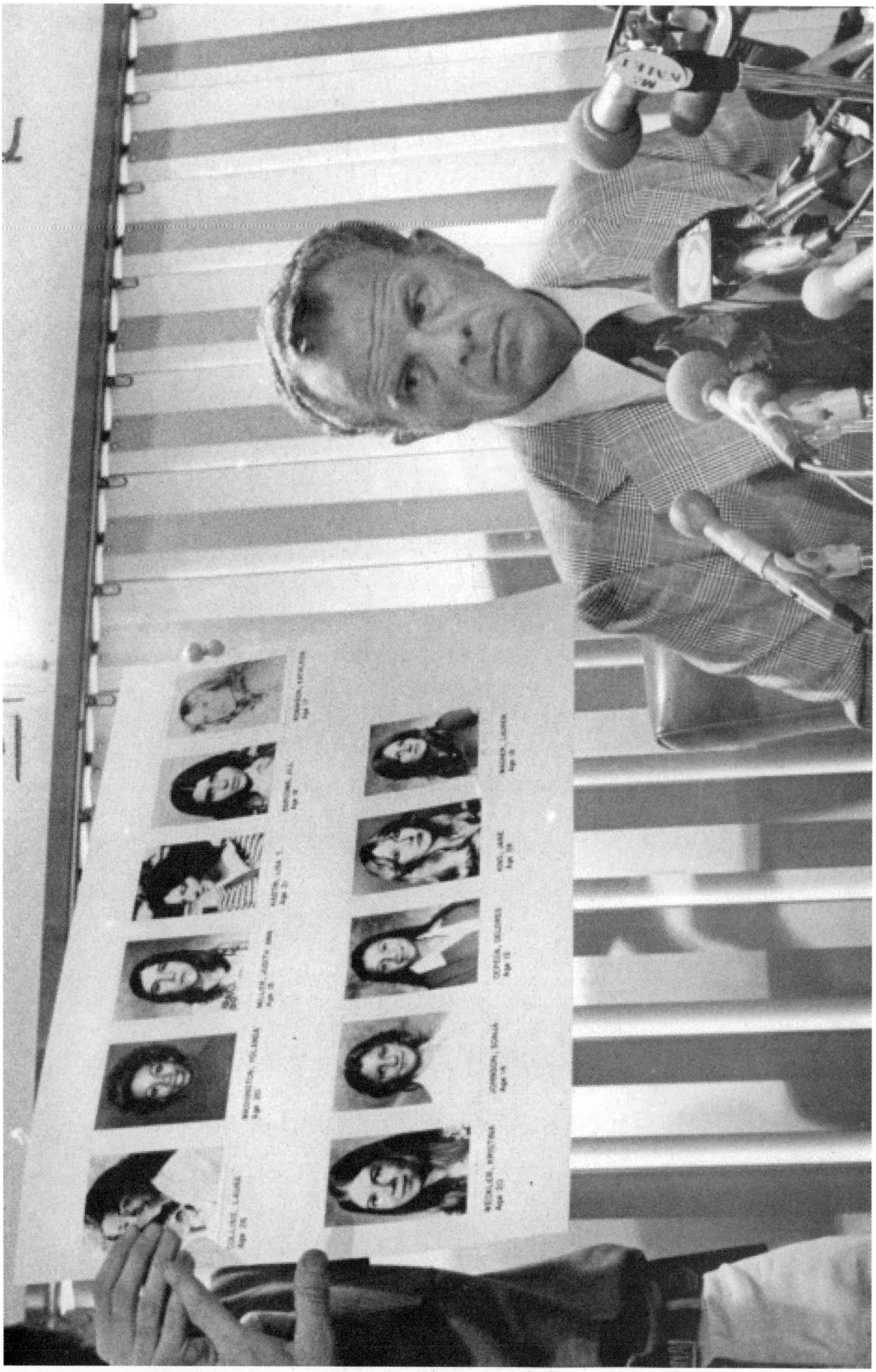

SEATTLE

On January 12, 1979, almost 11 months after Cindy Hudspeth's body was found in Los Angeles, two more bodies were discovered in Bellingham, Washington. Ken Bianchi was living in Bellingham at the time.

Western Washington University roommates Karen Mandic and Diane Wilder had taken on a housesitting job in Bayside for the weekend. They were responsible girls who could be trusted, but no one knew where they were.

Police tracked down the security company that worked the neighborhood where the girls were supposed to be housesitting. It was the same company that employed Ken Bianchi. The police spoke with him, but he claimed he had to attend a Sheriff's reserve meeting and could not talk at that time. Later, the police called the Sheriff's Reserve. Bianchi was not there, so they called him again. He claimed that he left the meeting because he was familiar with the topic being covered. Satisfied, the cops left him alone.

Soon thereafter, the police found a stranded car on the side of a road. Inside were the bodies of Mandic and Wilder. They had both been strangled. The police decided to take Bianchi into custody. They hoped that some tests could be run on the hair and fibers found in the car and at the Bayside home. While they had Bianchi in custody, they found a ton of stolen items in his home. Once again, he had been ripping people off under the guise of helping them. He was now much easier to keep in custody.

One of the officers remembered the uproar that happened the previous year in Los Angeles concerning the Hillside Stranglers. He sensed a similar pattern. He contacted Detective Frank Salerno of the Los Angeles Police Department and told him about Bianchi. When Salerno ran a check on Ken Bianchi, he took special notice of Ken's address: 809 East Garfield Avenue in Glendale, the same apartment complex as Kristina Weckler and right across the street from Cindy Hudspeth. It was all starting to come into focus. Salerno flew north to Washington. He conducted a search of Bianchi's new home where he found jewelry that belonged to Yolanda Washington and Kim Martin.

The Hillside Stranglers

CANARY KEN

Bianchi was tossed into the Whatcom County Jail. While there, he honed his skills of deception. First, he convinced his lawyer he suffered from amnesia. Then, he convinced a social worker that he was a wonderful, congenial, sensitive soul who could not harm a fly. The only possible way he could have committed these crimes, she surmised, was that he might have a split personality.

This was another light bulb moment for Ken. It was reinforced only a few days later while Ken was watching television. He watched the movie *Sybil*, starring Sally Field as a young girl with multiple personalities. The Hillside Strangler case became even stranger. Insanity was just around the corner.

Ken convinced a renowned amnesia and multiple personality syndrome (MPS) expert, Dr. John G. Watkins, that he suffered from MPS. The introduction of Steve Walker—Ken's evil twin—arose from the hypnosis sessions with Dr. Watkins. Steve Walker also happened to be the name that appeared on a fake psychiatric diploma used by Bianchi. "Steve" was Ken's own bad self, who smoked, cursed, and was a general all-around tough guy who didn't take shit from women. Bianchi's performance was so convincing that Dr. Watkins fell for it.

While the police were furious with Bianchi's testimonial behavior, they were pleased about one thing. He implicated his cousin, Angelo Buono, as an accomplice to the murders. Photographs of Buono were obtained and shown to witnesses in the Hillside Strangler murders. Two separate people implicated Buono as one of the men they had seen abducting women.

Ken resumed his therapy sessions. He soon convinced a second therapist, Dr. Ralph Allison, that he suffered from MPS. The police, however, would not consider an insanity plea from Bianchi. They brought in a therapist of their own, Dr. Martin Orne, who was ready to debunk Bianchi's claim of multiple personalities.

The doctor had his own scam for Bianchi. He told Ken that it was rare for a patient to only suffer from one extra personality. Sure enough, in no time, number three appeared. His name was Billy. Pretty soon there were two more personalities coming from Ken. He had enough personalities to field a basketball team.

The prosecution brought in a second therapist, Dr. Saul Faerstein. Dr. Faerstein feigned disinterest in Ken's claims. This reaction shocked Ken. Up to now, he had almost everyone fooled, or so he thought. Ken now began to worry.

On the basis of Dr. Orne and Dr. Faerstein's recommendation, Ken Bianchi could be brought to trial for the Hillside Strangler murders. A deal was struck, however, which spared Ken's life. If he admitted to the two Bellingham girls' deaths and some of the Los Angeles murders, he would not receive the death penalty.

Ken confessed. The police now went after Angelo Buono.

The Hillside Stranglers

ARRESTING ANGELO

The police arrested Angelo on October 22, 1979. For many reasons, the prosecution of Angelo Buono was extremely difficult. Bianchi's charges of murder in California were dropped as part of his deal. This was a big mistake. Bianchi became unreliable. He changed his story, making it seem as if Angelo was not involved in any of the stranglings.

Over time, the prosecution turned a corner and proceeded with charges against Buono. Though Bianchi had become undependable, they still used his original confessions against Buono. Furthermore, fibers found on the eyelid of Judy Miller matched the foam cushion couch inserts found in Buono's home. Also, two witnesses had positively identified the "Italian Stallion."

One problem.

Los Angeles prosecutor Roger Kelly developed cold feet. A political animal if ever there was one, Kelly sensed he would lose the case against Buono. So instead of doing everything in his power to assure a conviction, Kelly threw his hands up in defeat. When Bianchi stated from the stand that he made up the multiple personality syndromes, Kelly was ready to pack it in. He moved to dismiss all ten counts of murder against Angelo Buono.

Superior Court Judge Ronald M. George was not pleased. After a reasonable delay, Judge George returned with his ruling on Kelly's request for dismissal. The case would move forward. Most often, judges would side with the prosecution in a request for dismissal. Judge George, however, believed there was more than enough evidence to prove that Angelo Buono was indeed involved in the Hillside Stranglings. The D.A.'s response was unique. They actually withdrew from the case.

Judge George assigned State Attorney General George Deukmejian's office to take over Buono's prosecution. The trial began in November of 1981 and did not truly get rolling until the following spring. It turned into the longest trial in the history of the United States—over two years. On October 31, 1983, the jury returned with a guilty verdict on the murder of Lauren Wagner. A few days later, Buono was convicted of eight more of the murders. He was not convicted in the death of Yolanda Washington.

Judge Ronald George is now Chief Justice of the California Supreme Court.

Buono received life in prison. He is currently serving his time in Folsom. Ken Bianchi is serving a life sentence in Walla Walla in Washington.

The Hillside Stranglers

CHAPTER 11

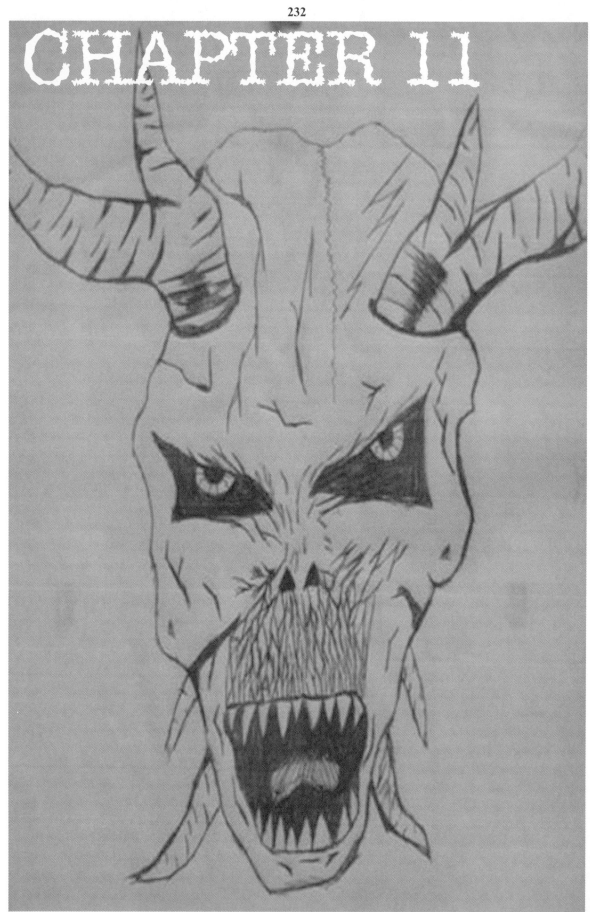

THE NIGHT STALKER

Just three years after the trial of the Hillside Stranglers, Los Angeles was thrown into another state of panic. During the spring and summer of 1985, a series of break-ins, rapes, and murders occurred. The crimes were being committed all across the vast area of Los Angeles County. People were being slaughtered regardless of their age, color, or sex. By the end of the summer, one man would be captured and paraded before the country.

Another Los Angeles serial killer. His name was Richard Ramirez.

RICHIE

Richard Ramirez was born on February 28, 1960 in El Paso, Texas. He was the youngest of seven children born to Julian and Mercedes Ramirez. His father was an illegal alien who worked in the local rail yard and later became a police officer. Supposedly, his father was verbally abusive to Richard and his siblings.

Ramirez's childhood was relatively normal, despite the tension with his father. He was a smart kid who seemed more interested in goofing off than going to school. Lack of attendance resulted in Ramirez having to repeat ninth grade. He also loved listening to heavy metal music by such hit bands as Judas Priest, Iron Maiden, Black Sabbath, and AC/DC. Some childhood buddies later claimed that Ramirez took the satirical Satanism espoused in these groups' music a little too far. He became a devout follower of Satanism and preached its "do for yourself" philosophy to anyone who was willing to listen. These beliefs were in direct contradiction to his Christian household upbringing.

Ramirez was also a petty thief. He was never busted as a juvenile, but the cops had their eyes on him. By the time he reached adulthood, he would get caught. He was nailed three times for possession of marijuana. He avoided prison, but was placed on probation. At the age of 20, his probation ended and Ramirez took off to Los Angeles.

While in Los Angeles, Ramirez became a more accomplished thief and even more of a loser. He would rip off cars and commit minor infractions. He also indulged in drugs and alcohol. The further down he slipped, the more he believed that he was a minion of Satan sent to Los Angeles to commit the Dark One's dirty work.

The Night Stalker

CRASH PADS

When Ramirez arrived in Los Angeles, he had a run-in with his sister-in-law. She despised Richard and demanded that his brother, Ruben, not let him stay with them. Broke and despondent, Ramirez stayed at some of the seediest locales in the city. These hotels were known hotbeds for drug dealers, prostitutes, and bums who hoped to score a $10 room after rolling some poor schlub over. Most of the hotels where Ramirez stayed were all in the general downtown area. They included the Hotel Rosslyn (112 W. 5th Street), the Frontier Hotel (111 W. 5th Street), the Cecil Hotel (640 S. Main Street), and the Hotel Huntington (752 S. Main Street).

Downtown Los Angeles

JENNIE VINCOW

The killing spree began on June 27, 1984. Richard Ramirez was hopped up on cocaine and cruising around in a stolen car. He cranked up the stereo system and blared out his favorite heavy metal tunes at maximum volume. He was rocking and rolling and feeling no pain. Ramirez cruised around aimlessly until he reached downtown Los Angeles. He got out of the car and strolled down a street. He found a dark alley in which to shoot up his remaining coke. He was coming down from his high and feeling frantic. He needed more cash.

He jumped back into his car and headed out with no particular destination. He wound up in Glassell Park on Chapman Street. He got out of the car again and walked around the neighborhood. He stopped in front of a rundown pink apartment complex. He assessed the situation and decided to go into apartment number 2, home of 79-year-old Jennie Vincow. He walked by her front window and noticed that it was open. He removed the screen and crept inside.

Once he looked around, Ramirez realized that the woman had no money and nothing worth stealing. This sent him into an internal rage. Ramirez spotted Vincow asleep in her bed. He walked up to the old woman, removed a half-foot long knife from his back pocket, and plunged it straight into her heart. She screamed. He continued slashing and stabbing. She attempted to resist, but he would not stop. He placed the blade on her throat and sliced her from ear-to-ear, nearly decapitating the elderly woman. He covered her up with a blanket and stabbed her three more times in the chest, even though she was already dead.

Richard Ramirez had his first taste of blood. Overcome with arousal, he masturbated for an hour before leaving the scene.

3330 Chapman Street #2   Glassell Park

DAYLE OKAZAKI

The murder of Dayle Okazaki was the first crime in Ramirez's reign of terror that grabbed people's attention.

An attractive young woman, Michelle Hernandez, was returning to her apartment on March 17, 1985. Unbeknownst to her, a man in black followed her. Hernandez parked her car in her garage. The man snuck under the garage door as Hernandez remained in her car. When she got out, the man confronted her. He held a gun to her face and pulled the trigger. Hernandez flinched and threw her hands to her face. Lucky for her, she had her keys in that hand. The keys deflected the bullet, but the man had no idea that she was still alive. Hernandez fell to the ground and played dead.

The man, assuming he killed the young girl, entered her apartment. Robbery was his intent. As he looked around the tiny apartment, he heard a noise. Hernandez's roommate, Dayle Okazaki, a 34-year-old Asian woman, came out to check the noise. The man in black saw her duck behind the kitchen counter. He decided to taunt her. Eventually, she rose from behind the counter. The man shot her directly in the forehead. She died instantly and the man took off.

He exited through the garage. He then spotted Hernandez, who screamed for her life. He did not kill her. Instead, he bolted out of the garage leaving behind a black baseball cap with the insignia of heavy metal rockers, AC/DC.

8510 E. Village Lane   Rosemead

VERONICA YU

Jacked up on adrenaline, the man in black took off in his stolen car. He eventually encountered another woman in her car on the freeway. He followed her from Rosemead all the way to Monterey Park. The woman, 30-year-old Veronica Yu, realized she was being followed. Instead of trying to evade her tailgater, she pulled her car around and confronted the man. She was furious.

The man got out of his car and walked up to her. He claimed he knew her, but she knew he was lying. She became angrier. She threatened to call the police. The man reached into her car and grabbed Yu. He tried to pull her out of the car window, but Yu violently resisted. The man suddenly jumped over the hood of her car and made a play for her unlocked passenger door. Once inside, he placed his gun next to her back and pulled the trigger. Bleeding, she ran into the street. He coldly aimed at her again, pulled the trigger a second time, and pegged her in the back. Yu fell over into a bloody heap in the middle of the street.

The man in black had killed his second victim of the night.

500 Block of N. Alhambra Ave. Monterey Park

THE ZAZARRAS

Eight days later, the man in black struck again, this time at the home of 64-year-old Vincent Zazarra and his 44-year-old wife, Maxine. Vincent, owner of two pizza restaurants, was asleep on the couch in the living room. He dozed off while watching television. His wife was asleep in the back bedroom.

The killer cased the house for a few moments and then made his move. Using a large can as a mini-stepladder, he entered through the bathroom window. Once inside, the intruder took off his shoes and crept towards the husband. He pointed the gun at the man and fired. Zazarra was hit, but not dead. He began to fight back. He was not successful. A geyser of blood squirted out of the helpless man.

Zazarra's dying screams woke his wife. The killer rushed into her bedroom and quickly put her at bay with the gun. He demanded all of their money. She demanded he leave. He was not going anywhere.

The killer hog-tied Maxine. He began to ransack the home, taking anything of value. Maxine, a church-going attorney, realized that she needed to save her husband, who was quickly dying in the front room. She remembered that her husband kept a shotgun under their bed. While the killer searched for valuables, she untied herself and made a play for the weapon. She retrieved the gun and stood up, pointing it directly towards the man in black. He turned around and faced the armed, diminutive woman. He lunged for her. She pulled the trigger.

Click!

Nothing happened. Maxine did not know that her husband had recently removed the .22 shells. The killer was furious. He screamed as he pulled the trigger of his own gun, killing Maxine Zazarra.

The madman was not done. He wanted to make the woman pay. He attempted to remove her heart, but his knife would not penetrate her ribcage. So, he moved to her face. He first sliced off her eyelids. He then removed both of her eyes. After pocketing the treasures, he took off.

He did, however, leave behind one important item.

An Avia shoeprint.

WILLIAM DOI

Two-and-a-half weeks later, on April 14, the killer returned to Monterey Park, where he had executed Veronica Yu. Under cover of rain, the prowler located the Doi residence and decided he found his newest target. William Doi, 66, an international sales manager, liked to protect himself and his family. He kept several handguns around the house. He also had a serious alarm system.

These protective measures did not keep the intruder from entering. The man in black prowled outside the home, trying to find a way in. He spotted a window with no alarm trigger. He cut the window screen, pushed the window up, and entered the home. Doi heard the window being opened and grabbed a gun of his own. The killer saw Doi reach for the weapon and shot him in the mouth. He shot again, but his gun jammed.

Lillian Doi, William Doi's wife, had suffered a debilitating stroke only two years earlier. She was practically an invalid. She could only lie still on the bed as the killer punched and kicked her husband. Lillian Doi screamed in agony for her husband's life but that only infuriated the killer. He cursed at her and put her thumbs in tiny thumb cuffs. He also ransacked their home.

The killer was overcome with sexual emotion by the scene. The blood and screams excited him. He returned to Lillian Doi and raped her while she was still cuffed. Then, the killer took off.

William Doi was still alive. He found his battered wife and called 911. He continually faded in and out of consciousness. The paramedics arrived and placed him in an ambulance, but they were too late. He died before they could reach the hospital.

1586 Trumbower Ave. Monterey Park

MABEL BELL

Mabel Bell, 83, was a tough cookie. She had lived by herself in a small home in Monrovia, just 20 miles north of downtown Los Angeles. A widow, she raised her two children by herself without complaint. In 1983, she had taken in her sister, Florence "Nettie" Lang, an invalid. Despite the burden, Bell made the most of her days, playing bridge with friends and generally getting out and about.

She was also a trusting woman. Bell always left her doors unlocked.

Perfect for the intruder.

On June 1, Ramirez made his way towards Monrovia and directly to Bell's home. It stood alone on a small, twisting road. The killer simply walked through the unlocked front door and began to scan for valuables. Not finding anything of worth, the killer went into the kitchen for a knife, since he had brought no weapon this night. He pulled out the kitchen drawers, yet could not find a knife. He did, however, find a hammer.

He took the weapon and proceeded into Lang's bedroom. He pummeled the old woman with the hammer, then bound her up, and headed for Bell's room. The man in black smashed Bell in the head with the hammer, waking her from her slumber. Frightened, she screamed at the man to get out of her house. He cussed her out and smashed her repeatedly with the hammer. He then packed all kinds of items into a bag, but he was not done yet. He returned to the invalid Lang's room. Excited by the blood, he raped her.

This time, the man left his mark. With a tube of red lipstick, he drew a pentagram on the inside of Bell's thigh and a large pentagram on Lang's bedroom wall.

A pentagram.

The sign of Satan.

The two old women were not discovered for another two-and-a-half days. They were still alive. Nettie Lang miraculously survived the attack. Her sister, Mabel Bell, did not. She never came out of her coma.

The man in black had killed again.

443 N. Alta Vista Ave. Monrovia

MARY CANNON

Ramirez became bolder each day. On July 2, the killer headed to the town of Arcadia, near Monrovia. He drove into the clean neighborhood and began to walk up the streets. He stopped in front of the residence of 75-year-old Mary Cannon. He wasted no time and immediately removed the screen from her front window. Ramirez lifted the window and entered her home.

Ramirez crept around her house and came upon the old woman asleep in her bedroom. Once again, he did not carry his own weapon, so he had to improvise. He grabbed a lamp from Cannon's dresser and aimed it towards her head. While the old cancer survivor slept soundly, he raised the makeshift weapon and smashed it forcefully down upon her head. She screamed, and he punched her in the mouth, knocking her unconscious. He needed another weapon to finish her off. Ramirez snuck into the kitchen and found a ten-inch butcher knife. He returned to Cannon's bedroom. He plunged the implement into her throat. Again. And again. And again.

Ramirez finished the murder, stole as many items as he could carry, and took off into the night.

310 E. Haven Avenue   Arcadia

JOYCE NELSON

By now, Ramirez's deeds were being reported throughout the media. He was mainly known as "The Valley Intruder." He was thrilled by the acclaim, even if he was not actually named in the press.

Flush with his new celebrity status, he decided to up the ante. He returned to the location of two earlier murders, Monterey Park. He parked his stolen car and walked to a new house. The humble abode belonged to 61-year-old Joyce Nelson. He tried the front door, but it was locked. He then tried the window next to it and easily gained entrance to Nelson's home.

Once inside, he noticed Nelson asleep on her couch in the living room. He quietly approached her and placed the muzzle of his gun to her forehead. Jolting awake, she screamed at him to leave her alone, but he merely told her that he would kill her if she made any more noise.

His blood lust rising, Ramirez attempted to drag Nelson to her bedroom. She attempted to fight him off, but only infuriated the intruder. He relentlessly kicked the woman, again and again. He actually spun her around in a circle with one of his kicks. He also stepped in her blood, leaving more distinctive Avia shoe prints.

By the time he was done with her, she was an unrecognizable mess.

"The Valley Intruder" had struck again. But this night, he was still not satisfied.

348 E. Arlight Street   Monterey Park

CHAINARONG KHOVANANTH

Ramirez's appetite was not yet sated. He jumped on the freeway until he hit the small town of Sun Valley. He parked the car on Schoenborn Street and began walking around the neighborhood. He wanted more blood.

He stopped in front of the home of Thailand immigrant Chainarong Khovananth and his wife, Somkid. They were parents of an eight-year-old son and a two-year-old daughter. Ramirez did not care who they were.

He walked up to the front of the Khovananth's house and attempted to open the front door. It was locked. He tried the front windows. They too were locked. He moved around to the back. He tried the sliding glass back door and it was open. Once again, the intruder was inside.

He noticed Somkid asleep on the couch. She immediately awoke and almost began to scream. Ramirez reached her before she could warn her family and used his large hands to cover her mouth. He warned her that if she made a noise "it was all over but the crying." She nodded in agreement. He removed his hand and began to case the house.

Ramirez walked into Chainarong's bedroom and found the man asleep in bed. He walked right up to the husband, placed his gun to the man's head, and pulled the trigger. It only took one bullet. Ramirez wrapped the dead man up in a blanket and left him on the bed. He was becoming aroused and returned for Somkid.

He noticed that she had removed her wedding ring. He ordered her to retrieve it, which she did. He then ripped off her nightgown and dragged her to the bedroom. He tied her up with a cord and raped her on the bed next to the body of her dead husband. Somkid's fear was an aphrodisiac for Ramirez.

Suddenly, an alarm clock sounded. It came from the little boy's room. Ramirez dismounted and went in the direction of the sound. He found the little boy. He tied him up, stuck a sock in his mouth, and returned to Somkid. He continued to rape and sodomize the tiny woman. He eventually stole all of her jewelry and made her swear allegiance to Satan.

13037 Schoenborn Street   Sun Valley

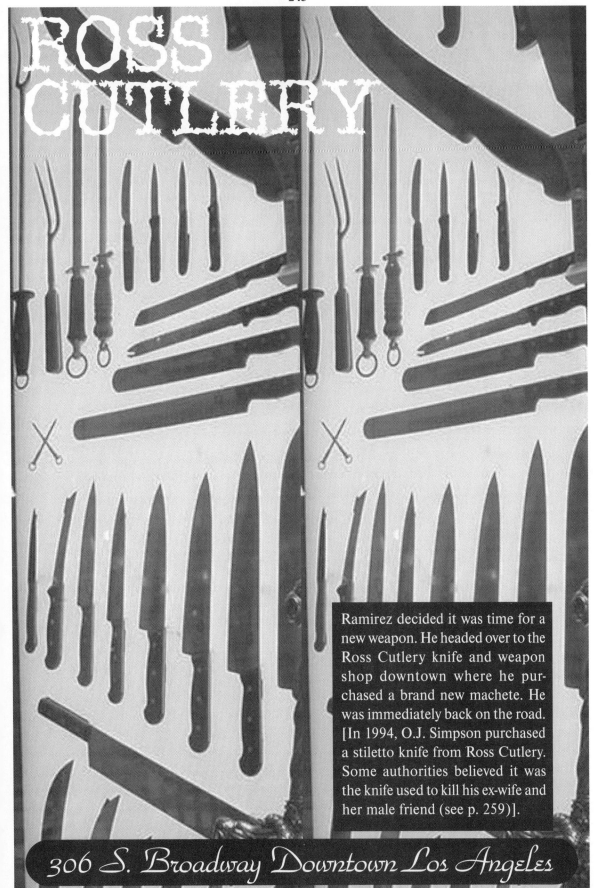

ROSS CUTLERY

Ramirez decided it was time for a new weapon. He headed over to the Ross Cutlery knife and weapon shop downtown where he purchased a brand new machete. He was immediately back on the road. [In 1994, O.J. Simpson purchased a stiletto knife from Ross Cutlery. Some authorities believed it was the knife used to kill his ex-wife and her male friend (see p. 259)].

306 S. Broadway Downtown Los Angeles

MAX & LELA KNEIDING

After Ramirez picked up the machete from Ross Cutlery, he headed to Hillside Strangler territory: Glendale. He drove another stolen car to the corner of Stanley Avenue and Zerr Court. He walked down the street until he reached the home of Max and Lela Kneiding.

Ramirez snuck around back, but was thwarted by locked windows. It seemed as if the citizens of Los Angeles were finally wising up and locking their doors and windows. Ramirez would not be deterred, however, as he approached the Kneiding's French doors. He slit the screen on the door, reached inside, and popped the door lock.

He was inside yet again.

Max, 68, and Lela, 66, together since high school, were asleep. Ramirez flicked on the bedroom light and walked up to their bed. He kicked it, waking the couple. Max would be the first to die. Ramirez swung the machete at the old man, striking him in the neck. It was not enough to kill him. Ramirez grabbed his .22 pistol and stuck it against Max's head. He pulled the trigger.

Click!

The gun did not fire. Lela was screaming at the top of her lungs for Ramirez to leave her husband alone. Ramirez calmly reloaded his pistol and aimed it at Max. Ignoring Lela's pleas, he pulled the trigger, ending her husband's life. Ramirez turned the gun on Lela. He rapidly fired three shots into the woman's face. She died instantly.

He was off again.

1431 Stanley Avenue   Glendale

ELYAS ABOWATH

On August 8, sixteen years after the followers of Charles Manson headed out to slaughter Sharon Tate and four others in Benedict Canyon, Richard Ramirez continued his much deadlier reign of terror. Detective Frank Salerno had called him a coward in the newspapers, sending Ramirez into a rage.

He stole yet another car and raced off to the small town of Diamond Bar, 30 miles from downtown Los Angeles. This time, he was packing some serious heat. He had a pair of handcuffs, a .25 automatic, a .38 pistol, and an Uzi machinegun. He was not going to take any more risks.

Once in Diamond Bar, he pulled the vehicle onto Pinehill Lane and killed the engine. As usual, he walked around the neighborhood until he found the perfect home. That home belonged to Elyas and Sakina Abowath. He immediately walked to the backyard and unsuccessfully attempted to gain entrance through the back door and windows. He was, however, able to pry open the sliding glass door and make his entrance.

Ramirez stalked the inside of the house. He came across a bedroom where the Abowath's two children, a three-year-old boy and a ten-week-old boy, slept. Leaving the children alone, he found the bedroom where the parents were sound asleep. Then, he did something unusual. He left. Ramirez went outside to move his new car right in front of the Abowath's driveway.

Ramirez returned to the house and headed directly for the parents' bedroom. He walked up to Elyas, stuck the .25 to his head, and squeezed the trigger. Elyas died instantly. The madman then jumped on Sakina and screamed at her at the top of his lungs. He blindfolded the petite mother with a shirt and gagged her mouth to the point of choking. She bit him and Ramirez responded with a flurry of kicks, slaps, and punches to the woman. He tied her up with another shirt and began looking for his bounty.

Ramirez became excited by the vandalism and murder. He turned his attentions back to Sakina. He raped and sodomized her. He forced her to perform fellatio on him while making her pledge her loyalty to Satan. He also fed from her milk-laden breasts.

Suddenly, her three-year-old son entered the bedroom crying for his father. Ramirez jumped over the mother, grabbed the little boy, tossed him on the bed. He tied him down and stuck a pillowcase over the boy's head to keep him quiet. He returned to raping Sakina.

When he finished, Ramirez told her that he had only knocked her husband out. Then, he took off. Sakina told her son to wake his daddy. The little boy attempted to stir his father, but the man was dead.

21303 Pinehill Lane   Diamond Bar

SAN FRANCISCO & PETER PAN

Ramirez felt that Los Angeles was too hot for him. The "Night Stalker" nickname had been bandied about all over the press. The entire county of Los Angeles was up in arms about this vicious killer and many would do whatever was necessary to defend their lives. He decided a new location was necessary, so he headed up north to San Francisco.

He checked into Room 315 of the Bristol Hotel on Mason Street in the Tenderloin District. He cruised the neighborhood, checked out a porno shop, smoked a joint, and followed women around, trying to determine who was going to be his next victim.

On August 18, Ramirez entered the home of Peter Pan, 66, and Barbara Pan, 62, in Eucalyptus. He found the Pans sound asleep in their upstairs bedroom. Sticking with his usual pattern when a man was present, he walked up to Peter and pointed a gun at his head. He squeezed the trigger and killed the man instantly. Ramirez then turned his attention to Barbara, who woke at the sound of the gunshot. He attempted to rape her, but she fought him off. Ramirez turned the gun on her and killed her as well.

Ramirez took as many possessions as he could carry and then decided it was time to leave another message. With a tube of Barbara's lipstick, he drew a large pentagram on the wall and wrote the phrase, "Jack The Knife."

The Night Stalker

DIANE FEINSTEIN

Current California United States Senator Diane Feinstein played an important role in the Richard Ramirez case. However, probably not one she wanted people to remember.

After the Peter and Barbara Pan murders, Los Angeles police detective Frank Salerno believed "The Night Stalker" had migrated to the Bay Area and commenced his killing spree. He flew up to San Francisco and was ready to track the killer down. Diane Feinstein, who was mayor of San Francisco at the time, threw a major kink into his plans.

One method used by detectives to obtain information on a murder case was the withholding of certain key facts from the press and the public, something only the killer or criminal would know. It also saved time on false confessions. The key fact withheld from the public in the Ramirez murder spree was the Avia shoeprints and the fact that the particular shoes were extremely rare.

Mayor Feinstein threw the investigation for a loop with a hastily called press conference after the Pan murders. She provided details about the reoccurrence of Avia shoeprints that had been collected at the Los Angeles crime scenes.

Richard Ramirez watched Mayor Feinstein's briefing on television. He was unaware that he had been leaving distinctive shoe prints at the sites. He knew what he had to do now. He drove to the Golden Gate Bridge, walked to the middle of it, and tossed his sneakers into the water. They were never discovered.

The Night Stalker

EVIDENCE

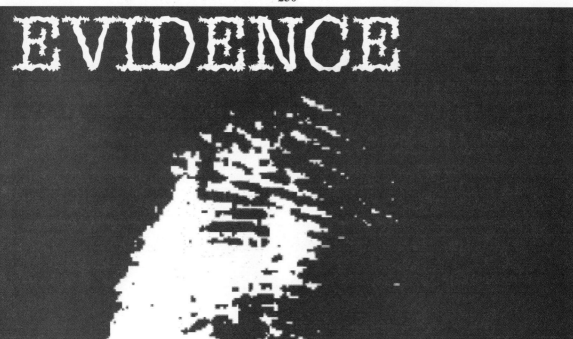

Ramirez blazed out of San Francisco. As soon as he returned to Los Angeles, he resumed his quest for blood. He stole another car and headed down south to Mission Viejo where he found the home of 29-year-old William Carns and his 27-year-old fiancée, Carole Smith.

He followed his usual modus operandi by trying the front door and windows then heading to the backyard. At the back of the house, he took off a window screen and crawled inside. He found the couple's bedroom and made his move.

He pointed a gun at Carns's face and pulled the trigger. He then moved around the bed and plugged Carns with two more bullets, sending the man to the floor. As Carns lay bleeding to death, he grabbed Smith and tied her up with her fiancée's ties. He screamed at her to hand over all of their valuables. He also made her swear allegiance to Satan. Similarly to almost every other female victim, he raped and sodomized the young woman.

When he was done with her, he gave her a gentle kiss and told her to tell everyone that "The Night Stalker" had been there. Both Carns and Smith survived their attacks.

Ramirez finally got careless.

A young man, James Romero III, had spotted Ramirez earlier in the evening. He did not recognize the prowler and became suspicious. He wrote down the first three digits of Ramirez's license plate number, just in case something bad happened.

Ramirez drove back to Los Angeles and dumped the stolen car at a shopping center at Sixth Street and Alexandria Avenue. He attempted to wipe the car down and remove any evidence, but he forgot one small thing—a single fingerprint on the car's rearview mirror.

It would lead to his arrest.

The Night Stalker

GO GREYHOUND

When the fingerprint was found on the stolen car after the Carns and Smith assaults, Los Angeles police were able to track down the perp who had stolen the automobile. It was Richard Ramirez. The fingerprint match led to a photo the police had on file for a previous arrest and was compared to police sketches of "The Night Stalker." The police believed they had found their serial killer.

At the end of August, Ramirez's photograph was sent to the media and displayed on every television news broadcast that night and plastered on the front of every newspaper in the area. The police assumed that Ramirez would attempt to flee the city once he knew that he was their primary suspect. Officers were sent to every major transportation hub in the city including airports, train stations, and bus stops.

The police did not know Ramirez was already gone. He had been in Arizona scoring some cocaine. He was, however, on his way back to Los Angeles on a Greyhound Bus. On August 30, Richard Ramirez pulled into the downtown Greyhound Bus Station. Armed officers were everywhere. As he glanced at the situation, he realized something unusual. The cops were not checking people coming in from out-of-town; they were only looking for passengers who were trying to get away. He counted his blessings and made a beeline for the backdoor.

He escaped yet again.

1716 E. 6th Street Los Angeles

CAPTURE & ARREST

Ramirez calmly walked out of the bus station. His resolve would soon be tested. He passed by Duke's Liquor store and spotted a newspaper rack. On the cover, his mugshot looked back at him. He glanced up and noticed several people staring at him and pointing. He realized what was going on.

Ramirez was now on the run.

He took off, but no matter which direction he turned, people spotted him. Overhead, police helicopters littered the sky like giant buzzing gnats. He eventually ended up in an East Los Angeles neighborhood. Still on foot, Ramirez realized he needed a getaway car. He approached a young woman driving her vehicle on Indiana Avenue. He grabbed her through the open window and tried to remove her from the vehicle. The girl's boyfriend saw the altercation and yelled at Ramirez to leave her alone. Even though Ramirez had a gun, he took off running.

He hopped over a fence of a house on Perry Street. He then crossed the street and ended up in the yard of woman who recognized his face from the newspaper. She began to scream and ran into her home. Ramirez changed directions and headed toward Hubbard Street. He

jumped another fence and landed in Luis Munoz's backyard. Munoz was preparing an outdoor barbecue. He looked up at Ramirez and asked what the hell was he doing. Ramirez did not respond, so Munoz slapped him with his spatula. Ramirez immediately took off again.

He noticed a car hoisted up on boxes with the engine running. Ramirez saw his opportunity and made a play for the automobile. As he headed toward the vehicle, the owner came out of his house. Ramirez got into the car, threw it in gear, and was ready to take off. The owner ran towards the car, grabbed Ramirez by the throat, and informed him that he was not going to steal *this* car. Ramirez got out of the car and somehow escaped the man's clutches. He began to run again.

He crossed the street and accosted a young woman. He demanded her car keys, but she refused. He gutpunched her, snatched her keys, and jumped into her car. Several neighbors saw this confrontation and rushed to the young girl's aid. They surrounded the car and

Near 3727 E. Hubbard Street Los Angeles

demanded that he get out. The woman's husband approached Ramirez with a steel pipe and angrily pulled the killer out of the car. He smacked Ramirez in the back of the head with the pipe, but Ramirez somehow managed to escape.

As he ran down Hubbard Street, more citizens spilled out of their homes. Ramirez was surrounded. He began to hiss like a serpent. The man with the pipe was not impressed. He again hit Ramirez in the back of the head, knocking him to the ground. Many people wanted Ramirez dead, but cooler heads prevailed.

Police officers soon showed up at the scene and arrested the serial killer. The reign of terror would finally come to an end.

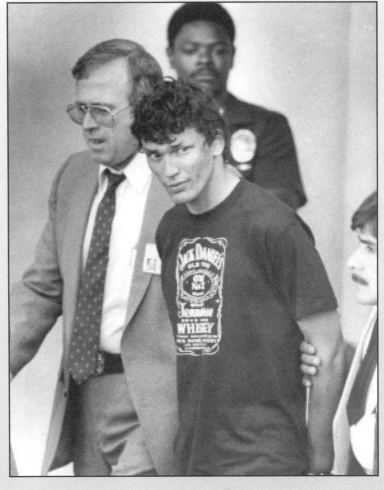

Ramirez's captors were awarded plaques from city officials for their bravery.

Near 3727 E. Hubbard Street Los Angeles

The Night Stalker

DEAD MAN TALKING

While Ramirez was being held at the Los Angeles County Jail, he was placed in extra-protective custody, due to the high level of his notoriety. His next-door cellmate was actor Sean Penn. Penn was in jail for punching a photographer.

At the time, Penn was still married to pop music icon and stalker victim, Madonna (see p. 21). It has been reported that Madonna came to see her husband in jail and noticed the charismatic killer. She also had no idea who he was. Madonna supposedly told her husband that Ramirez was extremely attractive, but Penn informed her of the crimes Ramirez was accused of committing.

Supposedly, Ramirez attempted to befriend Penn. He sent the actor a note asking for his autograph. Penn, in polite fashion, responded that he thought very little of the serial killer and that he should off himself.

Ramirez found his response humorous. He told Penn to "hit him again."

He signed the letter: "Satan 666."

441 Bauchet Street   Los Angeles

THE FARCE

The trial of Richard Ramirez would not start for almost three years after the final murder. The causes for this delay were numerous.

In his pre-trial hearings, Ramirez first came across as insolent, shamed, and quiet. Eventually, as he spent time in his holding cell reading numerous books on famous serial killers, Ramirez came out of his shell. He began to cause all sorts of disruptions. He would shout at the judge and prosecuting attorneys. He would praise Satan upon leaving the chambers. He once drew a pentagram on his hand and flashed it at the eager media photographers to be splashed all over the newspapers the following day. He reveled in his newfound celebrity.

In addition to Ramirez's outbursts, a political struggle occurred in relation to his representatives of the court. He disapproved of the court-appointed attorney he received in the beginning. His family hired an intelligent Hispanic attorney who was discovered to have committed a minor transgression early in his life, and subsequently was fired by the family. After several months, two inexperienced lawyers, Daniel Hernandez and Arturo Hernandez (no relation), were hired to represent the confessed serial killer. Neither one had ever tried a capital punishment case.

The Hernandez lawyers filed delay after delay. On January 10, 1989, the trial of one of the world's most notorious serial killers began. It was expected to last four to six months. It would go on for much longer.

Ramirez considered the whole concept of a trial to be a farce. He knew he was guilty and proudly admitted it. He had no idea why he was forced to sit through such a fiasco. He treated the proceedings as a joke. Ramirez would enter the courtroom wearing dark sunglasses. He would spend more time staring at his groupies than appreciating the solemnity of the occasion. He often cut up with his attorneys, and he would loudly laugh at crying witnesses who were describing the atrocious acts he committed. It was a joke and Ramirez constantly reminded everyone of that fact.

On September 20, 1989, the trial ended. Ramirez was found guilty on 46 charges including first-degree murder and robbery. He was sentenced to die in San Quentin's gas chamber.

111 N. Hill Street Los Angeles

SERIAL GROUPIES

Ramirez developed an unusual following while in court. Many women were drawn to his dark features and dangerous personality. Oftentimes in court, the first few rows would be filled with several women pining for Richard's attention. He received hundreds of letters from adoring female fans that wanted to redeem him, join him in future killing sprees, or marry him. Many wanted Richard to anoint them as Satanists. The adulation of this unrepentant serial killer ticked off numerous people. From the cops who brought Ramirez in, to the families of the victims, to the public at large, most were disgusted by this worship of a madman.

One of the eventual jurors, Cynthia Haden, fell in love with Ramirez. She even baked muffins for him on Valentine's Day. Haden caused concern for many involved in the conviction of Ramirez. Originally an alternate, she eventually ascended to juror, after another juror was murdered by her abusive husband during the determination phase.

Detective Frank Salerno believed that Haden would side with the killer and cause a mistrial. Haden, however, not only voted to convict him, but also to give him the death penalty. After the trial, Haden went to see Ramirez in prison and attempted to strike up a relationship. She argued that Ramirez had received horrible representation from his attorneys and that the decision should be overturned on appeal. She submerged herself in his case and even got to visit him as part of his defense team. She used these opportunities to engage in a little tête-a-tête with Ramirez.

Det. Frank Salerno worked on the Hillside Stranglers case and the Night Stalker case.

111 N. Hill Street Los Angeles

CHAPTER 12 THE PEOPLE V. O.J.

June 12, 1994. The mutilated bodies of Nicole Brown Simpson, ex-wife of former Heisman trophy winner and pro-football legend O.J. Simpson, and Ronald Goldman were found at Nicole's condo on Bundy Drive in Brentwood. It was a bloody murder scene. Nicole's body was found lying facedown in the fetal position, her hand clenched in a death grip, a pool of blood extending more than ten feet from where she was discovered. Directly across from her, Goldman was sitting up, eyes open, covered in blood.

There was blood everywhere. There were no eyewitnesses.

This case came to epitomize the dark underside of Los Angeles. It had fame, beauty, wealth, success, jealousy, abuse, drugs, questionable police work, racism, and a trial that would become the "top-rated miniseries" to come out of Hollywood in years.

There was no case quite like the *People v. O. J. Simpson*.

MURDER SCENE

On June 12, 1994, at approximately 10:30 PM, Steven Schwab was walking his dog near the Bundy Avenue residence of Nicole Brown Simpson. Schwab heard the whimpering of another dog. He found a stray Akita walking around, but there was something unusual about this animal. It was leaving bloody footprints. Schwab assumed that the dog might be injured. The Akita followed Schwab back to his home.

Around 11:40 PM, Schwab saw two acquaintances, Sukru Boztepe and Bettina Rasmussen. The couple offered to take the dog to their home to care for it. They took the Akita to their home, but the animal was restless. It constantly pawed at the couple's door, wanting to go somewhere. The couple let the dog out and followed it to Nicole Brown Simpson's condo on Bundy Avenue.

Even in the dark Sukru could see the blood. Looking for the source, Sukru noticed a dark figure near the stairs of the condo. It was the body of Nicole Brown Simpson. She was not moving. Sukru called the police who arrived near midnight. Upon closer inspection, they found the body of an unidentified man, later determined to be 25-year-old aspiring actor and model, Ronald Lyle Goldman. It would also be revealed that Goldman, a waiter at the trendy Italian restaurant Mezzaluna in Brentwood, was dropping

off a pair of eyeglasses that were left at the eatery by Nicole's mother earlier that evening.

Several officers reported to the crime scene and made cursory observations regarding the murders. One of those officers was Detective Mark Fuhrman. He was the seventeenth officer to log in. Fuhrman would notice several key bits of evidence at the scene. Among these items were a black knit cap, a bloody leather glove, and several drops of

1994: 875 S. Bundy Drive   Brentwood
Present: 879 S. Bundy Drive   Brentwood

blood. The blood drops seemed to indicate that the killer or killers had fled the crime scene through the walkway that runs alongside the home.

Fuhrman eventually ceded control of the investigation to senior robbery/homicide detectives Tom Lange and Philip Vannatter. Lange and Vannatter, after taking a quick look at the crime scene, decided to alert O.J. Simpson of his ex-wife's death and transfer his children, Sydney and Justin, to his custody. The two youngsters were found upstairs, asleep in their beds, when police arrived. They had slept through the entire ordeal.

PICTURED BELOW:
Nicole Brown Simpson's condo as it appears today. It is the entrance on the right hand side. The front has been redesigned and the address changed. They forgot, however, to change the curb number.

1994: 875 S. Bundy Drive Brentwood
Present: 879 S. Bundy Drive Brentwood

ROCKINGHAM

O.J. Simpson's estate was located a mere five minutes away from Nicole Brown Simpson's condo on Bundy. Detectives Lange, Vannatter, Furhman, and Ron Phillips made the short drive to the Rockingham estate. Upon arrival at the house, the officers noticed a white Ford Bronco parked askew on North Rockingham Avenue at the front gate of Simpson's house. The police decided to take a closer look.

Detective Fuhrman walked up to the Bronco. He noticed a red speck on the driver's side door. It was miniscule, but it stood out on the white paint of the Bronco. Fuhrman claimed that he believed the speck to be blood, so he took a look inside the vehicle. He claimed that he saw a package with Simpson's business name on the outside of it, a plastic bag, and a shovel in the back of the truck. Fuhrman also claimed that he noticed several specks of blood inside as well as on the running boards of the truck.

Then, Fuhrman supposedly found several drops of blood on the driveway leading to Simpson's estate. As Fuhrman allegedly uncovered this evidence, Lange and Vannatter attempted to contact Simpson inside his home. They rang the intercom several times, but no one answered. They contacted the Westec security team who came out to the site to investigate the commotion. The Westec representative was initially uncooperative, but eventually gave them a phone number. When they received no answer, Vannatter made a crucial decision. Given the scene at Bundy, he claimed that he believed O.J. Simpson could also be in danger. He was not sure if Simpson could have been kidnapped, tied up in his own home, or possibly even murdered.

Vannatter claimed that he was thinking in the best interest of Simpson when he ordered Fuhrman to scale the five-foot wall.

Fuhrman jumped over the wall and walked to the gate. He pressed an electronic buzzer that opened the gate and allowed the officers to enter the premises.

The legal troubles began here.

1994: 360 N. Rockingham Avenue   Brentwood
Present: 380 N. Rockingham Avenue   Brentwood

KATO & THUMPS

Upon entering the grounds, Fuhrman knocked on the guesthouse door. A sleepy-eyed, tousle-haired surfer dude, Brian "Kato" Kaelin, greeted him. Kaelin informed Fuhrman that O.J. was on a business trip to Chicago and had left late the night before. The officers claimed that they were worried for the safety of anyone that might still be in the house. They wanted to know if there were any persons inside. Kaelin informed them that Simpson's adult daughter, Arnelle, lived in the bungalow and that she was probably inside.

Vannatter and Lange approached the back bungalow and knocked on Arnelle's door. She, too, had been asleep, and was not clear about what was happening. She invited the officers into the home where they informed her of Nicole's murder. They expressed their fears for Simpson's well being.

Meanwhile, Fuhrman questioned Kaelin about his whereabouts the night before. Kaelin told Fuhrman that he and O.J. went to McDonald's to pick up some drive-thru hamburgers. He thought it was unusual, because he and Simpson almost never hung out together.

After their dinner, Kaelin retreated back to his bungalow. He claimed he spent most of the evening talking on the phone with his girlfriend. At approximately 10:45 PM, Kaelin claimed that he heard three loud thumps on his wall from outside. He believed, at first, that it might have been an earthquake, because a picture was visibly shaken on his wall. He did not rush out to check the noise right away, but eventually searched behind the bungalow. He did not notice anyone.

While Lange and Vannatter interviewed Arnelle, Fuhrman decided to look around the premises. He wanted to check the area behind Kaelin's bedroom. He thought he might see something that explained the three thumps. What he found would turn the city of Los Angeles on its head and eventually lead to one of the biggest travesties in American trial history.

Simpson's house was torn down in 1998. A new mansion has been erected at the same location and the address has been changed.

1994: 360 N. Rockingham Avenue   Brentwood
Present: 380 N. Rockingham Avenue   Brentwood

BLOODY GLOVE & CHICAGO

Mark Fuhrman returned to Lange and Vannatter with serious news. They had to see what he had discovered. He led them behind Kaelin's room, where he pointed out a leather glove—not just any glove, but a perfect match to the glove found at the Bundy crime scene.

According to Lange and Vannatter, two seasoned homicide detectives with over 50 years combined experience, this discovery marked the first time they suspected that maybe, just maybe, O.J. Simpson was involved in the brutal execution of his former wife and her male friend, Ron Goldman. They figured out where O.J. was staying in Chicago and called to inform him of the murder of his ex-wife. They wanted him back in Los Angeles.

Simpson never once asked anything about Nicole or what happened to her.

The People v. O. J. Simpson

BACK IN L.A.

O.J. Simpson flew back to Los Angeles. He arrived at the Rockingham estate at noon. He had a small bandage on the middle finger of his left hand. Officer Don Thompson, an African-American, immediately placed him into handcuffs. The cuffing was captured by television news crews and aired across the country. It was the first of many racially motivated arguments to come out of this story. Most people conveniently forgot that Officer Thompson was black and that Vannatter, a white police officer, was the one who later uncuffed the football legend.

Simpson was joined by his initial attorney Howard Weitzman. Vannatter and Lange wanted to interview Simpson. Simpson complied and headed downtown with the boys in blue. The officers drove him to the Parker Center. This is where the questionable interview/interrogation took place.

Vannatter and Lange insisted that the encounter between themselves and Simpson was simply an interview. Simpson was not an official suspect. They were merely trying to get as much information out of him as possible. Furthermore, they were able to photograph his cut finger and take blood samples from "The Juice."

Many other officers and lawyers criticized the lead detectives' efforts and considered this interview to be a major missed opportunity. They had total access to Simpson without the intrusion of a lawyer and they blew it. Simpson had waived his right to have an attorney present during questioning, and he told Weitzman that he had it under control.

Vannatter and Lange's interview lasted only 32 minutes and seemed to lack focus. Others believed that the statements extracted from Simpson were more than adequate to cast serious doubt on his innocence in the murder of his former wife. This interview, however, would not even be introduced in the criminal court trial.

150 N. Los Angeles St.   Downtown L.A.

RELEASE & SLOW SPEED CHASE

In an interesting decision, Vannatter decided to allow Simpson to go home. Vannatter then contacted Los Angeles District Attorney Marcia Clark to handle the murder case. Clark was well known for her prosecution of stalker John Bardo for the murder of television sitcom actress, Rebecca Schaeffer (see p. 20). Vannatter and Clark believed that the test results of the blood from Simpson, from the crime scene, and from Simpson's estate would provide them with sufficient ammunition to file murder charges against Simpson. Unfortunately, the blood test results took a few days to obtain. Hence, Vannatter released Simpson until the results were back.

By Thursday, Vannatter and Clark received those results. While Simpson attended the funeral of his ex-wife, Vannatter and Clark began to believe that Simpson killed both Nicole Brown Simpson and Ron Goldman. Vannatter made contact with one of O.J.'s new lawyers, Robert Shapiro. Shapiro, best known as a pleading attorney who worked on such high-profile cases as the Christian Brando murder and the John DeLorean drug bust, agreed to a pick-up time with Vannatter. The police decided to detain Simpson at 11:00 AM on Friday at Shapiro's estate.

When the time came around, O.J. Simpson was nowhere to be found. Shapiro claimed that O.J. never showed up and that he had no idea where to find his client. Police were sent to the home of Robert Kardashian, yet another Simpson attorney and best friend, but O.J. was not there. They also sent police to Simpson's Rockingham estate and to Ascension Cemetery where Nicole was buried.

San Diego (405) Freeway

Police feared that Simpson might attempt to commit suicide. They were almost right. Simpson and his long-time football teammate and best friend Al Cowlings had taken off in Cowling's white Ford Bronco to Nicole's gravesite. While there, Simpson informed Cowlings that he was going to end it all. Simpson, however, backed off of his suicide pledge and left the cemetery. He and Cowlings climbed back into the Bronco and began the slowest high-speed chase broadcast to more than 95 million viewers nationwide.

Several motorists pulled off the side of the San Diego (405) Freeway to let the procession pass. People from local neighborhoods lined the sides of the freeways to watch. Many cheered, while others booed, as the Bronco appeared in their midst. Some people even took the time to make signs proclaiming "The Juice's" guilt or innocence. It resembled a high-tech, low-speed version of a USC/UCLA football game.

O.J. Simpson was once again at the center of attention.

After two hours of the slow-speed crawl, Al Cowlings returned O.J. Simpson to his Rockingham estate where he was greeted by his family and friends. A SWAT team was there to greet him as well. Officials allowed Simpson to enter his home and say his goodbyes to his family. While he was in his house, a police search of Cowling's Bronco uncovered several interesting items. Officers located a revolver, a fake beard, glue, cash, and Simpson's passport.

Simpson was arrested, taken back to Parker Center, and charged with the murders of his ex-wife, Nicole Brown Simpson, and her friend, Ronald Goldman.

San Diego (405) Freeway

BK 4013970   06 17 94

LOS ANGELES POLICE   JAIL DIV

The People v. O. J. Simpson

DREAM TEAM

On June 20, a forlorn Simpson was dragged into court. He looked tired, beaten down, and resigned to his fate. Yet, he elected to proclaim that he was "Not Guilty" in the crimes. His new lawyer, Johnnie Cochran, supported him.

Cochran had a reputation as a flamboyant, flashy personality who liked nice cars and money. His record as a criminal defense attorney, however, was suspect. While he claimed that he had won several criminal trials, no one asked him to recount a past victory. Instead, he had developed a reputation as an attorney who took on high-profile celebrity civil matters. Cochran had represented celebrities such as superstar entertainer Michael Jackson. He also raised his name value after the Los Angeles riots in 1992 (see p. 128), when he sued the City of Los Angeles and its police department for moving *out* of high-risk areas during the riots. In that suit, Cochran claimed that the police's actions were racist and proved that they were unwilling to assist minorities in any way.

Cochran had experience in only one murder trial. In 1972, he represented former Black Panther Benjamin "Geronimo" Pratt when Pratt was accused of killing a white schoolteacher at a Santa Monica tennis court. Cochran lost that trial and Pratt was sentenced to life in prison.

Robert Shapiro's record of success was not much better than Cochran's. He had only worked on one murder trial, the Brando case. Shapiro pleaded Brando out with a ten-year sentence for the murder of Dag Drollet.

Simpson also hired famed criminal defense attorney, F. Lee Bailey. Bailey actually had a successful career as a criminal attorney, unlike Cochran and Shapiro, and had worked on several murder cases. He was most well known for the Dr. Sam Sheppard murder case, which was the basis for the television series and movie, *The Fugitive*. He also worked on the Boston Strangler case of Albert DeSalvo. His most recent high-profile case before the Simpson case involved the Patty Hearst bank robbery charge (see p. 118). Many analysts believed that the Hearst case was a slam-dunk. Bailey, however, lost that case and with it went most of his elevated profile. That was almost 20 years before the Simpson murder case.

The final piece of the Simpson defense team puzzle was famed appellate attorney Alan Dershowitz. The media mistakenly portrayed Dershowitz's importance in the case of Claus von Bulow and his attempted murder of his wife. The press reported that Dershowitz had represented von Bulow during the criminal trial, when the reality was that he only handled the appellate issues before the court. Dershowitz was not a criminal defense lawyer.

These were the four main characters that would make up Simpson's so-called "Dream Team." The concept seems to have risen out of journalistic laziness as opposed to proven track records.

The People v. O. J. Simpson

CRIMINAL TRIAL

The wacky spectacle began on January 24, 1995. The prosecution, led by Marcia Clark and Christopher Darden, would present, what they claimed to be, a mountain of evidence.

They introduced blood evidence that implicated Simpson. They introduced past abuse reports made against Simpson by Nicole and character witnesses that claimed Simpson was a violent individual. They had witnesses that had seen Simpson act strange throughout the evening, before and after the suggested times of the murders.

They also had Mark Fuhrman.

Fuhrman became the scapegoat for the defense attorneys. The case turned from a murder trial to an indictment of the entire Los Angeles Police Department. Throughout the trial, Fuhrman was accused of being a racist by the defense. He continually denied the charges. On August 10, the defense pulled the rabbit out of their hat. They introduced a series of audiotapes to Judge Lance Ito that contained the voice of Mark Fuhrman.

Fuhrman and aspiring screenwriter Laura Hart had met several times to discuss Fuhrman's fanciful take on the life of a police officer. Fuhrman claimed that he was attempting to recreate a hard-boiled life of a rough and tumble detective who took on the bad guys and kicked their asses on a daily basis. Sometimes the imagery was harsh, but so was life on the streets, he claimed. He also liked to use the word "Nigger"—not just once, but approximately 40 times. If Fuhrman was merely using creative license, this sin might have been forgiven. However, he stated in court that he had never used the inflammatory remark—ever.

Suddenly, the murders of Nicole Brown Simpson and Ron Goldman were pushed to the side. The Trial of the Century now focused on one rogue cop and how his potential racist attitude could have tainted the entire case. Johnnie Cochran took the ball and ran with it. He continually referred to Fuhrman as "The Devil" and Fuhrman and Vannatter as "the evil twins of deception." Subtle.

The complete Fuhrman Tapes were not played in front of the jury. Judge Ito only played two snippets of the tape, because he probably did not want Fuhrman's remarks about his own wife, Captain Margaret York, to become part of the trial. Fuhrman, who had an ongoing feud with York in his earlier days on the force, claimed that York had "sucked her way to the top." Ouch.

Detective Fuhrman had perjured himself. To avoid further castigation on the stand, Fuhrman pled the fifth, which meant that he did not have to answer any questions. The appearance of one of the main detectives not answering a question such as "Did you plant evidence at O.J. Simpson's house?" destroyed the case.

On October 3, 1995, after nine months of laborious testimony, the jury recessed to make their decision. The jury in the Angelo Buono murder trial (see p. 208) took weeks to reach all of its final verdicts. The jury in the Simpson matter took four hours.

Their verdict?

Not Guilty.

111 N. Hill Street Los Angeles

CIVIL TRIAL

The families of Nicole Brown Simpson and Ronald Goldman filed civil suits against O.J. Simpson one year after the murders. The charges were to find that Simpson, by a preponderance of the evidence, had caused the murders of Nicole and Ron. A civil trial would require a lesser percentage of votes, could only dole out fees, and required that the defendant take the stand. On

October 13, 1996, the second Simpson circus began in Santa Monica Civil Courthouse in Santa Monica, California.

Simpson, on the advice of his attorneys, did not take the stand in the criminal trial. It is a common tactic employed to prevent the defendant from saying something he may regret later. Simpson was not so lucky in the civil trial. Attorney Daniel Petrocelli put Simpson on the stand and relentlessly grilled him.

Simpson became a mass of quivering jelly under the intense scrutiny of Petrocelli. He would often contradict key testimony from the criminal trial. He even contradicted many of his own statements. He looked especially foolish when he repeatedly denied ever beating his wife while a huge picture of a bruised Nicole loomed over his shoulder.

Petrocelli was also able to provide key evidence that never made it to the criminal trial. In the earlier proceeding, Simpson denied ever owning a pair of Bruno Magli shoes that matched the bloody shoeprints found at the Bundy Drive residence. He claimed that he would never wear such "ugly ass shoes." Petrocelli had located over 30 photographs of Simpson wearing what appeared to be the same Bruno Magli shoes during a television broadcast of an NFL game in 1993.

Another aspect was different in the civil trial. Judge Hiroshi Fujisaki did not allow Detective Fuhrman to testify in the trial. The judge wanted to make sure that the civil trial was about O.J. Simpson, not racism.

In January 1997, the jury came back with their decision. Unanimously, O.J. Simpson was considered to be liable in the deaths of both Nicole Brown Simpson and Ronald Goldman. The jurors awarded the victims' families $8.5 million in compensatory damages and $12.5 million in punitive damages for each victim. Grand total = $33.5 million.

O.J. Simpson has vowed to never pay a single penny.

He can be seen playing golf quite often these days.

1725 Main Street   Santa Monica

Nicole Brown Simpson can be seen at Ascension Cemetery.

24754 *Trabuco Road Lake Forest*

CHAPTER 13
CELEBRITY
CEMETERIES

The cemeteries of Los Angeles provide a much-needed service for many fans. It provides them the opportunity to get within six feet of some of their most cherished entertainers. While it can be exciting to spot a grave of a famous celebrity, these memorial parks should be treated with reverence and respect for others.

FOREST LAWN GLENDALE

The mother lode of all celebrity cemeteries.

The sprawling, lush 300 acres contain more celebrity graves than almost all other cemeteries combined. With over 250,000 inhabitants, Forest Lawn Glendale can be a bear to maneuver. Furthermore, the staff here is less than courteous, as they tend to discourage celebrity grave hunters.

But, alas, do not be discouraged. Be polite, respectful, and prepared. Your payoff will be well rewarded. From too numerous graves to count, to gorgeous replica statues of *all* of Michelangelo's works, to multimedia displays of religious artifacts, Forest Lawn Glendale has something for everyone.

Ask for a map to the cemetery at the front desk upon your arrival. It will not contain specific locales of the stars' graves, but it will be necessary for you to get around this vast expanse.

Here is a partial list of famous persons interred in this majestic cemetery:

1712 S. Glendale Avenue Glendale

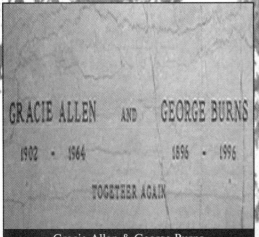

Gracie Allen & George Burns
Freedom Mausoleum - Sanctuary of Heritage

L. Frank Baum
Section G - next to the narrow road

Clara Bow
Freedom Mausoleum - Sanctuary of Heritage

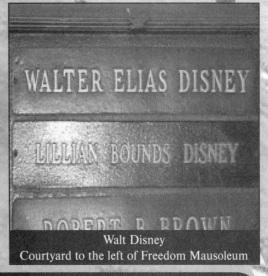

Nat "King" Cole
Freedom Mausoleum - Sanctuary of Heritage

Dorothy Dandridge (see p. 55)
Freedom Mausoleum - Columbarium of Victory

Walt Disney
Courtyard to the left of Freedom Mausoleum

1712 S. Glendale Avenue Glendale

Edward Doheny Jr. (see p. 78)
Temple of Santa Sabina - Sunrise Slope

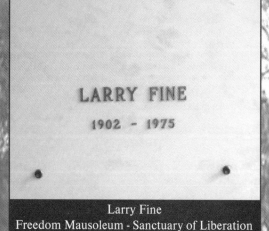

Larry Fine
Freedom Mausoleum - Sanctuary of Liberation

Errol Flynn
Garden of Everlasting Peace

Sid Grauman
Great Mausoleum - Sanctuary of Benediction

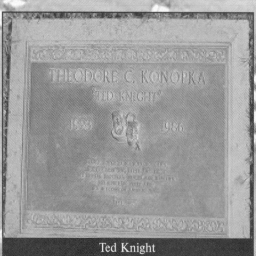

Ted Knight
Ascension Garden - Lot 9127

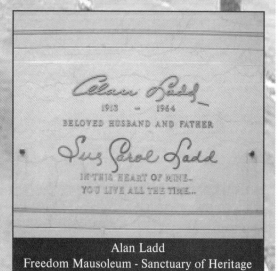

Alan Ladd
Freedom Mausoleum - Sanctuary of Heritage

1712 S. Glendale Avenue Glendale

Louis L'Amour
Courtyard outside of the Great Mausoleum

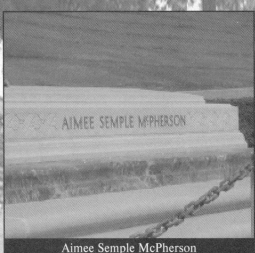

Chico Marx
Freedom Mausoleum - Sanctuary of Worship

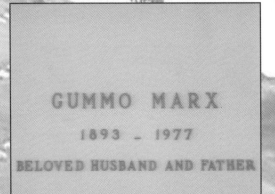

Gummo Marx
Freedom Mausoleum - Sanctuary of Brotherhood

Aimee Semple McPherson
Large crypt at back of Great Mausoleum

Clayton Moore
Everlasting Peace - Lot 5492

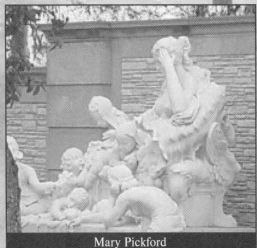

Mary Pickford
Garden of Memory on the North East Wall

1712 S. Glendale Avenue Glendale

Red Skelton
Great Mausoleum - Sanctuary of Benediction

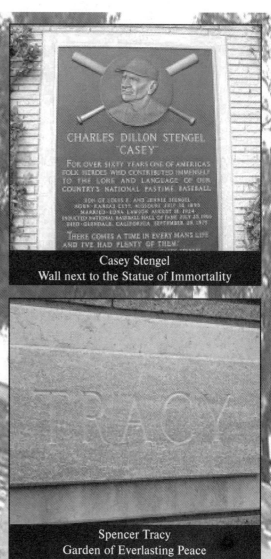

Casey Stengel
Wall next to the Statue of Immortality

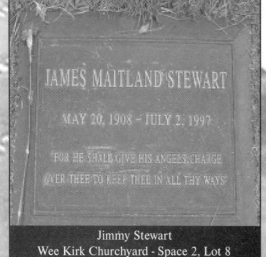

Jimmy Stewart
Wee Kirk Churchyard - Space 2, Lot 8

Spencer Tracy
Garden of Everlasting Peace

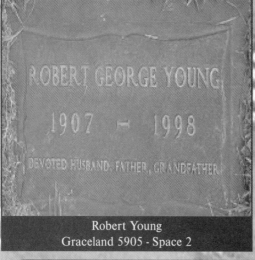

Robert Young
Graceland 5905 - Space 2

1712 S. Glendale Avenue Glendale

Even more celebrities are buried at Forest Lawn Glendale, however, their graves can be difficult to access. They include:

Theda Bara, Wallace Beery, Humphrey Bogart, William Castle, Lon Chaney Sr., Sam Cooke (see p. 2), George Cukor, Sammy Davis Jr., Don Drysdale, W.C. Fields, Clark Gable, Samuel Goldwyn, Jean Harlow, Carole Landis, Harold Lloyd, Carole Lombard, Ernst Lubitsch, Tom Mix, William Mulholland, Alexander Pantages, Marian Parker, Hugh T. Plunkett (see p. 78) David O. Selznick, Irving Thalberg, Jay Ward, Johnny "Guitar" Watson, Mary Wells, Roland West (see p. 106), James Whale (see p. 43), William Wyler, and Keenan Wynn.

1712 S. Glendale Avenue Glendale

FOREST LAWN HOLLYWOOD HILLS

Smaller than its Glendale sister cemetery, the Hollywood Hills version still holds an impressive array of movie stars beneath its surface. The décor here is more restrained than the Glendale cemetery with a focus on American heritage, highlighted by several statues of American presidents. The cemetery also overlooks Disney and Warner Brothers Studios.

A small sampling of its guests include:

6300 Forest Lawn Drive   Burbank

Morey Amsterdam
Court of Remembrance - furthest section North

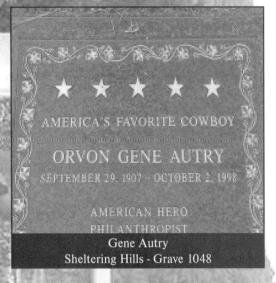

Gene Autry
Sheltering Hills - Grave 1048

Lucille Ball
Columbarium of Radiant Light

Albert "Cubby" Broccoli
Court of Remembrance

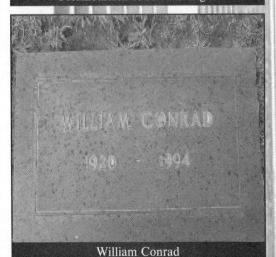

William Conrad
Lincoln Terrace - Plot 4448

Bert Convy
Court of Liberty - Lot 5281 - Left of sidewalk

6300 Forest Lawn Drive   Burbank

Scatman Crothers
Lincoln Terrace - Plot 4545

Bette Davis
Court of Remembrance

Brad Davis
Court of Remembrance - Columbarium of Valor

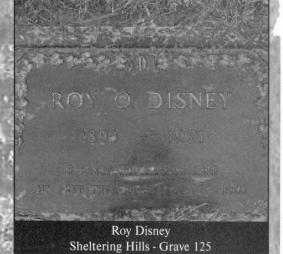

Roy Disney
Sheltering Hills - Grave 125

Marty Feldman
Garden of Heritage - Lot 5420

Andy Gibb
Court of Remembrance - 2534

6300 *Forest Lawn Drive* Burbank

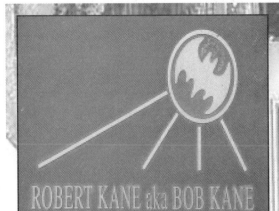

Bob Kane
Court of Liberty - Lot 1310

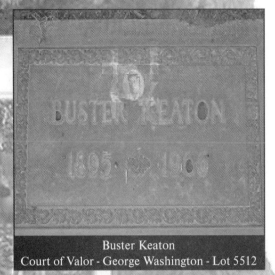

Buster Keaton
Court of Valor - George Washington - Lot 5512

Dorothy Lamour
Enduring Faith - Lot 387 - Space 2

Walter Lantz
Columbarium of Radiant Light

Charles Laughton
Court of Remembrance - 310

Stan Laurel
George Washington Section - 2nd Terrace - 910

6300 Forest Lawn Drive   Burbank

Liberace
Court of Remembrance

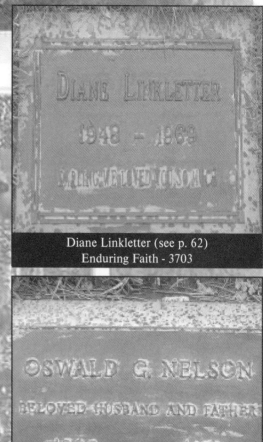

Diane Linkletter (see p. 62)
Enduring Faith - 3703

Harriet Nelson
Revelation - Lot 3540

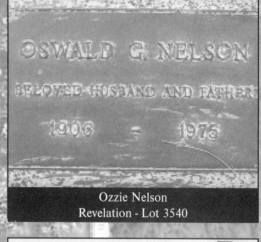

Ozzie Nelson
Revelation - Lot 3540

Ricky Nelson
Revelation - Lot 3538

Freddie Prinze (see p. 34)
Court of Remembrance - Sanctuary of Light - 2355

6300 Forest Lawn Drive   Burbank

George Raft (see p. 95)
Court of Remembrance - Sanctuary of Light

Telly Savalas
George Washington Section - 1281

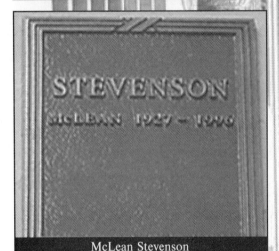

McLean Stevenson
Columbarium of Valor

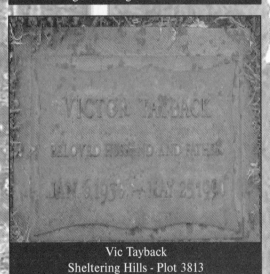

Vic Tayback
Sheltering Hills - Plot 3813

Lee Van Cleef
Court of Remembrance - Serenity Section - 156

Jack Webb
Sheltering Hills - 1999

6300 Forest Lawn Drive   Burbank

Forest Lawn Hollywood Hills is also the final resting place for Tex Avery, Ralph Bellamy, Leo Durocher, Bobby Fuller, Ernie Kovacs, Fritz Lang, Strother Martin, Dar Robinson, Helen Travolta, and Frank Wells.

6300 Forest Lawn Drive   Burbank

HILLSIDE MEMORIAL

One of Los Angeles's most beautiful cemeteries is this predominately Jewish graveyard. Located off the 405 Freeway in Culver City, and across the street from the Holy Cross cemetery (see p. 296), Hillside Memorial also has one of the most spectacular tombs ever seen. It is dedicated to famous silent movie/talkie actor/singer Al Jolson. Once you pull into the cemetery, you cannot miss it. It has a white canopy atop six pillars, fronted by a beautiful waterfall. It also has a large painting of the Ten Commandments.

Along with Al Jolson, be sure to greet the following:

6001 W. Centinela Avenue   Culver City

Jack Benny

Eddie Cantor

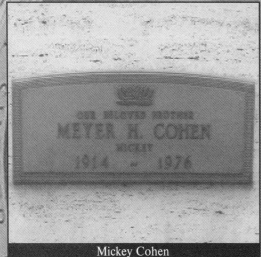

Mickey Cohen

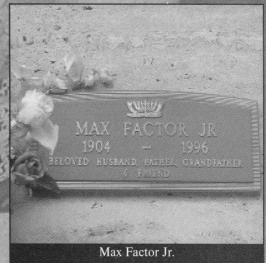

Max Factor Jr.

Max Factor Sr.

Mark Goodson

6001 W. Centinela Avenue   Culver City

Hank Greenberg

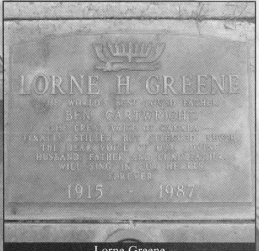

Lorne Greene

Moe Howard

David Janssen

George Jessel

Michael Landon

6001 W. Centinela Avenue   Culver City

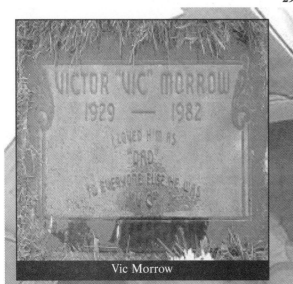

Vic Morrow

Dinah Shore

IRVING WALLACE
MARCH 19, 1916
JUNE 29, 1990

"LIFE IS NOT A DAILY DYING, NOT A POINTLESS
END, BUT A SOARING AND BLINDING GIFT
SNATCHED FROM ETERNITY."

Irving Wallace

6001 W. Centinela Avenue   Culver City

HOLLYWOOD FOREVER

One of Hollywood's oldest and most-recognized cemeteries is this huge complex located beneath the Hollywood sign in the backyard of Paramount Studios. Formerly known as Hollywood Memorial Park, Hollywood Forever features beautiful sprawling greenery, huge mausoleums, and tons of famous celebrity graves. The cemetery has been featured in numerous films including *L.A. Story* and Robert Altman's *The Player*.

Hollywood Memorial Park had fallen into a serious state of disrepair in the 90s. A young entrepreneur, Tyler Cassity, bought the cemetery and has undertaken major improvements, including replacing cracked tombstones, planting new greenery, and even creating a virtual cemetery.

The staff, under Cassity's understanding guidance, is the polar opposite of the Forest Lawn Glendale cemetery. The staff here is courteous, knowledgeable, and eager to assist people in locating famous gravesites. They even provide detailed maps in the flower shop with celebrity graves pinpointed.

Hollywood Forever is definitely worth the visit and is here to stay.

Be sure to say "Hello" to some of the following tenants:

Mel Blanc
Section 13 - Pineland Section - Lot 149 by road

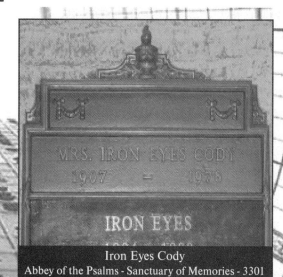

Iron Eyes Cody
Abbey of the Psalms - Sanctuary of Memories - 3301

Harry Cohn
Section 8 - Across from Cathedral Mausoleum

Marion Davies
Section 8 - East side of lake

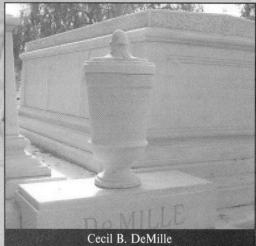

Cecil B. DeMille
Section 8 - North side of lake.

Nelson Eddy
Section - Lot 89

6000 Santa Monica Blvd. Hollywood

Douglas Fairbanks Sr.
Reflecting Pool beside Cathedral Mausoleum

Peter Finch
Cathedral Mausoleum - Corridor A - Crypt 1224

Victor Fleming
Abbey of the Psalms - Sanctuary of Refuge - #208

Janet Gaynor
Section 8 - Lot 193

Darla Hood
Abbey of the Psalms - Sanctuary of Light - G-4 - 7213

John Huston
Section 8 - Lot 6 - West side of lake

6000 Santa Monica Blvd. Hollywood

294

Peter Lorre
Cathedral Mausoleum - Corridor C - Niche 5 - Tier 1

Jayne Mansfield Cenotaph
Section 8 near lake. She is not buried here.

Jay Moloney
Section 8 - Lot 115 - Grave 21

Paul Muni
Section 14 - Grave 57

Tyrone Power
Section 8 - Bench near lake

Virginia Rappe
Section 8 - Lot 257

6000 Santa Monica Blvd. Hollywood

Edward G. Robinson Jr.
Abbey of the Psalms - Crypt 4386 - Corridor E-4

Benjamin "Bugsy" Siegel (see p. 95)
Beth Olam Mausoleum - M2 - 1087

Carl Switzer (see p. 24)
Section 6 - Grave 6 - Lot 26

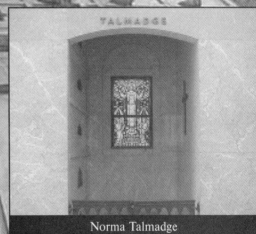

Norma Talmadge
Abbey of the Psalms - Shrine of Eternal Love -
Talmadge Room - Corridor G-7

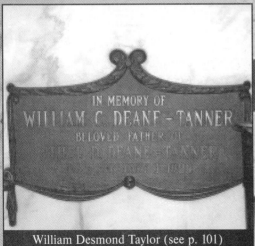

William Desmond Taylor (see p. 101)
Cathedral Mausoleum

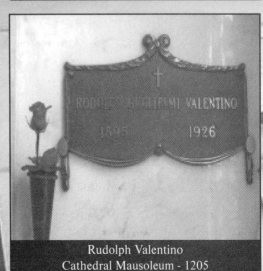

Rudolph Valentino
Cathedral Mausoleum - 1205

6000 Santa Monica Blvd. Hollywood

HOLY CROSS

This beautiful Roman Catholic cemetery is just across the street from Hillside Memorial. Holy Cross is one of the most immaculately kept, gorgeous resting places in the world. Replete with waterfalls, grottos, and white statues that depict various religious figures, Holy Cross offers a peaceful getaway for its residents and visitors.

Some of those that have decided to stay include:

5835 W. Slauson Avenue Culver City

Mary Astor
N-L 523-5

Ray Bolger
Mausoleum - Crypt F2 - Block 35

Charles Boyer
St. Ann Section - 5 - L186

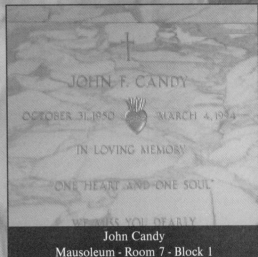

John Candy
Mausoleum - Room 7 - Block 1

MacDonald Carey
Grotto - 19 - L196

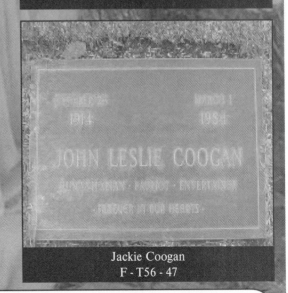

Jackie Coogan
F - T56 - 47

5835 W. Slauson Avenue Culver City

Darby Crash (see p. 29)
R - T8 - 114

Bing Crosby
Grotto - L119 - 1

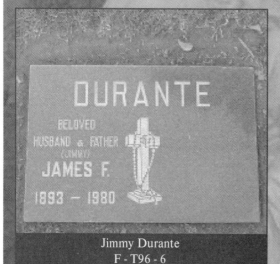

Jimmy Durante
F - T96 - 6

John Ford
M - L304 - 5

Mary Frann
CC-T 52 - 58

Jack Haley
Grotto - L196 - 2

5835 W. Slauson Avenue Culver City

Rita Hayworth
Grotto - L196 - 6

Bela Lugosi
Grotto - L120 - 1

Fred MacMurray
Mausoleum - Room 7 - D1

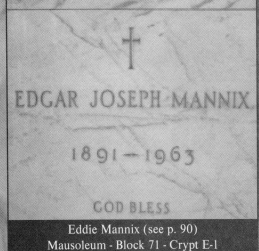

Eddie Mannix (see p. 90)
Mausoleum - Block 71 - Crypt E-1

Toni Mannix (see p. 90)
Mausoleum - Block 71 - Crypt E-2

Audrey Meadows
F - T29 - 58

5835 W. Slauson Avenue Culver City

Evelyn Nesbit
Section M - Lot 232 - Grave 2

Walter O'Malley
Section P - Lot 526 - Grave 5

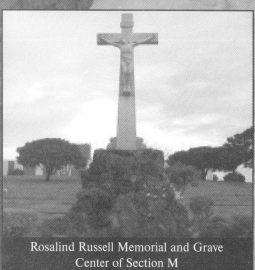

Rosalind Russell Memorial and Grave
Center of Section M

Gia Scala
Section M - Lot 542 - Grave 1

Sharon Tate (see p. 183)
St. Ann Section - L152 - 6

Lawrence Welk
Y - T9 - 110

5835 W. Slauson Avenue Culver City

5835 W. Slauson Avenue Culver City

MOUNT SINAI

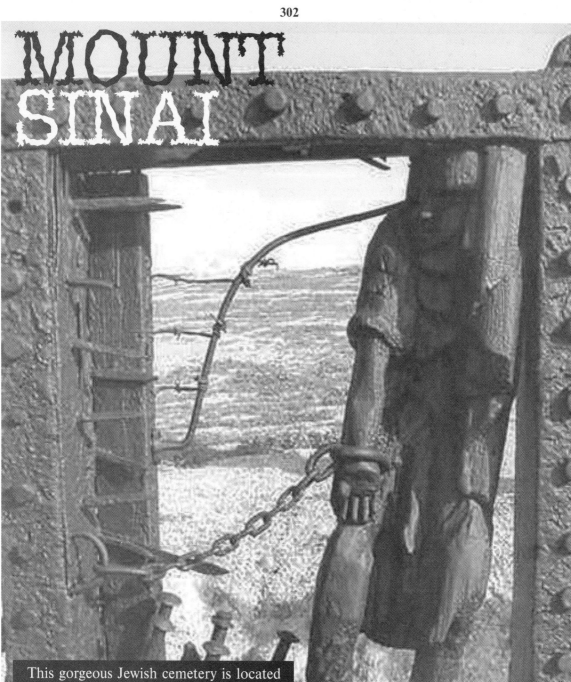

This gorgeous Jewish cemetery is located next to the Forest Lawn Hollywood Hills cemetery. It contains a living memorial to the six million Holocaust victims as well as a 150-foot long mural that tells the story of Jewish life in the United States. It is decorated with a quaint waterfall and contains some of the brightest Jewish stars to ever shine. Among them are the following:

5950 Forest Lawn Drive   Burbank

Irwin Allen
Heritage Courtyard - 2nd Floor - 39

Lee J. Cobb
Garden of Shemot - Lot 421

"Big Mama" Cass Elliot
Court of Tanach - Lot 5000 - Grave 2F

Norman Fell
Garden of Heritage - Columbarium of Tradition - Niche 1601A

Phil Silvers
Space 1004 - Front right of Heritage Mosaic

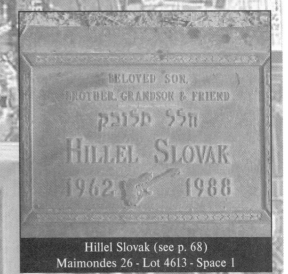

Hillel Slovak (see p. 68)
Maimondes 26 - Lot 4613 - Space 1

5950 Forest Lawn Drive Burbank

WESTWOOD MEMORIAL PARK

Another fascinating cemetery packed with tons of celebrities. If you only have a few hours to spare, this is the cemetery for you. Tucked away between a movie theater and several office buildings, Westwood Memorial is easily accessible and small enough to wander around and find the final resting places of some of the world's most well known celebrities. It has a circular driveway that you can drive on with no problem. It is also landscaped with several nice touches including gardens, benches, and beautiful trees.

Westwood Memorial also has the dubious distinction of being the cemetery to several female movie stars who died before their prime, including Marilyn Monroe, Natalie Wood, Dorothy Stratten, and Dominique Dunne.

Check out these women and more celebrities including:

MARILYN MONROE
1926 – 1962

1218 Glendon Avenue   Westwood

Eve Arden
Section D - 81

Jim Backus
Section D - 203

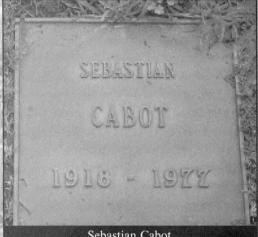

Sebastian Cabot
Urn Garden near office - Top Row - Nine from right

Truman Capote
Wall near Armand Hammer Mausoleum

John Cassavetes
Lot 308 - In front of Armand Hammer Mausoleum

Dominique Dunne (see p. 5)
Section D - 189

1218 Glendon Avenue   Westwood

Eva Gabor
In front of Armand Hammer Mausoleum

Armand Hammer
On left upon entering cemetery

BRIAN KEITH

1921 – 1997

DAISY KEITH

1969 – 1997

Brian Keith (see p. 33)
Garden of Serenity - New Memorial Garden

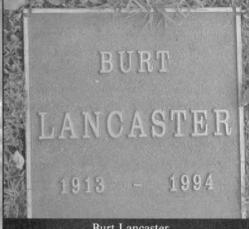

BURT

LANCASTER

1913 – 1994

Burt Lancaster
Across from Sanctuary of Love - Next to curb

LAZAR

IRVING   MARY

1907 – 1993   1932 – 1993

BELOVED BAA

Irving "Swifty" Lazar
Between Truman Capote and Armand Hammer

DEAN MARTIN
JUNE 7, 1917 – DECEMBER 25, 1995
EVERYBODY LOVES SOMEBODY SOMETIME

Dean Martin
Sanctuary of Love

1218 Glendon Avenue   Westwood

Marilyn Monroe (see p. 83)
Corridor of Memories - 24

Roy Orbison
Section D - 97 - Unmarked

Heather O'Rourke
Wall next to Truman Capote

Donna Reed
Section D - 142

Buddy Rich
Sanctuary of Tranquility

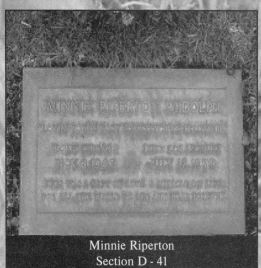

Minnie Riperton
Section D - 41

1218 Glendon Avenue   Westwood

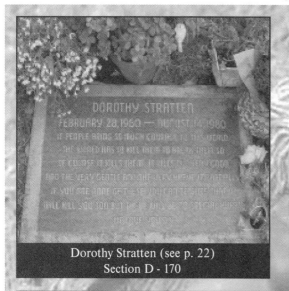

Dorothy Stratten (see p. 22)
Section D - 170

Mel Torme
Between Armand Hammer and Truman Capote

Carl Wilson
Section D - Just left of Minnie Riperton

Natalie Wood (see p. 114)
Section D - 60

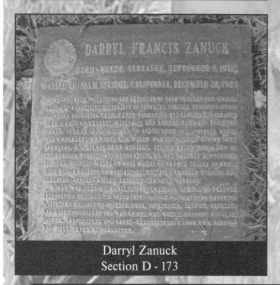

Darryl Zanuck
Section D - 173

Frank Zappa
Section D - 100 - Unmarked - Next to Lew Ayres

1218 Glendon Avenue Westwood

CHAPTER 14 MACABRE MARGINALIA

Some locations in Los Angeles are not easily categorizable. These locations, however, are excellent for exploring the worlds of murder and mayhem in the City of Angels.

1-800 AUTOPSY

"The deceased must be protected and given a voice." — Vidal Herrera

Need a crime scene cleaned up? How about sperm removed from your deceased husband? Think the doctors botched up your grandmother's surgery? Have no fear. Vidal Herrera and his unique Johnny-on-the spot autopsy service can help.

Formed in 1988, four years after Herrera suffered a debilitating back injury while lifting a large corpse for his job at the county coroner, 1-800 AUTOPSY provides a much-needed service. According to records, autopsies are only performed on 5% of all dead persons. Furthermore, Los Angeles coroners have come under intense scrutiny for their botched results in several high profile cases. Hence, the need for a mobile autopsy service such as this.

1-800 AUTOPSY provides a litany of services: full autopsies, disinterment, toxicology analyses, decomposition clean up, DNA banking, and HIV testing. Herrera runs a smooth ship that picks up the bodies and transports them to either a hospital or funeral home, whatever your need. They do not, however, perform autopsies at the customer's home or at his office. Herrera and his staff are friendly, efficient, and respectful, exactly what the majority of his clientele expect when they require his services.

Be sure to check out their website and peruse the unique gift catalog which includes t-shirts, femur bone pens, and vertebrae key rings.

http://www.1800autopsy.com

COLORADO STREET SUICIDE BRIDGE

This beautiful 1,467 foot concrete bridge is the scenic gateway into central Pasadena, just northeast of downtown Los Angeles. It is also known as the "Suicide Bridge."

Constructed in 1913, the 150-foot high structure crosses the dry Arroyo Seco riverbed. Rumor has it that a construction worker toppled over the side of the bridge and plunged headfirst into a vat of wet concrete below. Assuming he could not be saved, workers left his body in the quick drying mix to die. Allegedly, his soul cries out for other desperate beings. This may explain why the bridge became a hot spot of sorts during the Depression when 95 people jumped to their deaths from 1919 to 1937.

One of the most famous suicide attempts occurred on May 1, 1937, when a despondent mother threw her little baby girl over the railing and then jumped over herself. The mother died, but miraculously, the little girl survived the plunge. Her mother had inadvertently tossed her into some nearby trees, and she was later recovered from the thick branches.

The "Suicide Bridge" underwent a $27 million renovation in 1993, which included the installation of suicide prevention rails and spikes. The bridge has also received a Civil Engineering Landmark designation and is listed on the National Register of Historic Places.

Colorado Street Bridge Pasadena

CORONER'S GIFT SHOP

"We're dying for your business." – gift shop slogan

Be sure to check out "Skeletons In The Closet" when you are in Los Angeles for all of your macabre needs. Located on the second floor of the Los Angeles County Coroner's Office, this store contains over 100 items of death-related merchandise. They have everything from toe tags to beach towels emblazoned with chalk body outlines to a small-scale replica of the 1938 coroner's hearse known as "The Black Mariah."

Created in 1993, the coroner's gift shop now makes upwards of $500,000 in annual sales. Though considered in bad taste by some, proceeds of the sales help several worthwhile causes for the coroner. Money has been used to buy new equipment and has even led to a purchase of a new coroner's vehicle.

The best usage of the funds, however, goes towards the office's Youthful Drunk Driver Visitation Program. The program is an alternative to punishment for teens that get arrested for driving while intoxicated. Offenders must attend

the program that offers up a sober reality to the dangers of drunk driving. Over 2,000 kids a year have taken the tour that leads them into the dark world of the coroner's office. Kids observe a day in the life of a coroner that includes viewing several dead bodies and even a glimpse of an actual autopsy. Officials claim that their success rate is through the roof. They also believe that if the kids do not learn their lesson, they will return to the coroner's office—as clients.

1102 N. Mission Road #208 Los Angeles

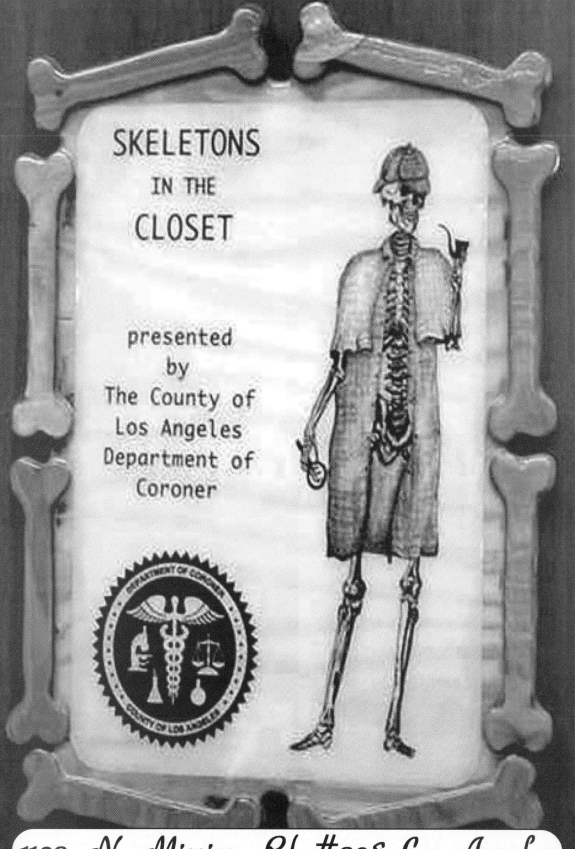

1102 N. Mission Rd. #208 Los Angeles

MUSEUM OF DEATH

With over 2,000 feet of space and nine rooms, the Museum of Death is the place to see every facet of death in all of its gory...errr, glory. Relocated in 2000 from San Diego, the Museum of Death contains all sorts of macabre memorabilia and offers a historical look at everyone's inevitable fate.

Proprietor Cathee Schultz is one of the happiest-go-lucky individuals in Hollywood and relishes her role as curator of death. She states "Death is her life" and that the exhibits in the museum make her appreciate her life more and more each day.

The holdings here are expansive:

*Crime scene photos of "The Black Dahlia" and the Helter Skelter murders;
*An electric chair replica complete with a real-life executed prisoner's bloody t-shirt;
*A Día de los Muertos (Day of the Dead) display;
*Ancient embalming equipment;
*Newspaper headlines of numerous tragic events from all over the world;
*Ancient lynching photographs;
*An immense wall display of car accident victims;
*Letters and artwork from serial killers such as Henry Lee Lucas, Ottis Toole, Lawrence Bittaker, Richard Ramirez, and John Wayne Gacy;

*A Heaven's Gate suicide cult diorama complete with an actual bunk bed from the compound purchased at an auction;
And much, much more.

The Museum of Death can be a bit of a sensory overload at times, but if you come in with a clear head, an open mind, and an empty stomach, you may leave here having learned more about yourself and your fellow future dirt-pushers than you may have hoped.

6340 Hollywood Blvd. #2 Hollywood

MUSEUM OF TOLERANCE

This self-guided, interactive museum spotlights the horrors of hatred and prejudice, with an emphasis on the Holocaust.

Hosted by a televised figure known as "The Manipulator," you can traverse through a series of rooms where different facets of racism are displayed. *The Other America* exhibit contains a 16-screen video wall that shows historic footage of civil rights struggles. A wall-sized, computerized map tracks several existing hate groups currently in operation in the United States.

The *Holocaust Section* has the most impact. When you enter, you are given an identification card of a real-life Jewish child who lived during the Holocaust. As you progress through the tour, you will be given updates on the child. By the end of this portion, you will learn whether your child lived or died at the hands of the Nazis.

While awaiting your child's fate, you can see numerous sights in the *Holocaust Section*. A re-creation of a 1930s street café depicts its patrons discussing the looming Nazi invasion. At the reenactment of the Wannsee Conference, the Nazis agree to exterminate all Jews. The Hall of Testimony resembles a high-tech version of a death shower, and you can view video-taped stories of courage and woe from survivors. A Multimedia Learning Center gives the museumgoer the opportunity to research thousands of stories on the Holocaust, as well as access a photo archive that contains over 50,000 photographs. The museum also houses actual artifacts from Auschwitz, a bed from the Majdanek death camp, and original letters from Anne Frank.

9876 W. Pico Blvd. Los Angeles

QUEEN MARY

The *Queen Mary* ocean liner, docked in Long Beach since 1967, is allegedly haunted. Even more fascinating is that it is also the site of a large-scale mass murder. Of course, that is not how the keepers of this beautiful ship, which is larger than the *Titanic*, wish to portray her.

The *Queen Mary* has a guided tour called "Ghosts and Legends." For the regular ticket price, which allows you to wander about the majestic seagoing vessel, you can also take the haunted tour inside the belly of the ship. Energetic guides, who seem to be hoping that some big-name Hollywood producer in the crowd will whisk them off to movie stardom, narrate an entertaining, if slightly cheesy, tour.

The tour takes you into the bowels of the ship and shows "ghostly" locations. Included sights are a haunted swimming pool where mysterious footprints appear in the bottom of the pool, engine room #13 where a ship worker was supposedly crushed to death and returned to haunt that region, and the most fascinating, realistic part of the ship—the bow.

What is so significant about the front of a ship?

In 1942, during World War II, the *Queen Mary* was painted a camouflage grey and re-christened the *Grey Ghost*. Its mission was to transport thousands of sailors at a time; sometimes up to 10,000 troops were crowded on board. The *Grey Ghost* was highly successful in its mission and was also greatly feared by its enemies. Adolf Hitler offered up a bounty of $250,000 and an Iron Cross for any submarine captain who could capture her.

On October 2, 1942, the *Grey Ghost* was transporting several troops from Ireland back to the United States. It was escorted by a British cruiser, the *H.M.S. Curacoa*. The ships began to perform a routine zigzag maneuver when the *H.M.S. Curacoa* crossed in front of the massive boat. The *Grey Ghost* sliced directly through the *H.M.S. Curacoa*, cutting it into two pieces. Barely a dent was put in the *Grey Ghost*. Three hundred thirty-eight sailors were killed by the impact. The *Grey Ghost*, on direct orders from the government, did not stop and render aid.

Be sure to check out some of the museums on board the *Queen Mary*. Tucked away, in a little corner on the upper deck, are a painting and a few newspaper articles about the collision. It is so small that the murder of 338 sailors aboard the *H.M.S. Curacoa* appears to be merely an irritating footnote in the history of the *Queen Mary*.

1126 Queens Highway North Long Beach

SERIAL KILLER AUTO GRAVEYARD

In a secluded spot in Santa Ana lies a bizarre collection of murderous memorabilia. Hidden from sight in a non-descript, razor fenced junkyard is a collection of automobiles from famous murders. Several cars that are tied to bloody crimes lie dormant in the lot. Authorities claim that well over 100 deaths are tied to these automobiles.

For example, a gray Toyota pickup lies in a corner. This truck belonged to an enraged postal worker by the name of Mark Robert Hilbun. Hilbun went on a murderous rampage in 1993 at the Dana Point postal office and killed two employees, after he had already killed his mother and their dog.

A faded red pickup truck that belonged to Thomas Francis Edwards can also be found here. In 1981, Edwards committed an inexplicable murder in the Cleveland National Forest while in this truck. Edwards noticed two 12-year-old girls, who were walking towards a picnic spot. He pulled his truck up beside them and shot them both in the head.

The true highlights of this graveyard, however, come in the form of two beaten up old pieces of junk. These heaps belonged to the overlapping "Freeway Killers" who were killing young boys and men and dumping their bodies all across the Los Angeles Freeway system: William Bonin and Randy Kraft.

Here you will find the dilapidated green Econoline van that William Bonin (see p.163) used to pick up young boys and men in his killing spree. The van still has the 70s-themed sticker "C.B. Trucker" on its rear door. If you take a look inside, you can see that there are no door handles in the back of the van. Bonin removed these to keep his victims from escaping. You can also see some of the rare carpet fiber that was found on several bodies and used to track Bonin down.

The other high-profile automobile is a beat-up brown Toyota Celica. This heap of junk belonged to Randy Kraft (see p. 175). While in this car, he was pulled over on the San Diego Freeway for suspected drunk driving. When police looked inside this car, they found a half-naked dead Marine. A further search turned up 47 photographs of unconscious or dead males, as well as a "Death List" that was found in the trunk. If Kraft's list was legitimate, he could be America's most prolific serial killer.

Authorities keep these cars in the event that they are needed as evidence. While most evidence has been collected, introduced into trial, then tagged and bagged, the need may arise for these cars to be included. Although this possibility is unlikely, the police would rather be safe than sorry. Therefore, this locale is the only one in the book that will not have an address provided.

So, you are going to have to find this one for yourself.

Santa Ana

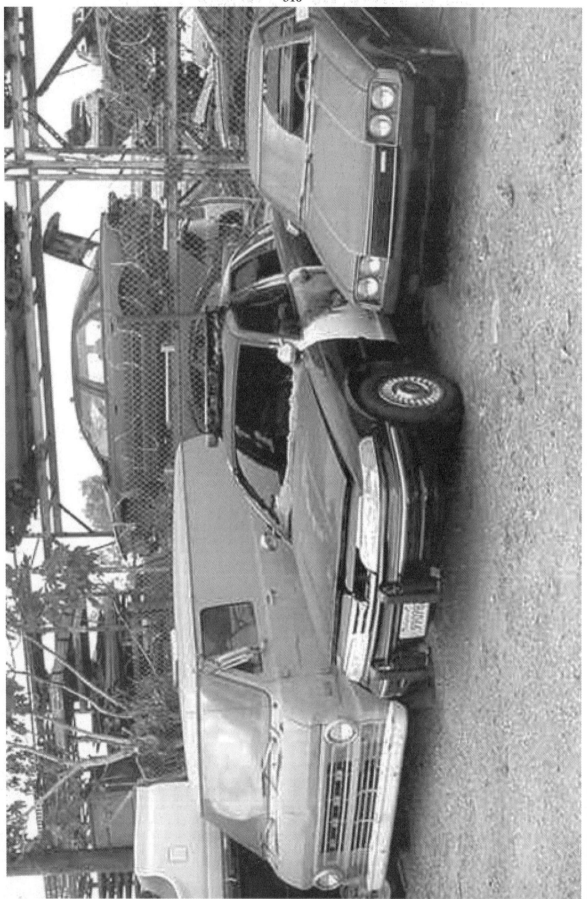

IN MEMORIAM

Mae Williford
Marjorie Yarbrough
J.D. Hollan

WEBSITE INFORMATION

---

http://www.hollywooddeathscenes.com

For more information, please log on to Corey Mitchell's website *http://www.hollywooddeathscenes.com*. There you will find updates of cases that appear in *Hollywood Death Scenes*, color photographs, and postings of cases that have surfaced since the publication of this book.

---

http://www.truecrimewriter.com

For more information on the true crime industry, please log on to Corey Mitchell's website *http://www.truecrimewriter.com*. There you will find interviews with top true crime authors, tools of the trade, important research links, and the latest information on current crimes.

INSIDE PHOTOS

1- Sam Cooke Star - Corey Mitchell (CM)
2- Sam Cooke - Courtesy of Starworld Collections
3- Polaris Motel - CM;
   Polaris Motel side - CM
4- Ennis Cosby Street Signs - CM;
   Ennis Cosby Death Site - CM
5- Dominique Dunne - Courtesy of Starworld Collections
6- Dominique Dunne in *Poltergeist* - Courtesy of Starworld Collections and MGM;
   Dominique Dunne House - CM
7- Marvin Gaye - Courtesy of Starworld Collections
8- Marvin Gaye House - CM
9- Phil Hartman - Courtesy of Starworld Collections
10- Phil Hartman House - CM
11- Sal Mineo - Courtesy of Larry Edmunds Collections;
   Sal Mineo Apartment - CM
12- Pacific Ocean - CM
13- Charlie Minor House - CM;
   Charlie Minor Window - CM
14- Haing S. Ngor - Courtesy of Larry Edmunds Collections
15- Haing S. Ngor Apartment - CM;
   Downtown Los Angeles - CM
16- Notorious B.I.G. - Courtesy of Starworld Collections;
   Petersen Automotive Museum Sign - CM
17- Petersen Automotive Museum - CM
18- Ramon Novarro - Courtesy of Larry Edmunds Collections
19- Ramon Novarro House - CM;
   Ramon Novarro House Close-up - CM
20- Rebecca Schaeffer - Courtesy of Larry Edmunds Collections;
   Rebecca Schaeffer Apartment - CM
21- Rebecca Schaeffer Door - CM;
   Theresa Saldana in *Victims for Victims: The Theresa Saldana Story* - Courtesy of Larry Edmunds Collections and NBC;
   Madonna - Courtesy of Larry Edmunds Collections;
   Steven Spielberg - Courtesy of Larry Edmunds Collections and Warner Bros.
22- Dorothy Stratten - Courtesy of Larry Edmunds Collections
23- Dorothy Stratten Apartment - CM
24- Carl Switzer - Courtesy of Larry Edmunds Collections
25- Carl Switzer's Death House - CM
26- Noose - CM
27- Museum of Death Entrance - CM
28- Ray Combs - Courtesy of Starworld Collections and LBS Communications;
   Glendale Adventist Medical Center - CM
29- Darby Crash House - CM
30- Hollywood Sign - CM
31- Margaux Hemingway in *Over the Brooklyn Bridge* - Courtesy of Larry Edmunds Collections and MGM/UA and Cannon Group
32- Margaux Hemingway Apartment - CM
33- Brian Keith - Courtesy of Larry Edmunds Collections;
   Malibu Colony - CM
34- Freddie Prinze and Jack Albertson - Courtesy of Starworld Collections
35- Plaza Hotel - CM
36- Plaza Hotel - CM
37- Savannah – Photographer: Brad Willis. Courtesy of Nancy Pera.
38- Savannah House - CM
39- Del Shannon House - CM
40- Jason Thirsk House – CM
41- Herve Villechaize and Ricardo Montalban - Courtesy of Larry Edmunds Collections
42- Herve Villechaize House - CM
43- *Bride of Frankenstein* - Courtesy of Larry Edmunds Collections
44- James Whale House - CM;
   James Whale Address Sign - CM
45- Rozz Williams - Photographer: Cecelia Trevejo. Courtesy of Nico.
46- Rozz Williams Apartment - CM;
   Rozz Williams Apartment Interior - Photographer: Cecelia Trevejo. Courtesy of Nico;
   Rozz Williams Suicide Door - CM
47- Chemical Imbalance - CM
48- John Belushi in *1941* - Courtesy of Larry Edmunds Collections and Universal City Studios
50- Chateau Marmont - CM
51- Chateau Marmont Bungalow Doors - CM;
   Chateau Marmont Sign - CM;
   Gilda Radner - Courtesy of Larry Edmunds Collections;
   Chris Farley - Courtesy of Larry Edmunds Collections;
   Phil Hartman – United Press International
52- Lenny Bruce - Courtesy of Starworld Collections
53- Lenny Bruce Gate Phone - CM
54- Lenny Bruce Gate - CM;
   Lenny Bruce House - CM
55- Dorothy Dandridge - Courtesy of Larry Edmunds Collections
56- Dorothy Dandridge Apartment - CM
57- William Holden - Courtesy of Larry Edmunds Collections and Universal Pictures
58- William Holden Address Sign - CM;
   William Holden Apartment - CM
59- Janis Joplin - Courtesy of Starworld Collections
60- Highland Gardens Sign - CM
61- Highland Gardens - CM
62- Shoreham Towers - CM;
   Shoreham Towers Address Sign - CM
63- River Phoenix - Courtesy of Larry Edmunds Collections
64- River Phoenix in *Stand By Me* - Courtesy of Larry Edmunds Collections
65- Viper Room - CM;
   Viper Room - CM
66- Don Simpson - Courtesy of Larry Edmunds Collections and Paramount Studios
67- Don Simpson House - CM
68- Hillel Slovak Apartment - Lisa Mitchell (LM)
69- Lupe Velez - Courtesy of Larry Edmunds Collections
70- Lupe Velez House - CM
71- Dennis Wilson - Courtesy of Starworld Collections
72- Dennis Wilson Marina Gate - CM;
   Dennis Wilson Boat Dock - CM
74- Nick Adams and Deborah Walley in *The Young Lovers* - Courtesy of Larry Edmunds Collections and Metro-Goldwyn-Mayer
75- Nick Adams House - CM
76- Albert Dekker and Susan Hayward in *Among The Living* Courtesy of Larry Edmunds Collections and Universal Studios
77- Albert Dekker Apartment - CM
78- Greystone Mansion - CM;
   Greystone Mansion Address Sign - CM
79- Greystone Mansion Courtyard - CM;
   Greystone Mansion Interior - CM

80- Greystone Mansion Interior – CM
82- Menendez House – CM
83- Marilyn Monroe – Courtesy of Larry Edmunds Collections
84- Marilyn Monroe House – CM
86- Marilyn Monroe – Courtesy of Larry Edmunds Collections;
Marilyn Monroe Garage – CM
87- Jack Nance in *Eraserhead* – Courtesy of Larry Edmunds Collections and Libra Films
88- Winchell's Donuts Parking Lot – CM
89- Winchell's Donuts – CM;
Jack Nance Apartment – CM;
Jack Nance Apartment Address Sign – CM
90- George Reeves – Courtesy of Larry Edmunds Collections
91- George Reeves House – CM
92- George Reeves – Courtesy of Larry Edmunds Collections
93- Elizabeth Short – Courtesy of the Museum of Death
94- Elizabeth Short Body – Courtesy of the Museum of Death;
Elizabeth Short Murder Site – CM
95- Benjamin "Bugsy" Siegel – Herald Examiner Collection/Los Angeles Public Library
96- Benjamin "Bugsy" Siegel Death Scene – CM
97- Benjamin "Bugsy" Siegel Corpse – Herald Examiner Collection/Los Angeles Public Library
98- Laurence Austin Corpse – Los Angeles County Court Archives;
Silent Movie Theater circa 1997 – Los Angeles County Court Archives
99- James Van Sickle Line-up Photo – Los Angeles County Court Archives;
Christian Rodriguez Line-up Photo – Los Angeles County Court Archives
100- Silent Movie Theater circa 1999 – CM;
Silent Movie Theater Grand Re-Opening – CM
101- William Desmond Taylor – Courtesy of Larry Edmunds Collections and A&E/Juniper Entertainment
102- Mabel Normand in *Caught in a Cabaret* – Courtesy of Larry Edmunds Collections and A&E/Juniper Entertainment;
Mary Miles Minter – Courtesy of Larry Edmunds Collections and A&E/Juniper Entertainment
103- Mary Miles Minter and Charlotte Shelby – Courtesy of Larry Edmunds Collections and A&E/Juniper Entertainment;
Pic 'n' Save Parking Lot – CM
104- City of Bradbury Sign - LM
105- Woodlyn Road Sign – LM;
Mickey Thompson Neighborhood Gate – LM
106- Thelma Todd – Courtesy of Larry Edmunds Collections and Metro-Goldwyn-Mayer
107- Thelma Todd's Roadside Café – CM;
Thelma Todd Corpse – Herald Examiner Collection/Los Angeles Public Library
108- Castillo del Mar Garage – CM;
Castillo del Mar – CM
109- Lana Turner – Courtesy of Larry Edmunds Collections
110- Lana Turner, Johnny Stompanato, and Cheryl Crane – Herald Examiner Collection/Los Angeles Public Library;
Lana Turner House – CM
111- Wonderland Bloody Wall – Los Angeles Police Department Video;
John Holmes – Courtesy of Starworld Collections
112- Wonderland Murder Victim – Los Angeles Police

Department Video
113- Wonderland Murder Location – CM
114- Natalie Wood – Courtesy of Larry Edmunds Collections
115- Natalie Wood and Robert Wagner – Courtesy of Larry Edmunds Collections
116- Natalie Wood – Courtesy of Larry Edmunds Collections
117- Los Angeles City Hall – CM
118- Patty Hearst – Courtesy of the Crime Lab
119- Bill Harris – Courtesy of the Crime Lab;
Emily Harris – Courtesy of the Crime Lab; ·
SLA House Fire – © Bettmann/CORBIS
120- New House on SLA Location – CM
121- Ambassador Hotel – CM
122- Robert Kennedy Assassination – © Bettmann/CORBIS
123- Police Cars – CM
124- Popeye's – CM
125- Lori Gonzalez Murder Site – CM
126- Rodney King Beating Site – CM
127- Rodney King Beating Site – CM
128- Riot Epicenter – CM
130- Blue Castle – CM
132- 76 Gas Station – CM
133- Margaret Mitchell Death Scene – CM
134- Margaret Mitchell Death Scene – CM
135- Mass Hysteria Bomb – CM
136- Southcoast Early Childhood Learning Center Playground – CM
137- Southcoast Early Childhood Learning Center – CM;
Commemorative Plaque – CM
138- Cal-State Fullerton Sign – CM;
Cal-State Fullerton Library Basement Door – CM
139- Commemorative Trees – CM;
Cal-State Fullerton Library – CM
140- Cal State Fullerton Library Basement – CM
141- David Alvarez – Courtesy of FBI Wanted List;
David Alvarez House – CM
142- Harvard Terrace Apartment Address – CM
143- Harvard Terrace Apartments – CM
144- Edward Charles III – Orange County Court Archives;
Edward Charles III House – CM
145- Los Coyotes Middle School – CM;
Edward Charles III Murder Weapon – CM
146- Edward Charles III Victims – Orange County Court Archives;
Charles Family Burnt Car – Orange County Court Archives
147- Former Dorothy Mae Apartment Location – CM
148- Marjorie Street Sign – CM
149- Flores House – CM
151- Sandi Nieves House – CM
152- Ronald Taylor House – CM
153- California Employment Development Department – CM
154- California Employment Development Department Hallway – CM;
James O'Brien Murder Scene - CM
155- Alan Winterbourne Death Scene – CM
156- SoCal Serial Killers – CM
157- SoCal Serial Killers – CM
158- Lawrence Bittaker – Courtesy of the Museum of Death
159- Glendora Ridge Motor Way Gate and Road – CM
160- San Dimas Canyon – LM
161- Shirley Ledford Dump Site – CM
162- Roy Norris House – CM;
Scott Motel – CM
163- William Bonin Mugshot – Orange County Court

Archives
164- William Bonin Van - Orange County Court Archives;
William Bonin Van Interior - Orange County Court
Archives
165- William Bonin House - CM;
William Bonin Couch - Orange County Court
Archives;
William Bonin Van Interior - Orange County Court
Archives
166- William Bonin Arrest Site - CM
168- Cindy Chandler and Gina Marano Dump Site - LM;
Chevron Gas Station - LM
169- Former Sizzler Location - CM;
Exxie Wilson's Head - Courtesy of the Museum of
Death;
Exxie Wilson Head Dump Site - CM;
170- Former Little Nashville Club Site - CM;
Jack Murray Murder Site - CM
171- Valley Plaza Doctors Hospital - CM
173- Harvey Glatman House - CM
174- Patrick Kearney House - CM
175- Randy Kraft - Orange County Court Archives;
Randy Kraft's Car - Orange County Court
Archives
176- Terry Gambrel - Orange County Court Archives;
Randy Kraft's House - CM
177- Kevin Green's Neighborhood - CM;
Gerald Parker - Orange County Court Archives
178- Bedroom Bashed by Gerald Parker - Orange County
Court Archives;
DNA Chart Used in Gerald Parker Conviction -
Orange County Court Archives
179- Glendale Adventist Medical Center Sign - CM
180- Glendale Adventist Medical Center - CM
182- Brandon Tholmer House - CM
183- Charles Manson - Herald Examiner Collection/Los
Angeles Public Library
184- Charles Manson - Herald Examiner Collection/Los
Angeles Public Library
185- Beach Boys - Courtesy of Starworld Collections;
Dennis Wilson House - CM
186- Former Yellow Submarine Location - CM
187- Spahn Ranch - CM;
Manson Family at Spahn Ranch - Herald Examiner
Collection/Los Angeles Public Library
188- Terry Melcher - Herald Examiner Collection/Los
Angeles Public Library;
Land of Paradise Sign - CM
190- Bernard Crowe - Herald Examiner Collection/Los
Angeles Public Library;
Bernard Crowe Shooting Location - CM
191- Bobby Beausoleil - Herald Examiner Collection/Los
Angeles Public Library;
Gary Hinman House - CM
192- Sharon Tate - Courtesy of Larry Edmunds Collections;
Sharon Tate House - Herald Examiner Collection/Los
Angeles Public Library
193- Abigail Folger - Herald Examiner Collection/Los
Angeles Public Library;
Jay Sebring - Herald Examiner Collection/Los Angeles
Public Library;
Patricia Krenwinkel - Herald Examiner Collection/Los
Angeles Public Library
195- Cielo Drive Sign - CM;
Villa Bella Gate - CM;
Villa Bella - CM;
Cary Grant - Courtesy of Larry Edmunds
Collections;

Henry Fonda - Courtesy of Larry Edmunds
Collections;
Candice Bergen - Courtesy of Larry Edmunds
Collections and Fox Broadcasting Company;
Trent Reznor - Courtesy of Starworld Collections and
nothing records
196- Villa Bella - CM
197- LaBianca House - CM
198- Charles "Tex" Watson - Herald Examiner Collection/
Los Angeles Public Library;
Patricia Krenwinkel and Leslie Van Houten - Herald
Examiner Collection/Los Angeles Public Library
199- Barker Ranch - Herald Examiner Collection/Los
Angeles Public Library
200- Sybil Brand Institute Cells - CM
201- Susan Atkins - Herald Examiner Collection/Los
Angeles Public Library
202- Sybil Brand Institute Sign - CM;
Sybil Brand Institute Cell - CM
203- Charles Manson - Herald Examiner Collection/Los
Angeles Public Library;
Vincent Bugliosi - Herald Examiner Collection/Los
Angeles Public Library
204- Los Angeles Superior District Court - CM;
Susan Atkins, Patricia Krenwinkel, and Leslie Van
Houten - Herald Examiner Collection/Los Angeles
Public Library
205- Manson Girls - Herald Examiner Collection/Los
Angeles Public Library;
Linda Kasabian - Herald Examiner Collection/Los
Angeles Public Library
206- Susan Atkins in Court - Herald Examiner Collection/
Los Angeles Public Library
207- Charles Manson - Herald Examiner Collection/Los
Angeles Public Library
208- Hillside Strangler Dump Site - LM
209- Kenneth Bianchi - © Bettmann/CORBIS;
Angelo Buono - Herald Examiner Collection/Los
Angeles Public Library
210- Kenneth Bianchi High School Graduation Photo -
Courtesy of the Museum of Death
211- Angelo Buono's Mother's House - CM
212- A&M Auto Repair - CM
213- Angelo Buono's Former House Location - CM;
Kenneth Bianchi's Former Apartment Courtyard
- CM
214- Yolanda Washington - Herald Examiner Collection/Los
Angeles Public Library;
Forest Lawn Hollywood Hills Sign - LM
215- Judith Miller - Herald Examiner Collection/Los
Angeles Public Library;
Judith Miller Dump Site - LM
216- Chevy Chase Country Club Sign - CM
217- Lissa Kastin Dump Site - CM
218- Kristina Weckler - Herald Examiner Collection/Los
Angeles Public Library
219- Kristina Weckler Dump Site - CM
220- Jane King - Herald Examiner Collection/Los Angeles
Public Library
221- Jane King Dump Site - CM;
Freeway Exit Sign - CM
222- Dolores Cepeda and Sonja Johnson Dump Site - CM
223- Lauren Wagner Corpse - Herald Examiner Collection/
Los Angeles Public Library
224- Hollywood Public Library - CM;
Tamarind Place Apartments - CM
225- Kim Martin Corpse - Herald Examiner Collection/Los
Angeles Public Library;

Kim Martin Dump Site – LM
226- Cindy Hudspeth Apartment – CM;
   Cindy Hudspeth Corpse in Trunk - © Reuters/
   CORBIS
227- Detective Edwin Henderson with Poster of Potential
   Strangler Victims - Herald Examiner Collection/Los
   Angeles Public Library
230- Police Outside of Angelo Buono's House - Herald
   Examiner Collection/Los Angeles Public Library
231- Judge Ronald George - Herald Examiner Collection/
   Los Angeles Public Library;
   Angelo Buono in Handcuffs - Herald Examiner
   Collection/Los Angeles Public Library
232- Devil Sketch Drawn by Richard Ramirez – Courtesy of
   the Museum of Death
233- Richard Ramirez - Herald Examiner Collection/Los
   Angeles Public Library
235- Hotel Rosslyn – CM
236- Jennie Vincow Apartment – CM
237- Dayle Okazaki Garage – CM
238- Veronica Yu Murder Street – CM
239- Zazarra House – CM
240- William Doi House – CM
241- Mabel Bell House – LM
242- Mary Cannon House – CM
243- Joyce Nelson House – CM
244- Chainarong Khovananth House – CM
245- Ross Cutlery – CM
246- Max and Lela Kneiding - Herald Examiner Collection/
   Los Angeles Public Library;
   Max and Lela Kneiding House – CM
247- Elyas Abowath House – CM
248- Golden Gate Bridge – LM
249- Golden Gate Bridge – LM
251- Greyhound Bus Station Address Sign – CM;
   Greyhound Bus – CM
252- Richard Ramirez Arrest Site – CM
253- Richard Ramirez Arrest - Herald Examiner Collection/
   Los Angeles Public Library;
   Richard Ramirez Captors Receive Award - Herald
   Examiner Collection/Los Angeles Public Library
254- Richard Ramirez Mugshot - Herald Examiner
   Collection/Los Angeles Public Library
255- Sean Penn in *Dead Man Walking* - Courtesy of Larry
   Edmunds Collections and Gramercy Pictures;
   Los Angeles County Jail – CM
256- Richard Ramirez Flashes Pentagram - Herald
   Examiner Collection/Los Angeles Public Library
257- Los Angeles Superior District Court – CM;
   Detective Frank Salerno - Herald Examiner Collection/
   Los Angeles Public Library
258- Richard Ramirez - Herald Examiner Collection/Los
   Angeles Public Library
259- O.J. Simpson Hall of Fame Jersey – CM
260- O.J. Simpson and Family – © Reuters/CORBIS;
   Nicole Brown Simpson Condo circa 1994 – Courtesy
   of the Crime Lab
261- Nicole Brown Simpson Condo circa 1994 – Courtesy
   of the Crime Lab;
   Nicole Brown Simpson Condo circa 2001 – CM
262- O.J. Simpson House circa 1994 – Courtesy of the
   Crime Lab
263- O.J. Simpson Former Location circa 2001 – CM
264- Downtown Chicago – LM
265- Parker Center – CM
266- O.J. Simpson in *The Naked Gun* - Courtesy of Larry
   Edmunds Collections and Paramount Studios
267- San Diego (405) Freeway – CM

268- O.J. Simpson Mugshot – Courtesy of the Museum of
   Death
269- Robert Shapiro and Johnnie Cochran – Photo
   Collection/Los Angeles Public Library
271- Santa Monica Civil Courthouse – CM
272- Nicole Brown Simpson Grave – CM
273- Hollywood Forever – CM
274- Statue of Immortality – LM
275- Gracie Allen and George Burns – CM;
   L. Frank Baum – LM;
   Clara Bow – CM;
   Nat "King" Cole – CM;
   Dorothy Dandridge – CM;
   Walt Disney - LM
276- E.L. Doheny Jr. – LM;
   Larry Fine – CM;
   Errol Flynn – LM;
   Sid Grauman – LM;
   Ted Knight – LM;
   Alan Ladd - CM
277- Louis L'Amour – CM
   Chico Marx – CM;
   Gummo Marx – CM;
   Aimee Semple McPherson – LM;
   Clayton Moore – LM;
   Mary Pickford – LM
278- Red Skelton – LM;
   Casey Stengel – LM;
   Jimmy Stewart – LM;
   Spencer Tracy – LM;
   Robert Young - LM
279- Statue Near Errol Flynn's Grave – LM
280- George Washington Statue – LM
281- Morey Amsterdam – CM;
   Gene Autry – LM;
   Lucille Ball – LM;
   Albert "Cubby" Broccoli – LM;
   William Conrad – LM;
   Bert Convy - LM
282- Scatman Crothers – LM;
   Bette Davis – LM;
   Brad Davis – CM;
   Roy Disney – LM;
   Marty Feldman – LM;
   Andy Gibb - LM
283- Bob Kane – LM;
   Buster Keaton – LM;
   Dorothy Lamour – LM;
   Walter Lantz – LM;
   Charles Laughton – CM;
   Stan Laurel - LM
284- Liberace – LM;
   Diane Linkletter – LM;
   Harriet Nelson – LM;
   Ozzie Nelson – LM;
   Ricky Nelson – LM;
   Freddie Prinze – LM
285- George Raft – LM;
   Telly Savalas – LM;
   McLean Stevenson – CM;
   Vic Tayback – LM;
   Lee Van Cleef – LM;
   Jack Webb - LM
286- Statue Near Walter Lantz's Grave – LM
287- Al Jolson Memorial – LM
288- Jack Benny – LM;
   Eddie Cantor – LM;
   Mickey Cohen – LM;

Max Factor Jr. – LM;
Max Factor Sr. – LM;
Mark Goodson - LM
289- Hank Greenberg – LM;
Lorne Greene – CM;
Moe Howard – LM;
David Janssen – LM;
George Jessel – LM;
Michael Landon - LM
290- Vic Morrow – LM;
Dinah Shore – CM;
Irving Wallace - LM
291- Hollywood Forever Lake – LM
292- Mel Blanc – LM;
Iron Eyes Cody – LM;
Harry Cohn – LM;
Marion Davies Crypt– LM;
Cecil B. DeMille – LM;
Nelson Eddy - LM
293- Douglas Fairbanks Sr. – LM;
Peter Finch – CM;
Victor Fleming – LM;
Janet Gaynor – LM;
Darla Hood – CM;
John Huston - LM
294- Peter Lorre – CM;
Jayne Mansfield Cenotaph – LM;
Jay Moloney – LM;
Paul Muni – LM;
Tyrone Power – LM;
Virginia Rappe - LM
295- Edward G. Robinson Jr. – CM;
Benjamin "Bugsy" Siegel – CM;
Carl Switzer – LM;
Norma Talmadge – LM;
William Desmond Taylor – CM;
Rudolph Valentino - LM
296- Holy Cross Mausoleum – LM
297- Mary Astor – LM;
Ray Bolger – LM;
Charles Boyer – LM;
John Candy – CM;
MacDonald Carey – LM;
Jackie Coogan - LM
298- Darby Crash – CM;
Bing Crosby – LM;
Jimmy Durante – LM;
John Ford – CM;
Mary Frann – LM;
Jack Haley - LM
299- Rita Hayworth – LM;
Bela Lugosi – LM;
Fred MacMurray – CM;
Eddie Mannix – LM;
Toni Mannix – LM;
Audrey Meadows - LM
300- Evelyn Nesbit – CM;
Walter O'Malley – LM;
Rosalind Russell – LM;
Gia Scala – CM;
Sharon Tate – LM;
Lawrence Welk - LM
301- Holy Cross Mausoleum Mural – LM
302- Holocaust Memorial – CM
303- Irwin Allen – CM;
Lee J. Cobb – CM;
"Big Mama" Cass Elliot – CM;
Norman Fell – CM;

Phil Silvers – CM;
Hillel Slovak - CM
304- Marilyn Monroe Crypt – LM
305- Eve Arden – LM;
Jim Backus – LM;
Sebastian Cabot – LM;
Truman Capote – LM;
John Cassavetes – LM;
Dominique Dunne - LM
306- Eva Gabor – LM;
Armand Hammer – LM;
Brian Keith – LM;
Burt Lancaster – LM;
Irving "Swifty" Lazar – LM;
Dean Martin – LM
307- Marilyn Monroe – LM;
Roy Orbison – LM;
Heather O'Rourke – LM;
Donna Reed – LM;
Buddy Rich – LM;
Minnie Riperton - LM
308- Dorothy Stratten – LM;
Mel Torme – LM;
Carl Wilson – LM;
Natalie Wood – LM;
Darryl Zanuck – LM;
Frank Zappa - LM
311- Colorado Street Bridge – CM
312- Coroner's Gift Shop – CM;
Los Angeles County Coroner's Building – CM
313- Skeletons in the Closet Sign – CM
314- Museum of Death Sign – CM;
Museum of Death Entrance - CM
315- Museum Of Tolerance – CM
316- Queen Mary Ghosts and Legends Mural – CM
318- William Bonin's Van and Randy Kraft's Car circa 2001 – CM
319- Sign at the Ambassador Hotel - CM

*Celebrity photos used for editorial purposes only.
**All photos listed as "CM" are ©2001 Corey Mitchell.
***All photos listed as "LM" are ©2001 Lisa Mitchell.
****All backgrounds drawn, photographed, sketched, and/or designed by author and are © 2001 Corey Mitchell.

COVER PHOTOS

Hollywood Sign - © 2001 Corey Mitchell
Phil Hartman - United Press International
Charles Manson - Herald Examiner Collection/Los Angeles Public Library
Marilyn Monroe - © Bettmann/CORBIS
Richard Ramirez - Herald Examiner Collection/Los Angeles Public Library
John Belushi - © Lynn Goldsmith/CORBIS

CREATIVE TOOLS

Dell Dimension 4100 PC, Sony Digital Mavica FD-85, Photoshop 5.5, and Pagemaker 6.5
Thank you Ray-Dog and Ted Jr. for the heads up.

ACKNOWLEDGEMENTS
AKA
KUDOS, HUZZAHS, &
COULDN'T-HAVE-DONE-IT-WITHOUT-CHAS

I would like to thank two amazing professionals who bent over backwards to walk me through the landmine-filled terrain that is publishing: Dennis McDougal and Poppy Z. Brite. Dennis, who hired me to help research the Cary Stayner story for his book *The Yosemite Murders*, has been the ultimate mentor. His insight and wisdom into the Byzantine structure of the industry are topped only by his humor and humanity. Poppy, whom I met at a book signing several years ago in Austin, Texas, is the example I hope to emulate in my career. Her willingness to take my annoying phone calls and talk with me about everything from true crime, to the horror industry, to the NBA amazes me. Thank you for reading my proposal and passing it along to Richard Curtis.

I send my gratitude to the aforementioned Mr. Curtis who has made this union with my publisher possible. Despite representing many of the biggest names in the business, he *always* takes my calls and answers my e-mails. I look forward to a long and bountiful relationship for years to come.

The staffs at Olmstead Press and LPC Group for taking on this project. Especially, David Wilk for believing in the concept. My editor, Maureen Owen, who brings a smile to my face every time I pick up the phone and speak with her. Curt Akin, who walked me through the torturous process of the book layout.

A book such as this requires extensive research. Therefore, it was of the utmost importance for me to work with competent individuals whom I did not know. Much to my surprise, I found most of the staffs at the Southern California court systems to be a pleasure. Knowledgeable, eager to assist, and friendly. Specifically, Geoff Christison and Bill Cook at the Orange County Superior Court Exhibits for their enthusiasm and easy-going attitude. I look forward to returning to your pit and working on future cases. Tracy and the lovely ladies of the Los Angeles Hall of Records for getting my requests right the first time and doing it with smiles on their faces. Norvel Armor in the Los Angeles Criminal Courts Exhibits for assistance on the Silent Movie Murder case.

Another pleasant surprise was working with the Recorder's Offices. Thanks to George Rodriguez in the Norwalk office and Sherie Hampton and Eryn Brown of the Riverside County Recorder's Office.

The people who deal in death bring an amazing sense of humor to their jobs, yet somehow simultaneously respect those affected by such horrible tragedies. This is best exemplified by Scott Carrier of the Los Angeles County Coroner's Office. Good luck on all of your projects. Also, Museum of Death curators J.D. Healy and Cathee Schultz. Have a great life.

Special thanks go out to Donna Muleady and Jim Amormino for the private trip to the serial killer auto graveyard. It is a sight few will ever see. I am glad I was one of the few.

Another pleasant surprise has been working with the courteous library staffs in West

Hollywood and Beverly Hills. My most financially draining, yet pleasant library transaction was with Caroline Cole of the downtown branch. The expense was worth every penny. Also, Matthew Mattson who salvaged my CD-R.

Photographs played a big part in the concept of this book. In addition to the wonderful *Los Angeles Herald-Examiner* collection, I was privileged to work with other professionals in the world of photography. Katie Walker of Corbis was enthusiastic. Pete Bateman of the Larry Edmunds Bookshop was a massive help in garnering the majority of the celebrity headshots. Marvin Henriquez of Starworld was a huge help with many of the musician headshots. Archivist extraordinaire Marc Wanamaker of Bison Archives solved a major issue for me and helped make the book what it is today. Nancy Pera provided the gorgeous shot of Savannah and is nice to boot. Also, Cecelia Trevejo and Nico for the amazing headshot of Rozz Williams and the interior shot of his apartment.

Thank you to Lesley Stevenson of the Cal-State Fullerton library for answering my questions regarding the massacre of 1976.

Anyone who knows me knows that music is a major part of my life. Of all the years I worked in the music business and all of the people I worked with I am glad to call two men my friends: Adam Grossman and Mark Gage. Good luck with your art and keep forging onward. Several musicians were also instrumental in making my writing more enjoyable. These are a few of the acts I listened to while working on the book. Vapourspace, Cusp, Phylr, here, Aphex Twin, Luke Vibert, Plug, Wagon Christ, P.J. Harvey, *Run Lola Run* s/t, Plastikman, *Requiem for a Dream* s/t, Tangerine Dream, Beethoven, Skylab, human mesh dance, *Twin Peaks* s/t, Prototype 909, Satoshi Tomiie, Fuse, Autechre, Juno Reactor, *Immortal Beloved* s/t, Fat Boy Slim, Talvin Singh, orb, Polygon Window, AFX, Orbital, Moby, Revolting Cocks, Ministry, NIN, Goldie, Roni Size, The Future Sound of London, Shellac, Metallica (pre-*TBA*), Seefeel, Consolidated, Mouse on Mars, *PI* s/t, Chemical Brothers, David Helfgott, Black Dog Productions, Intermix, and, of course, the soundtrack for *To Live and Die in L.A.*

A special thank you to my chiropractor, Dr. Scott Onoda, for fixing my neck and shoulder after my nasty accident. I enjoyed your recollections of true crime in L.A. Also Vickie and Reena for their bright smiles.

Special acclaim to two excellent writers who helped me with my craft. Brian Taggert and Dennis Etchison, two of the funniest, most intelligent, hardworking men that I have met. Spread the fear.

Teachers are severely underpaid and underappreciated. I would like to recognize the ones that had a strong impact on my life. Darlene Gartrell from my elementary school days. Margaret Fox from junior high. Richard Ramirez-Berg from the University of Texas and Michael Ariens from St. Mary's School of Law. Thank you for opening up new doors and encouraging me to step through them.

The value of friendship almost surpasses everything. I have been blessed to meet and befriend several amazing, skilled, intelligent people throughout my life. Dana Holliday, AKA Astrowoman, you amaze me with your breadth of knowledge of true crime, Hollywood, and the stars. But your energetic demeanor is even more impressive. Keep rattling your chains and rapping on the table. Aphrodite Jones, a talented writer with more spunk and drive than ten men combined. Thank you for the opportunity. Chris Goldrup and Beverly Rubin-Goldrup, two special friends on the West Coast. Stay strong and never stop fighting. My college roomie Vince Garcia. Always have a good time. Kevin and Shauna Fowler for all of their support.

Jimmy Mansour, one of the few people who I actually enjoyed working for. To the two legal eagles who are also my friends, Rob Carter and David Schaefer. Both are perfect examples that lawyers can actually be decent human beings and trustworthy friends.

A special acknowledgement must go out to my lifelong friends from P-ville, Lupe Garcia, Rick Butler, Knox Williams, Michael Sheppard, and Peter Soria. I have learned more about life from each one of you than I care to admit. Thank you for your support, laughter, and friendship that has lasted since first grade. May it continue for another 30 years, and then another 30. Bet it all and leave the driving to Mike!

My best friend and co-conspirator, the Dog, Ray Seggern merits special notice. Thanks for helping me get this book off the ground. This would not have been possible without your help. One day we will work on a project together, I can assure you of that. Keep concocting.

Next to friendship, nothing means more to me than family. I recently inherited a new tribe and I want to thank them for their belief in me. Warm wishes go out to my in-laws, Donna and Ted Popp. My sisters-in-law Lynn and Leane. My brother-in-law Ted Jr. Also, Mike Whalen and Connie Popp. My nieces Sara, Stephanie, and April. My nephews Tres and Craig. I look forward to being a part of your family for decades to come.

My own family, who have stood by me through all of my unusual career choices. You can all relax now, I found my niche. For my aunt Renee Runyan, who loves to read. Dick Yarbrough, the kindest man on the planet. My nephew, Ronnie Mitchell, who will rule the world one day. To my brothers Kyle and Darrin. Thanks for showing me the ropes and putting up with my pestering behavior. To their wives, Ramona (who is the sister I never had), and DeDe (welcome to the family). My parents, Carol and Don Mitchell, who always encouraged me to read anything I wanted, thank you. Your unconditional love and support have always made me realize that I can try anything and always come out on top. Thank you for years of laughter, warmth, and love. I am one lucky man.

And finally, to the one person who makes me realize just how lucky I am, my wife Lisa. Nothing compares to your charm, beauty, intelligence, humor, and general all-around goodness. Thank you for being the light that always shines bright for me. I only hope that I can bring you one-tenth the amount of happiness over our lifetimes that you have already given me in such a short time. Yours eternally.

Corey Mitchell
5/10/2001

Next trip—NYC